LISTEN to the MAX 1

K&Y English Lab

James Kapper	B.A. Linguistics, The University of North Dakota M.A. Linguistics, The University of Illinois Faculty, Ansan College in the Department of Tourism English
Lucia Barrimore	B.A. English literature and History, University of Queensland, Australia Full-time teacher, Heathfield High School, Australia
Nathan Kim	B.A. Political Science, The University of Michigan, High Honor M.A. Social Studies, HKUST, High Honor
Elaine Cho	B.A. Economics, Indiana University Director, IU English Academy

Listen to the MAX ❶

Thirteenth published in January 2023
By Darakwon, Inc.
Darakwon Bldg., 211, Munbal-ro, Paju-si, Gyeonggi-do 10881
Republic of Korea
Tel: 82-2-736-2031 (Ext. 250)
Fax: 82-2-732-2037

Author: K&Y English Lab
Publisher: Kyudo Chung
Editors: Myungjin Kim, Guembalmi Kim
Proofreader: Michael A. Putlack
Illustrator: Illumania
Interior design: Jieun Yun, Soyeon Park
Cover design: F205

Price: ₩15,000

ISBN 978-89-5995-921-1 58740
      978-89-5995-927-3 (set)

www.darakwon.co.kr
Visit the Darakwon homepage to learn about our other publications and promotions, and to download the MP3 files.

[Components] Main Book / Answer Book / Free MP3 Download

LISTEN to the MAX

K&Y English Lab

DARAKWON

Introduction

<Listen to the MAX> is a series of books for students who are preparing for the foreign language high school entrance examination as well as other high-level listening tests. It contains three training books, which allow students to practice multiple choice questions and various topics, words, and expressions, and it also contains three books that are very similar to the actual listening tests for foreign language high schools.

As the topics covered on listening tests are becoming more and more varied, this <Listen to the MAX 1~3> covers a wide range of topics and expressions. Students can learn the essential phrases and sentences they need to understand the passages on each topic. As they study from book 1 to book 3, they will experience longer and more complicated listening passages, and they can get used to the various styles of questions in each book.

Also, by solving the problems and filling in the blanks in the Dictation Tests section, they can repeatedly check what they heard and see if they understood properly. This will help students improve their comprehension and concentration on the long and high-speed recordings on the listening tests.

We hope that students who study with this series of books will be confident and successful when taking a foreign language high school entrance exam or other high-level listening tests so that they will be able to assure themselves of a future with more chances and potential.

How to Use this Book

Key Expressions

This part is designed to prepare you for the key expressions the unit covers. You will be given several exercises about useful words and phrases and will learn their applications in the sentences or dialogues.

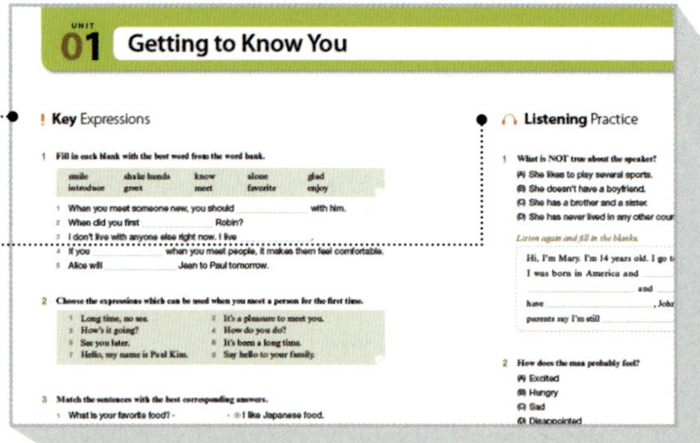

Listening Practice

In this part, you'll be given two short passages(a conversation and a monologue). The multiple choice exercise for each passage will be good practice before you get used to longer passages with complicated questions.

You can confirm your understanding of the pa -ssages by filling in the blanks after listening a second time.

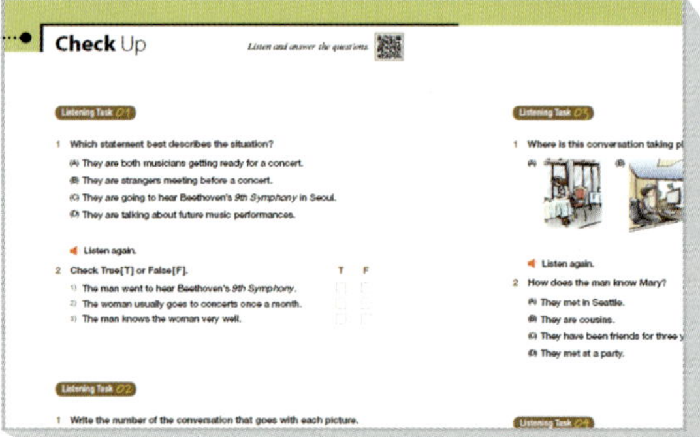

Check Up

You'll be given longer and more complicated passages here. For the passages with multiple questions, the passage will be repeated to allow you to understand it better.

Listening Test

This part gives you a chance to experience 8 passages that are similar to the actual listening test. The topics are similar to those on the actual test, as are the questions.

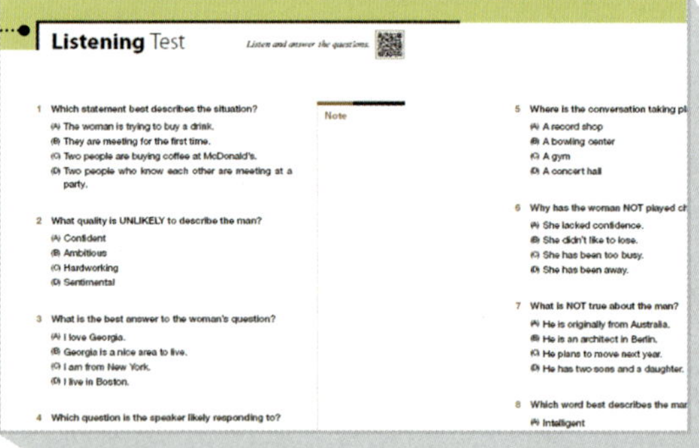

Dictation Test

In this part of the book, you will hear those 8 passages which you practiced in the Listening Test section. You can check to see if you can write exactly what you hear.

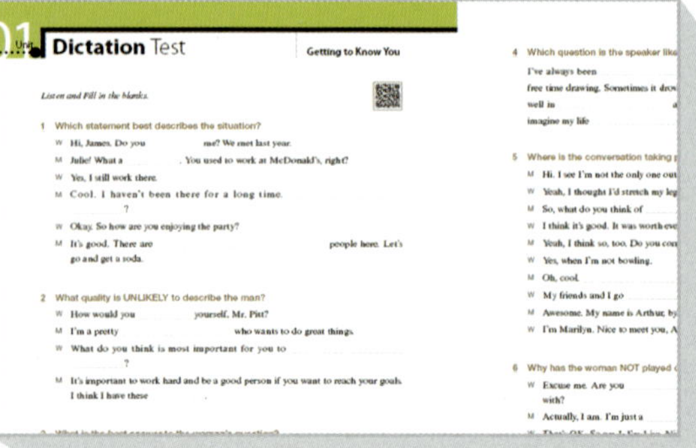

Contents

! Key Expressions

1 **Fill in each blank with the best word from the word bank.**

smile	shake hands	know	alone	glad
introduce	greet	meet	favorite	enjoy

1   When you meet someone new, you should _________________ with him.

2   When did you first _________________ Robin?

3   I don't live with anyone else right now. I live _________________.

4   If you _________________ when you meet people, it makes them feel comfortable.

5   Alice will _________________ Jean to Paul tomorrow.

2 **Choose the expressions which can be used when you meet a person for the first time.**

1 Long time, no see.	2 It's a pleasure to meet you.
3 How's it going?	4 How do you do?
5 See you later.	6 It's been a long time.
7 Hello, my name is Paul Kim.	8 Say hello to your family.

3 **Match the sentences with the best corresponding answers.**

1   What is your favorite food? •   • ⓐ I like Japanese food.

2   Hello, my name is Jane. •   • ⓑ Good to meet you. My name is Jane.

3   Hey, what's up? •   • ⓒ Hi, Jane. I'm Jason.

4   Hi, I'm Hideo. •   • ⓓ Oh, yeah. We have met. How are you?

5   Where are you from? •   • ⓔ Nothing much.

6   How do you know Alan? •   • ⓕ We were at college together.

7   Tim, have you met Paul? •   • ⓖ Actually, I am from Boston.
Paul, this is Tim.

 Listening Practice

1 **What is NOT true about the speaker?**

(A) She likes to play several sports.

(B) She doesn't have a boyfriend.

(C) She has a brother and a sister.

(D) She has never lived in any other countries.

Listen again and fill in the blanks.

Hi, I'm Mary. I'm 14 years old. I go to a school in Boston where I am in grade 9. I was born in America and _____________________ there all my life. I like _____________________ and _____________ as well as some other games. I have _____________________, John and Paul. I have lots of good friends, but my parents say I'm still _____________________ to date.

2 **How does the man probably feel?**

(A) Excited

(B) Hungry

(C) Sad

(D) Disappointed

Listen again and fill in the blanks.

W1 Sally, _________________ my friend Pete. We are in the English club together.

W2 Hi, Pete. Are you waiting for a table, too?

M Actually, I'm _________________ my friends. We're _________________ meet here.

W2 Really? Well, I hope they'll get here soon.

M I hope so, too. I _________________ all day.

Check Up

Listening Task 01

1 Which statement best describes the situation?

(A) They are both musicians getting ready for a concert.

(B) They are strangers meeting before a concert.

(C) They are going to hear Beethoven's *9th Symphony* in Seoul.

(D) They are talking about future music performances.

🔊 **Listen again.**

2 Check True[T] or False[F].   T   F

1) The man went to hear Beethoven's *9th Symphony*.

2) The woman usually goes to concerts once a month.

3) The man knows the woman very well.

Listening Task 02

1 Write the number of the conversation that goes with each picture.

1)

[   ]

2)

[   ]

3)

[   ]

1 Where is this conversation taking place?

(A)  (B)  (C)  (D) 

🔊 Listen again.

2 How does the man know Mary?

(A) They met in Seattle.

(B) They are cousins.

(C) They have been friends for three years.

(D) They met at a party.

1 What did the man NOT enjoy doing in Hawaii?

(A) Hanging out with his friends

(B) Swimming in the ocean

(C) Surfing at the beach

(D) Shopping at Waikiki

Listening Test

1 Which statement best describes the situation?

(A) The woman is trying to buy a drink.

(B) They are meeting for the first time.

(C) Two people are buying coffee at McDonald's.

(D) Two people who know each other are meeting at a party.

2 What quality is UNLIKELY to describe the man?

(A) Confident

(B) Ambitious

(C) Hardworking

(D) Sentimental

3 What is the best answer to the woman's question?

(A) I love Georgia.

(B) Georgia is a nice area to live.

(C) I am from New York.

(D) I live in Boston.

4 Which question is the speaker likely responding to?

(A) Why do you like art?

(B) What was your major?

(C) What made you become an artist?

(D) Who is your favorite artist?

Note

5 **Where is the conversation taking place?**

(A) A record shop

(B) A bowling center

(C) A gym

(D) A concert hall

6 **Why has the woman NOT played chess lately?**

(A) She lacked confidence.

(B) She didn't like to lose.

(C) She has been too busy.

(D) She has been away.

7 **What is NOT true about the man?**

(A) He is originally from Australia.

(B) He is an architect in Berlin.

(C) He plans to move next year.

(D) He has two sons and a daughter.

8 **Which word best describes the man?**

(A) Intelligent

(B) Unsure

(C) Unlucky

(D) Enthusiastic

Note

❗ **Key** Expressions

1 **Fill in each blank with the best word from the word bank.**

| skill | umpire | dribble | goal | gold medal |
| penalty kick | score | tournament | court | tackle |

1 The chief ________________ called, "Foul ball!"

2 The ________________ is five to zero in our favor.

3 He won a ________________ at the 2004 Olympic games.

4 The referee gave them a ________________ for the severe foul.

5 You should know how to pass, shoot, and ________________ the ball in basketball.

2 **Find the words related to each picture below.**

| serve | ground | court | assist | racket |
| bat | diamond | strike | the first half | shoot |

1 ________________
   ____
   ____

2 ________________
   ____
   ____

3 **Match the sentences with the best corresponding answers.**

1 How often do you go to baseball games? •   • ⓐ No, but I enjoy watching it.

2 Do you play on any teams? •   • ⓑ I'm fond of Manchester United.

3 What's your favorite soccer team? •   • ⓒ I jog every morning.

4 What do you do for exercise? •   • ⓓ About once a month.

5 Do you like wrestling? •   • ⓔ Yes, I'm a member of the basketball team.

6 Have you ever tried snowboarding? •   • ⓕ Yes, it was so exciting.

7 What's the most popular sport in your country? •   • ⓖ Definitely soccer.

🎧 **Listening** Practice

1   **Which sport does the man describe?**

(A) Cricket

(B) Tennis

(C) Soccer

(D) Badminton

Listen again and fill in the blanks.

> The basic rules of this game are _______________________________. There are
> _______________________ playing against each other. Each team must try to get control
> of the ball and _______________________ the other team's net. Whoever
> kicks the most balls into the net _______________________. The players
> may not touch the ball _______________________.

2   **What is NOT true about the conversation?**

(A) They are talking about a baseball game.

(B) The man expects the Yankees to win the game.

(C) The man believes the Dodgers deserved to win last year.

(D) They have the same opinion on the winner of the game.

Listen again and fill in the blanks.

> W   Hey, Jim. _______________________ about tonight's game?
>
> M   I think the New York Yankees _______________________ to the LA Dodgers
> _______________________.
>
> W   Me, too. I think the Dodgers will _______________________ the World Series.
>
> M   Actually, they should have won last year, but their best pitcher was out with an
> injury during the playoffs.
>
> W   Yeah. _______________________.

Check Up

Listening Task 01

1 **What is the man talking about?**

(A) His new hobby

(B) The reason he likes golf

(C) How to hit a golf ball

(D) The reason he plays golf

🔊 **Listen again.**

2 **Which statement shows his feeling about his golf ability?**

(A) He is improving rapidly.

(B) He is improving, but not quickly.

(C) He will never be a good golfer.

(D) He is a naturally good golfer.

Listening Task 02

1 **Write the number of the talk that goes with each picture.**

1) 
[   ]

2) 
[   ]

3) 
[   ]

Listening Task 03

1 **How does the fans' noise affect the player?**

(A) She doesn't hear them at all.

(B) She thinks they are too noisy.

(C) They sometimes encourage her.

(D) They make her lose focus.

🔊 **Listen again.**

2 **What is NOT true about the conversation?**

(A) The fans' cheering can affect her performance.

(B) The woman mostly doesn't hear the crowd.

(C) The woman isn't superstitious at all.

(D) The woman listens to music before playing.

Listening Task 04

1 **What does the man DISLIKE about sports such as soccer and baseball?**

(A) He has to play with a friend.

(B) He has to compete with other people.

(C) He cannot play early in the morning.

(D) His legs will hurt afterwards.

Listening Test

Listen and answer the questions.

1 What is true about the speaker?

(A) He hates basketball, but he is a good player.

(B) He loves basketball, but he is a bad player.

(C) He likes basketball but doesn't think he's a good player.

(D) He hates basketball, and his team thinks he's a bad player.

2 What is true about the conversation?

	Popular sports in the UK	Popular sports in Korea
(A)	Boxing	Baseball
(B)	Boxing	Boxing
(C)	Soccer	Baseball
(D)	Soccer	Boxing

3 What does the speaker think will happen?

(A) The Lions will have a hard time winning.

(B) The Lions will not be able to win.

(C) The Lions have a chance to win this game.

(D) The Lions have talent, but it will be too difficult to win.

4 How did the man feel about the game?

(A) It was outstanding.

(B) It wasn't interesting until the end.

(C) The end of it was a shame.

(D) No one played very well.

5 What is the speaker talking about?

(A) How watching sports is boring

(B) People who watch sports too much

(C) The problem with sports channels

(D) What he enjoys doing with his friends

6 How many goals did their team score during the second half of the match?

(A) One

(B) Five

(C) Seven

(D) None

7 What is true about the talk?

(A) Hong Man does not play his original sport.

(B) Hong Man is the biggest man in Korea.

(C) Hong Man created new interest in ssireum.

(D) Training is more important to Hong Man than the match.

8 Why does the man say that he had better start playing properly?

(A) He thinks he is playing badly.

(B) He does not want the woman to win the match.

(C) He is not enjoying the game.

(D) He has not been practicing.

Note

! **Key** Expressions

1   **Fill in each blank with the best word from the word bank.**

| residence | hold on | | wrong number | answer | hang up |
| contact | take a message | | text message | call center | receiver |

1   Is this Mr. Kim's _________________?

2   I'm afraid he's out at the moment. May I _________________?

3   Is there somebody we can _________________ in an emergency?

4   Don't _________________. I still have something to tell you.

5   Sorry, but you called the _________________.

2   **Match each situation with the correct expression.**

1   The volume is too low   •   • ⓐ "Hold on, please!"

2   Put through to someone else   •   • ⓑ "The number is no longer in service."

3   Another caller is on the line   •   • ⓒ "I can hardly hear you!"

4   Cell phone is beyond service range •   • ⓓ "The signal is too week."

5   The phone number has changed   •   • ⓔ "I'm sorry. This line is busy."

3   **Match the sentences with the best corresponding answers.**

1   Any messages for me?   •   • ⓐ I think you've got the wrong number.

2   Could you please call me back?   •   • ⓑ Of course. Go ahead.

3   Isn't this 523-6397?   •   • ⓒ Thank you. It's very important.

4   I'll make sure he gets the message. •   • ⓓ Yes, there is one from Mark.

5   Let me repeat that just to be sure.   •   • ⓔ Okay, I'll call back later.

6   Who's calling please?   •   • ⓕ It's Peter.

7   Sorry, the person you've called is not available.   •   • ⓖ OK. When is a good time?

 **Listening** Practice

1   **What is NOT true about the talk?**

(A) Mark called Chris.

(B) Chris is not available to talk on the phone.

(C) Mark is inviting Chris to the amusement park.

(D) Mark will call again to get an answer.

Listen again and fill in the blanks.

> Hello, Chris. ________________ Mark. I ________________ to ask if you can join us this weekend. My sister and I are going to the amusement park, and we have four tickets. You can ____________ your little brother if you want. Anyway, give me a phone call ________________ you listen to this message! Bye!

2   **What will the man probably say next?**

(A) Well, it's big and brown. My name is on the inside.

(B) I think I left it on the seat.

(C) The woman next to me was talking, and I got confused.

(D) Never mind. I'll find it myself.

Listen again and fill in the blanks.

> W   ____________. City Subway Lost and Found. ________________?
>
> M   Hi, I lost my bag today at City Hall Subway Station. I ________________ know if someone found it.
>
> W   OK, ________________ describe it for me?
>
> M   ________________________________

Check Up

Listening Task *01*

1   Why does the woman probably ask the man to hold on?

(A) She is angry because they cannot have lunch.

(B) She is busy because she is having lunch.

(C) She is checking her diary to see if she is free.

(D) She is asking her father whether she can go out in the evening.

🔊 **Listen again.**

2   When will they probably meet?

(A) After lunch

(B) In the evening at 6 p.m.

(C) In the evening at 7 p.m.

(D) The next day at lunchtime

Listening Task *02*

1   Check True[T] or False[F].

		T	F
1)	The woman wants a small pizza with extra cheese and sausage.	☐	☐
2)	She will have the pizza in fifteen minutes.	☐	☐
3)	They will deliver her pizza.	☐	☐

Listening Task *03*

1 **Why does the woman think she has the correct number?**

(A) She is from Canada.

(B) She looked up the code herself.

(C) She has called the number before.

(D) She worked as an operator before.

🔊 **Listen again.**

2 **Check True[T] or False[F].**   T   F

1) There is no extra charge if the operator puts her call through.   ☐   ☐

2) The operator thinks that the woman has the wrong city code.   ☐   ☐

3) The operator is about to put her call through.   ☐   ☐

Listening Task *04*

1 **What is the man going to get next time?**

(A) More charges

(B) An itemized bill

(C) The man's file

(D) A new phone number

Test

Listen and answer the questions.

1 **What will the woman probably say next?**

(A) Terrific. I will see you then.

(B) I knew you would like that.

(C) Sorry to hear that.

(D) I don't have a test.

2 **What is the correct information according to the conversation?**

	Arriving time	Number of people
(A)	6	6
(B)	6	7
(C)	7	6
(D)	7	7

3 **Why does the man ask the woman where Marvin is?**

(A) He wants to visit Marvin.

(B) He urgently needs to speak to Marvin.

(C) He thinks that Marvin is in danger.

(D) He is a good friend of Marvin's.

4 **How many calls did she make today?**

(A) 5

(B) 6

(C) 7

(D) 8

Note

5 **Why is the man calling?**

(A) He wants to help Anna out.

(B) He needs to get his book back from her.

(C) He is asking for help for his assignment.

(D) He is busy and wants some help.

6 **Which question does the talk try to answer?**

(A) How do you meet your old friends?

(B) How do you relax with your old friends?

(C) Why do you prefer calling your friends to meeting them?

(D) Why do you meet your friends in a coffee shop?

7 **What is a reason for having voicemail?**

(A) To send messages to an annoying friend

(B) To avoid talking directly to people

(C) To talk to your mother

(D) To avoid meeting other people

8 **Which statement agrees with the man's advice?**

(A) Her best friend doesn't like her that much.

(B) She should choose another best friend.

(C) She should hang up on her best friend.

(D) She should find some new friends.

Note

! **Key** Expressions

1 **Fill in each blank with the best word from the word bank.**

casual	fashionable	take off	out of fashion	in style
try on	hairstyle	magazines	influence	dress up

1 Do you like your new _______________?

2 You should _______________ when you go to parties.

3 No one wears this style anymore. It's gone _______________.

4 At every house I go to, I have to _______________ my shoes before entering.

5 Some people only wear new kinds of clothes. They like clothes that are _______________.

2 **Match each word with the picture describing it.**

briefs	trousers	pajamas	undershirt	suit

1 _______________   2 _______________   3 _______________   4 _______________   5 _______________

3 **Match the sentences with the best corresponding answers.**

1 Can I help you?   •   • ⓐ It's a small.

2 What size is the T-shirt?   •   • ⓑ It's nice, but I think it's too short.

3 Is it on sale?   •   • ⓒ At the department store.

4 Do you like this dress?   •   • ⓓ What's the problem?

5 I'd like to return these pants.   •   • ⓔ Yes. It's only five dollars.

6 Do you like wearing formal suits? •   • ⓕ No, I like casual styles.

7 Where do you usually buy your clothes?   •   • ⓖ Yes, I'm looking for children's clothes.

🎧 **Listening** Practice

1 **What is the speaker's father wearing?**

(A)  (B)  (C)  (D) 

Listen again and fill in the blanks.

My dad always ________________ funny clothes. Today, he has on a ________________ suit with a ________________________ shirt and a pink tie. He always makes sure that his shirt and tie ________________. His shoes are very shiny. I think my dad's clothes have ____.

2 **What is the problem?**

(A) Dad doesn't like Sally's skirt.

(B) Sally's friends wear skirts.

(C) Her father likes long skirts.

(D) Sally doesn't like pants.

Listen again and fill in the blanks.

M   Sally, you can't go to school ________________________________.

W   Why not, Dad?

M   It's ________________________________. It's very cold today.

W   But, Dad, my friends can wear skirts like this.

M   No, you have to ________________________________.

W   Okay. I will wear pants today.

Check Up

Listening Task 01

1   What is the main idea of the talk?

(A) Sometimes clothing goes out of fashion.

(B) Sometimes kids can wear their mother's clothing.

(C) Sometimes old fashions become popular again in the future.

(D) Bright colors are in fashion again.

🔊 Listen again.

2   Check True [T] or False [F].   T   F

1) Kids are not allowed to wear their parents' clothing.

2) Kids are wearing what their parents wore before.

3) Styles from the 1970s are not popular anymore.

Listening Task 02

1   Write the number of the talk that goes with each picture.

1)    2)    3) 

[   ]   [   ]   [   ]

1 Which word best describes the boy's feeling?

(A) Glad

(B) Upset

(C) Tired

(D) Happy

 Listen again.

2 What is the biggest difference between the speakers?

(A) The way they make holes in jeans

(B) The way they put jeans in the garbage

(C) The way they choose new jeans

(D) The way they see fashion

1 Which is the woman's wedding photo?

(A)  (B)  (C)  (D) 

1 Why does the boy NOT like the shirt?

(A) He doesn't like its color.

(B) He thinks he doesn't look good in it.

(C) Dark colors are too boring.

(D) He hates to wear the same colors as others.

2 What is the woman likely to buy?

(A)

(B)

(C)

(D)

3 What will the boy probably do after this conversation?

(A) Buy the expensive shirt.

(B) Buy the black shirt.

(C) Buy the blue shirt.

(D) Go to another store.

4 What is NOT true about Sally?

(A) She wants to be a shop owner.

(B) She learns about fashion from TV and magazines.

(C) She has many good clothes.

(D) She doesn't like her friends wearing her clothing.

Note

5 **Which question does the talk try to answer?**

(A) Why do actors and singers wear nice clothes?

(B) How do young people learn about fashion?

(C) Why do young people wear similar clothes?

(D) Why are young people interested in TV programs and movies?

Note

6 **What is true about the conversation?**

(A) The woman has a lot of money.

(B) The man likes nice clothes.

(C) The woman doesn't like nice clothes.

(D) Trendy clothes are expensive.

7 **What does the woman NOT want?**

(A) To wear makeup

(B) To look like a pop star

(C) To look like a circus clown

(D) To look nice

8 **Who is the woman they are talking about?**

! **Key** Expressions

1 **Fill in each blank with the best word from the word bank.**

greedy	ambitious	lazy	outgoing	imaginative
hardworking	generous	friendly	shy	bossy

1 It's difficult to talk to strangers when you are _______________.

2 If you tell others what to do all the time, they will call you _______________.

3 Gina always has lots of creative ideas; she is very _______________.

4 He's really _______________ and is always giving things away.

5 Amy loves being with people. She's incredibly _______________.

2 **Circle the words that describe positive characteristics.**

patient	honest	polite	nasty	offensive
enthusiastic	friendly	indolent	mean	vain

3 **Match the sentences with the best corresponding answers.**

1 Isn't that being a bit negative? •

2 Don't be so fussy. •

3 Careful with that quick temper. •

4 Don't be so shy. Everyone likes you. •

5 She's so absentminded these days. •

6 Are you a very sociable person? •

7 I think your son's a little stubborn. •

• ⓐ It's because she's very busy at work.

• ⓑ Sorry, but I'm not very outgoing.

• ⓒ But I want everything to be perfect.

• ⓓ Okay, I'll calm down.

• ⓔ No, I think it's being realistic.

• ⓕ Yes, he has a very strong will.

• ⓖ Yes, I love going out and meeting new people.

🎧 **Listening** Practice

1 **Which word does NOT describe the speaker's brother?**

(A) Conservative

(B) Hardworking

(C) Successful

(D) Helpful

Listen again and fill in the blanks.

I have an ________________. I really admire him. He's very ________________ and ________________. He never takes a vacation, but he doesn't ________________. Whenever he has free time, he helps his brother with his homework. Sometimes he ________________, too. I study hard so that I can be ________________ like him.

2 **Which statement best describes Carl?**

(A) He is very diligent.

(B) He isn't outgoing.

(C) He is not punctual.

(D) He is reliable.

Listen again and fill in the blanks.

M Carl said he'd be here ________________ ago.

W It seems like he forgot as usual.

M Well, he's got a lot on his plate. You know he is preparing for his ________________.

W Yeah, but this isn't ________________. He always does this. I'll give him ________________.

M I've already ________________. He's not answering.

Check Up

Listen and answer the questions.

Listening Task *01*

1 Which word best describes the speaker's personality?

(A) Outgoing

(B) Kind

(C) Talkative

(D) Timid

🔊 **Listen again.**

2 Check True[T] or False[F].

		T	F
1)	She doesn't like meeting new people.	☐	☐
2)	She has plenty to say to strangers.	☐	☐
3)	She finds it difficult to speak to people.	☐	☐

Listening Task *02*

1 How do they think Jeremy should change?

(A) He should talk more.

(B) He should become less self-centered.

(C) He should talk to everyone.

(D) He should become more self-centered.

Listening Task *03*

1 **What are the speakers talking about?**

(A) How to help their son become an important man

(B) How irresponsible their son is

(C) When they will fetch her letters from the office

(D) When the father will talk to his son

🔊 **Listen again.**

2 **Which statement is true about the conversation?**

(A) The man will speak to his son.

(B) The woman will speak to her son.

(C) The woman is going to cry.

(D) The woman isn't worried about her son.

Listening Task *04*

1 **What is it that shocks the speaker?**

(A) When people act in cunning ways

(B) Her friends' dishonesty

(C) When people she knows are kind-hearted

(D) When people she knows change how they behave

Listening Test

Note

1 Which word best describes Bill?

(A) Courageous

(B) Shy

(C) Arrogant

(D) Confident

2 Who is the speaker talking about?

(A) Her brother

(B) Her ex-husband

(C) Her current boyfriend

(D) Her new boyfriend

3 Which word best describes Tom?

(A) Impolite

(B) Honest

(C) Generous

(D) Unreliable

4 Which word does NOT describe Dan?

(A) Patient

(B) Lucky

(C) Helpful

(D) Dedicated

5 **What does the speaker feel for the coach?**

(A) Jealousy

(B) Affection

(C) Admiration

(D) Disappointment

6 **Why was the man surprised?**

(A) Because Steve made some noise

(B) Because Steve comes home late

(C) Because Steve is different from how he looks

(D) Because Steve doesn't care about other people

7 **What is true about the conversation?**

(A) The woman is serious.

(B) The woman is emotional.

(C) The man is considerate.

(D) The man is romantic.

8 **According to the speaker, what kind of person is Ben?**

(A) An ambitious person

(B) A humble person

(C) A quiet person

(D) An uncultured person

Note

06 Parties

! **Key** Expressions

1 **Fill in each blank with the best word from the word bank.**

variety	invitation	sense of humor	present	buffet
anniversary	celebrates	firework	guests	dance floor

1 This party is by ________________ only.

2 When is your parents' wedding ________________?

3 Treat ________________ and their spouses with respect.

4 His ________________ pleased everyone at the party.

5 Chuseok is a traditional Korean holiday that ________________ a good harvest.

2 **Match each party with its characteristics.**

1 potluck party •   • ⓐ A pregnant woman receives many presents.

2 surprise party •   • ⓑ A bride receives lots of gifts.

3 dinner party •   • ⓒ Participants are supposed to bring food.

4 bridal shower •   • ⓓ An even number of people are usually invited.

5 baby shower •   • ⓔ Someone at the party will be surprised.

3 **Match the sentences with the best corresponding answers.**

1 It's a benefit dinner for cancer research. •   • ⓐ Yes. I already sent my RSVP.

2 Did you get the invitation? •   • ⓑ Thanks, I made them myself.

3 Does Tom know about the party? •   • ⓒ That's a good cause. I'll buy 2 tickets.

4 The decorations are very delicate. •   • ⓓ Of course not. It's a surprise.

5 What should I wear? •   • ⓔ Sure, why not?

6 Would you like to dance? •   • ⓕ Casual dress is okay.

7 Isn't the food fabulous? •   • ⓖ Incredible! Have you tried the oysters?

🎧 **Listening** Practice

__1__ **What is the main idea of the talk?**

(A) The speaker is introducing his new house.

(B) The speaker is talking about a party.

(C) The speaker is feeling really bored.

(D) The speaker is describing the rooftop.

Listen again and fill in the blanks.

_______________________________________ about last night at Jim's house. He prepared
a buffet, big fireworks, and even a live music band. On the rooftop, there was a
_______________. Isn't that _______________? You should have joined us. Some people
might say it's too _______________, but I feel my life seems so boring now!

__2__ **What is true about the conversation?**

(A) They are choosing between a café and a restaurant to have a party.

(B) They want to get noisy in the cafe.

(C) They want to go around the neighborhood.

(D) They are wondering if a restaurant is too fancy for a party.

Listen again and fill in the blanks.

M   Hey, Jane. Do you know any good place for my _______________________?

W   You mean like a _______________?

M   Not really. Somewhere _______________ and a little _______________.

W   I think any _______________________________ would be okay.

M   A café may be a _______________________. Actually, there's the Italian café on Main
Street. What do you think about it?

W   That's a good idea. They have two floors for _______________________. And they're
okay about people getting noisy.

Check Up

1 **What can be inferred about the party?**

(A) There were very few people at the party.

(B) The party was very boring.

(C) The party was perfect until the middle of it.

(D) Halfway through the party, many people left.

🔊 Listen again.

2 **What did NOT happen?**

(A) The heating system stopped working.

(B) Many people went to the party.

(C) About 50 people went on a journey.

(D) The evening was very busy.

1 **Write the number of the talk that goes with each picture.**

1)   2)   3)

[   ]   [   ]   [   ]

Listening Task *03*

1   **What food did the kids NOT have at the party?**

(A) Cake

(B) Ice cream

(C) Candy

(D) Soda

🔊 **Listen again.**

2   **What ruined the party?**

(A) The children did not have a good time.

(B) The weather was bad.

(C) There was no cake at the party.

(D) Her daughter was scared of the clown.

Listening Task *04*

1   **What is a fun place for businesspeople to make connections?**

(A) A business meeting

(B) A network

(C) A dinner party

(D) A coffee shop

Listening Test

Listen and answer the questions. 

1 **Why will the woman NOT be able to go to the party?**

(A) She is working the next day.

(B) She has no invitation.

(C) Her boss is very generous.

(D) She is working until 10 p.m.

2 **What will the man wear at the event?**

(A) 

(B) 

(C) 

(D) 

3 **What is the purpose of the talk?**

(A) To invite someone to a party

(B) To express thanks for a party invitation

(C) To talk about her favorite things

(D) To complain

4 **When did the speaker eat?**

(A) He ate at the beginning of the party.

(B) He ate all throughout the party.

(C) He ate at the end of the party.

(D) He didn't eat anything at all.

5 Why does the man say, "Be careful when living in a house on the coast"?

(A) He knows that she doesn't like the water.

(B) He thinks the oceans will rise from global warming.

(C) He prefers living in the mountains.

(D) Scientists have shown that living on the coast is dangerous.

6 What are the two things the women need before the prom?

(A) New hairstyles and partners

(B) A car and partners

(C) Jobs and partners

(D) Dresses and partners

7 Which sentence can go at the end of the talk?

(A) Therefore, you should enjoy an office party.

(B) Therefore, think of the office party as an extension of your business.

(C) Therefore, you should bring your family to the office party.

(D) Therefore, you can make friends at the office party.

8 Which food will NOT be eaten at the party?

(A) Snacks

(B) Salads

(C) Desserts from another country

(D) Traditional foods from the guests' own countries

Note

! Key Expressions

1 **Fill in each blank with the best word from the word bank.**

salad	appetizer	dessert	another cup	well-done
main dish	seasoning	ingredient	beverage	allergic

1 Could I have _______________ of coffee?

2 The _______________ was really fresh and crisp.

3 I am _______________ to seafood.

4 Roast beef is the _______________.

5 Would you like some ice cream for _______________?

2 **Choose the foods that vegetarians don't eat.**

roast turkey	a baked potato	strawberry jam	cucumbers
broiled salmon	a Caesar salad	roast pork	mushroom soup

3 **Match the sentences with the best corresponding answers.**

1 I won't have dessert. I'm too full. •　　• ⓐ Let's have it here. I'm not in a hurry.

2 Should we split the bill? •　　• ⓑ We'd like a table by the window, please.

3 Should we get it to go or eat it here? •　　• ⓒ How about a piece of cake or pie?

4 Where would you like to sit? •　　• ⓓ Me, too. That was a big dinner.

5 Could I get a refill on my drink? •　　• ⓔ No, I'll pay since it was my idea.

6 I would like some dessert. •　　• ⓕ Yes, I'll pour you some.

7 May I take your order? •　　• ⓖ Yes, I'd like some soup with a salad.

 **Listening** Practice

1   **What is NOT true about the speaker?**

(A) She traveled all over the world.

(B) She likes Europe the best.

(C) She wants to stay in Europe for the rest of her life.

(D) She loves French and German dishes best.

Listen again and fill in the blanks.

I'm Jane, a chef. I've _______________ all over the world to learn different _______________ techniques and dishes. Europe is my favorite place, and my favorite ethnic foods to prepare are _______________________________. Both foods are rich and filled with so many _______________.

2   **What is true about the conversation?**

(A) The two speakers both like French food.

(B) The man and woman are comparing their favorite Italian dishes.

(C) The woman loves spaghetti with chicken.

(D) The man prefers spaghetti with seafood.

Listen again and fill in the blanks.

M   What is your _______________________?

W   I love _______________ food. I'm a big fan of pasta.

M   What is your favorite dish then?

W   I love spaghetti with _______________________, especially shrimp.

M   I see. My favorite is spaghetti with roasted _______________.

W   That's _______________, too!

Check Up

Listen and answer the questions. 

1 What does the woman care about the most?

(A) The steak

(B) The salad

(C) The sour cream

(D) The dessert

🔊 Listen again.

2 Check True[T] or False[F].

		T	F
1)	The female customer wanted a medium-sized New York steak.	☐	☐
2)	She only wanted a little bit of sour cream on her potato.	☐	☐
3)	She also ordered a beverage.	☐	☐

1 What is NOT the reason the speaker dislikes this restaurant?

(A) The poor service

(B) The unimpressive food

(C) The high prices

(D) Its staff

Listening Task 03

1 **How did the woman's emotions change during the conversation?**

(A) Sad → Glad

(B) Uncomfortable → Satisfied

(C) Satisfied → Disappointed

(D) Disappointed → Excited

🔊 **Listen again.**

2 **What is true about the conversation?**

(A) The woman doesn't want to pay.

(B) The man wants the woman to pay.

(C) Both of them want to pay, but the man wins.

(D) The dinner was free.

Listening Task 04

1 **What is true about the conversation?**

(A) The woman thinks eating Chinese food in the morning is a good idea.

(B) The restaurant never closes.

(C) The food at the restaurant is expensive.

(D) They've never been to the restaurant.

Listening Test

Listen and answer the questions.

1 Which question is the speaker likely responding to?

(A) How do restaurants prepare their foods?

(B) What is a good restaurant?

(C) How can we find a successful restaurant?

(D) What makes a restaurant successful?

2 What best describes the situation in the picture?

(A)   (B)   (C)

3 What is the right order of the situation?

(A) ⓐ - ⓑ - ⓒ

(B) ⓑ - ⓐ - ⓒ

(C) ⓑ - ⓒ - ⓐ

(D) ⓒ - ⓑ - ⓐ

4 What is true about the conversation?

(A) The woman will get the shrimp dish.

(B) The man wants a piece of pie.

(C) The man will have the shrimp.

(D) The man thinks the woman has bad taste in food.

49

5 **What does the woman probably say next?**

(A) It is none of your business.

(B) You're welcome.

(C) No problem. The wait was worth it.

(D) I am glad to hear that, too.

6 **What is the main idea of the talk?**

(A) He hates working at the restaurant.

(B) He is good at his job.

(C) He learned responsibility from this job.

(D) He wants to work there for three more years.

7 **What was the reason she mentioned fish in her talk?**

(A) To explain why she became a vegetarian

(B) To describe how difficult it is to be a vegetarian

(C) To stress that she is a vegetarian

(D) To highlight that being on a meatless diet is a challenge

8 **What does the woman NOT ask about the restaurant?**

(A) Its location

(B) The service

(C) The quality of the food

(D) Its cleanliness

Note

! **Key** Expressions

1   **Fill in each blank with the best word from the word bank.**

go to a movie	concert	performance	sold out	plot
opening night	up-to-date	review	hanging out	front row

1   I always check online for the most _______________ movie information.

2   The show is so popular that the tickets have already _______________.

3   Can you follow the _______________ of this movie?

4   I don't want to sit in the _______________. It's too close.

5   If you like classical music, you shouldn't miss this _______________.

2   **Match each kind of movie with the best description on the right.**

1   romance •   • ⓐ A movie that tells a love story

2   horror •   • ⓑ A movie that tries to scare the audience

3   action •   • ⓒ A movie that tries to make people laugh

4   comedy •   • ⓓ A movie with a fast-moving story that is full of danger and excitement

3   **Match the sentences with the best corresponding answers.**

1   I got your ticket already. •   • ⓐ Wow. It must have been good.

2   We all clapped for about 10 minutes. •   • ⓑ Really? I haven't followed the awards for two years now.

3   Dramas are too boring these days. •   • ⓒ How about going to the river park?

4   The Oscars are on tonight. •   • ⓓ I usually go out with my friends.

5   What do you do on Friday nights? •   • ⓔ Yes, there's too much crying.

6   Which do you like better, seeing a movie or a play? •   • ⓕ I don't know. I like them both.

7   What do you have in mind for tomorrow's picnic? •   • ⓖ Thanks. When are we going?

🎧 **Listening** Practice

1 **What best describes how the boy is feeling now?**

(A) Angry

(B) Disappointed

(C) Excited

(D) Tired

Listen again and fill in the blanks.

> There is going to be a _________________ this Saturday night. I can't wait for it. My
> _________________ is going to be playing. I saved up _________________
> for a few months so that I could buy _________________. My father is going to take
> my best friend and me to the hall. I have all of the group's CDs, but this is the first
> concert for me to go to. This is going to be _____________.

2 **What is the father likely to say at the end?**

(A) I liked the movie.

(B) The last part was good.

(C) It was better than average.

(D) No, it was okay.

Listen again and fill in the blanks.

> W So, how did you enjoy _____________________, Dad?
>
> M I thought it was really ___________. And the soundtrack was pretty good, too.
>
> W Yeah, I agree. And I really loved the chase scenes. They seemed to be totally
> _________________.
>
> M I thought that the _________________ were well done, too.
>
> W Exactly. What did you think of the _________________?
>
> M _________________.

Check Up

Listening Task 01

1 Which music does the speaker NOT like?

(A) Rap

(B) Pop

(C) Rock

(D) Classical

🔊 Listen again.

2 What is NOT mentioned in the talk?

(A) Why he likes listening to music

(B) His favorite kinds of music

(C) The reason he listens to classical music

(D) The reason he dislikes rap music

Listening Task 02

1 Write the number of the talk that goes with each picture.

1)

[   ]

2)

[   ]

3)

[   ]

Listening Task 03

1   Why did the woman stay up all night?

(A) She wasn't tired.

(B) The next day was a holiday.

(C) She had to go to school that day.

(D) She was reading a book.

🔊 Listen again.

2   What is the best description of the woman?

(A) A couch potato

(B) A walking dictionary

(C) A bookworm

(D) An athlete

Listening Task 04

1   What were the speakers doing before going out in the snow?

(A) They were sleeping.

(B) They were eating dinner.

(C) They were watching television.

(D) They were taking pictures.

Listening Test

Listen and answer the questions.

1 **What will the speakers probably do after the conversation?**

(A) Take a ride on the flume

(B) Wait for the next roller coaster

(C) Get in line for the bumper cars

(D) Try to go on all of the rides

2 **Why will the man see the show at 8:30 p.m.?**

(A) The comedy show at 6 p.m. is not so good.

(B) He does not want to sit in the back at the 6 p.m. show.

(C) He won't be on time for the 6 p.m. show.

(D) The show at 8:30 p.m. is better.

3 **How did the woman feel about the movie?**

(A) Pleased

(B) Excited

(C) Bored

(D) Scared

4 **What is the woman talking about?**

(A) How she forgot to pay for the play

(B) A plan to go and see a play

(C) A play she is watching

(D) A good play to see

Note

5 **What will they do together on Saturday?**

(A) They will go to the beach.

(B) They will go to a music concert in the park.

(C) They will watch the baseball game.

(D) They will have lunch in the park.

6 **How does the man feel about the program?**

(A) He wants to see it again.

(B) He's tired of seeing it.

(C) He thinks it's funny.

(D) He thinks it is interesting.

7 **What does the woman NOT want?**

(A)  (B) 

(C)  (D) 

8 **How much does the woman have to pay?**

(A) Three dollars

(B) Seven dollars

(C) Eight dollars

(D) Ten dollars

Note

09 Transportation

! **Key** Expressions

1   **Fill in each blank with the best word from the word bank.**

traffic jam	speeding	driver's license	seatbelt	layover
accident	flat tire	fee	highway	intersection

1   The man is quickly crossing the ________________.

2   I got a ticket for ________________ on the way home.

3   I was caught in a rush hour ________________.

4   Please fasten your ________________.

5   I got in an ________________ yesterday, but I didn't get hurt at all.

2   **Choose the phrase you need to explain the way to the school on the map.**

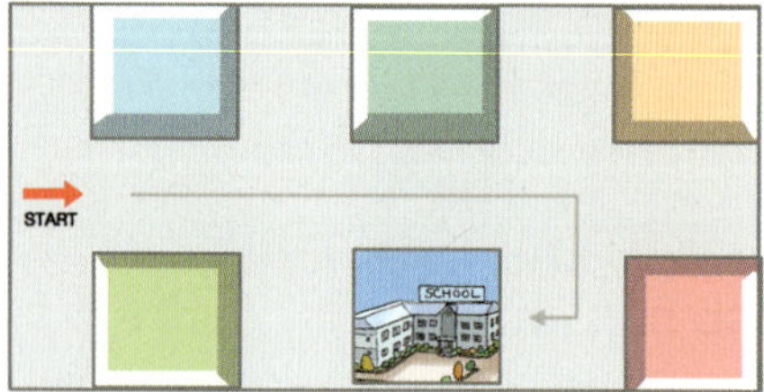

go two blocks	turn left	turn right
on the corner	go straight	on your right
on your left	the opposite side	

3   **Match the sentences with the best corresponding answers.**

1   How much is the ticket?   •   • ⓐ It should be half an hour by bus.

2   How many stops before we get off?   •   • ⓑ About 900 won.

3   How do I get to the library from here? •   • ⓒ Not on this street.

4   I'm sorry I was late.   •   • ⓓ You have to take Bus No. 93.

5   Is there a parking space?   •   • ⓔ We get off at the seventh stop.

6   Where's the bus stop?   •   • ⓕ Over there by the corner.

7   How long does it take from Itaewon •   • ⓖ That's okay. There was a traffic
    to the airport?   jam today.

 Listening Practice

1 **What is the main topic of the talk?**

(A) How to take a bus to school

(B) How to spend his time while going to school

(C) Why he listens to audio books

(D) How to learn a new language

Listen again and fill in the blanks.

Hi, I'm James Park. I'm in my senior year of ___________ . I've been going to school ___________ for three years. My house is an hour away from school. When I was younger, I ___________ talk with my friends all the time. But these days, I have to study. It's also the ___________ to listen to audio books. I listen to books about history or politics, and I'm even learning ___________ .

2 **What is true about the conversation?**

(A) They are discussing how to get to their destination.

(B) The man says that the subway is worse than the bus.

(C) The restaurant is within walking distance.

(D) The woman likes the subway.

Listen again and fill in the blanks.

M   How should we go to the ___________?

W   I don't know. Where is it again?

M   It's ___________.

W   Well, then, we can get there by ___________.

M   Let's take the subway. ___________.

W   True, but I like the bus better since you can see where you are.

M   Well, it's ___________.

Check Up

Listen and answer the questions.

1   How does the woman feel about her car?

(A) Satisfied

(B) Indifferent

(C) Sad

(D) Disgusted

🔊 **Listen again.**

2   The man is surprised by the car because of its…

(A) size

(B) common color

(C) unusual color

(D) type

1   What best describes how the man is feeling?

(A) Disappointed

(B) Frustrated

(C) Angry

(D) Desperate

Listening Task 03

1 What is true about the conversation?

(A) They have a flat tire, and they have to call a tow truck.

(B) The man will change the tire by himself.

(C) The woman and man will change the flat tire together.

(D) The spare tire is flat.

🔊 Listen again.

2 Why is the woman going to help the man?

(A) Because she wants to

(B) Because she is good at it

(C) Because then things will get done faster

(D) Because she is getting paid

Listening Task 04

1 What is the man going to do?

(A) He will drive home from work.

(B) He will start taking the subway.

(C) He will wait in traffic for a long time.

(D) He will stay at work until the evening.

Listening Test

Listen and answer the questions.

1 What is the main idea of the talk?

(A) George is preparing for his driver's license test.

(B) He is having trouble with parking.

(C) The parking part of the test is worth less than twenty-five percent.

(D) He is a twenty-year-old man.

2 What is the total cost of the tickets to Seoul Land?

(A) Ten thousand won

(B) Twenty thousand won

(C) Fifteen thousand won

(D) Fifty thousand won

3 What did the woman NOT do on the airplane?

(A)  (B) 

(C)  (D) 

4 Where is the conversation taking place?

(A) A train station

(B) A bus station

(C) A gas station

(D) A movie theater

Note

5 **Why does the woman think cards are better?**

(A) Because they're lighter to carry around

(B) Because they're cheaper and can be used on buses

(C) Because she owns the card company

(D) Because she hates tickets

6 **Which is NOT true about the conversation?**

(A) The man doesn't know where the Coex Mall is.

(B) Samsung Station is on the green line, which is line number 2.

(C) The woman says the trip will last more than fifty minutes.

(D) They are at Sadang Station.

7 **Which question is the talk responding to?**

(A) What is the cheapest form of transportation?

(B) What is the best form of transportation in big cities?

(C) What is a better way to travel than buses and planes?

(D) What is the safest form of transportation?

8 **How many flights will the man take before he arrives in Boston?**

(A) Two

(B) Three

(C) Four

(D) Five

Note

! **Key** Expressions

1 **Fill in each blank with the best word from the word bank.**

outdoor	exercise	surfing the Internet	comic books	garden
collect	interests	hobby	concert	draw

1 I love doing ________________ activities like hiking, camping, and fishing.

2 We grow vegetables in the ________________.

3 I love to read novels, ________________, and poetry.

4 Nowadays, many young people seem to prefer ________________ to reading books.

5 Recently, I've found a new ________________.

2 **Choose the activities you do in your free time.**

gardening	cooking	playing in a band
hiking	surfing the Internet	watching movies
shopping	playing computer games	listening to music
reading books	exercising	chatting

3 **Match the sentences with the best corresponding answers.**

1 Do you like cooking? • • ⓐ Yes, he plays golf.

2 What kind of magazines do you like? • • ⓑ I've never tried it.

3 Do you like playing soccer? • • ⓒ I like *News Weekly*.

4 Does your father have a hobby? • • ⓓ I usually read books.

5 What do you do in your free time? • • ⓔ No, I don't like sports.

6 My friend has the same hobby as I do. • • ⓕ That's great.

7 Do you prefer outdoor activities • • ⓖ Definitely the latter.
   or indoor activities?

🎧 **Listening** Practice

1 **What is the topic of the talk?**

(A) How to relax

(B) Ways to learn a new hobby

(C) The benefits of having a hobby

(D) Why you should meet new people

Listen again and fill in the blanks.

Most people have some sort of ______________. Hobbies help people to relax and give them opportunities to meet ______________________. They can also give people things to talk about. In addition, ______________ something new is good for keeping the mind ____________. There are many ______________________ to develop a hobby that interests you.

2 **What does the man think about the woman's new hobby?**

(A) He wants the same hobby, too.

(B) He thinks it's not proper for her to do.

(C) He thinks it's too dangerous for himself.

(D) He is afraid of riding a motorbike.

Listen again and fill in the blanks.

W   I have a lot of ____________________ these days.

M   So, what are you going to do?

W   I am thinking of __________________ a motorbike.

M   Oh yeah? Isn't it too ________________ for women?

W   I don't think so as long as I ________________.

Check Up

Listening Task 01

1 What is the speaker talking about?

(A) What she enjoys doing

(B) Why she can't do the things he likes

(C) Why she likes listening to music

(D) How she will become a great photographer

🔊 **Listen again.**

2 Check True[T] or False[F].

		T	F
1)	She doesn't like music.	☐	☐
2)	She wants to learn about photography.	☐	☐
3)	She can't afford a nice digital camera right now.	☐	☐

Listening Task 02

1 Why did the woman NOT want to go hiking?

(A) She is very busy at work.

(B) She enjoys climbing mountains more than hiking.

(C) She is out of shape.

(D) She doesn't know the man very well.

Listening Task 03

1 **What is "pretty scary" according to the conversation?**

(A) Skydiving

(B) The woman's brother

(C) Ordinary things

(D) Jumping again

🔊 **Listen again.**

2 **What can be inferred from the woman's last words?**

(A) She won't go skydiving with her brother.

(B) She doesn't enjoy exercise.

(C) She will definitely go skydiving with her brother.

(D) Her brother is not serious about skydiving.

Listening Task 04

1 **Why does the man NOT have a cat now?**

(A) He has other hobbies.

(B) His job keeps him busy.

(C) He already has many pets.

(D) He travels every week.

Listening Test

Listen and answer the questions.

1 Which of the following talks is about how to enjoy one's hobby with others?

(A)   (B)   (C)

2 Which statement best describes the situation?

(A) They are talking about Laurie's hobby.
(B) They are talking about money.
(C) The woman is asking to borrow some money.
(D) The man is looking for some old money.

3 According to the talk, how can you make money from your hobby?

(A) Collect stamps and sell them
(B) Teach other people how to do it
(C) Spend a little money on it
(D) Take up even more hobbies

4 Why will the man NOT give the woman flowers this year?

(A) He is not good at gardening.
(B) His garden is too new.
(C) His garden is too small.
(D) He just doesn't want to.

Note

5 **What can help you become good at DIY furniture making?**

(A) Learning from the experts

(B) The right materials

(C) Information on the Internet or in books

(D) Your neighbors

6 **What will the speakers do this weekend?**

(A) They will go shopping.

(B) They will go biking.

(C) They will go to the museum.

(D) They will see *Star Wars*.

7 **How much will the woman pay?**

(A) 60 dollars

(B) 125 dollars

(C) 131 dollars

(D) 185 dollars

8 **What is one topic the workshop probably will NOT talk about?**

(A) Differences between men and women's hobbies

(B) What an "interest" is

(C) Common hobbies worldwide

(D) How to develop good language habits

Note

❗ **Key** Expressions

1 **Fill in each blank with the best word from the word bank.**

historic	snake park	festival	hot springs	amusement park
lake	gallery	ski resort	museum	zoo

1 My son enjoys going on the rides at the _______________.

2 I took many photographs of the elephants and monkeys at the _______________.

3 Let's take a boat ride across the _______________ this afternoon.

4 I sometimes go to the _______________ for relaxation.

5 My daughter was frightened at the _______________.

2 **What do you do when you visit a new city? Choose from the phrases below.**

visit museums	visit churches or temples	take a bus tour
try the local food	go to the zoo	buy souvenirs
go shopping	attend local cultural events	

3 **Match the sentences with the best corresponding answers.**

1 Let's relax in one of the pools. •
2 I went to the museum yesterday • with my boyfriend.
3 I have two free passes for the • amusement park.
4 Why don't we go to the cinema? •
5 My favorite activity is to ride my • bicycle in the park.
6 How much is the entrance fee? •
7 Shall we climb the mountain? •

• ⓐ Sounds charming.
• ⓑ There are too many people waiting.
• ⓒ But there are too many other cyclists there in summer.
• ⓓ I'd love to. I'll book the tickets.
• ⓔ Can I go there with you? I love the rides.
• ⓕ I think it is ten dollars for children.
• ⓖ Sure, I want to see the view from the top.

🎧 **Listening** Practice

1 **What is the talk about?**

(A) One person's trip to an amusement park

(B) The story of the first amusement park

(C) A description of an amusement park

(D) Why amusement parks are so much fun

Listen again and fill in the blanks.

> This is a _______________________________ for children and adults. Customers can go
> on lots of different rides at this place. The most exciting ride for most people is the
> _______________. This goes up and down very fast and _______________ even makes
> loops. There are also other rides like bumper cars, the haunted house, and merry-go-
> rounds.

2 **What is true about the conversation?**

(A) The woman likes to go skiing.

(B) The man is very good at skiing.

(C) The man likes to take his family to the ski resort.

(D) The man does not really enjoy skiing.

Listen again and fill in the blanks.

> W _______________________ do you go to the ski resort?
>
> M In winter, I go almost every _______________________.
>
> W You must be really good at _______________________.
>
> M Not really. But it's very pretty in winter. My family enjoys walking in the snow.
>
> W Maybe I will take my family to visit the ski resort _______________________.
>
> M You should go because they would really _______________________.

Check Up

Listening Task *01*

1 Which question is the speaker probably responding to?

(A) Why do you shop at department stores?

(B) What is your favorite place to shop?

(C) Can you tell me about the history of department stores?

(D) When was the last time you visited a department store?

🔊 Listen again.

2 Check True [T] or False [F].

		T	F
1)	Department stores had many different goods for sale.	☐	☐
2)	Other merchants liked the new department stores after all.	☐	☐
3)	Customers didn't like the new department stores.	☐	☐
4)	The department stores were more expensive than other stores.	☐	☐

Listening Task *02*

1 Write the number of the talk that goes with each picture.

1)

[   ]

2)

[   ]

3)

[   ]

Listening Task 03

1 **Why was the man NOT able to go up the tower?**

(A) He did not want to.

(B) He is afraid of heights.

(C) He had no film left in his camera.

(D) The weather was bad.

🔊 **Listen again.**

2 **What best describes how the man felt about seeing the Eiffel Tower?**

(A) He was very disappointed.

(B) He was surprised by how small it is.

(C) He was amazed by it.

(D) He was shocked by how huge it is.

Listening Task 04

1 **What is the topic of the conversation?**

(A) How to make an ice sculpture

(B) Famous events around the world

(C) Crowds at the ice festival

(D) Visiting the ice festival

Listening Test

Listen and answer the questions.

1 When will the speakers go to Seoul Tower?

(A) The following day

(B) In the afternoon

(C) The next week

(D) The day before the man leaves Korea

2 Why did the speaker mention pizza delivery cars?

(A) To show that pizza is popular in Hawaii

(B) To describe how to surf in Hawaii

(C) To show how strong Hawaii's surfing culture is

(D) To explain why surfing is popular in Hawaii

3 Jane is going to visit the Seoul Metro Museum this Friday with her parents and her three younger brothers. Two of her brothers are younger than 10 years old. How much will they pay altogether?

(A) 80 dollars

(B) 90 dollars

(C) 100 dollars

(D) 108 dollars

4 Why is it difficult to get a ticket for a game?

(A) The stadium is not big enough.

(B) It is too expensive.

(C) There are many season ticket holders.

(D) There are too many people around.

Note

5 **What does the man want the woman to take pictures of?**

(A) The beach in Cape Town

(B) The valley where they make wine

(C) The famous Table Mountain

(D) The hotel in Cape Town

6 **Why does the speaker say that this show isn't for those who get nervous very easily?**

(A) He's worried people may not like the show.

(B) He thinks people are getting tired of seeing it.

(C) He thinks the show may be overwhelming.

(D) He thinks the show is too loud.

7 **What is NOT true about the Inca Trail trek?**

(A) The course was built on rocks.

(B) You can experience an old market during the trek.

(C) A lot of people visit the place each year.

(D) You can experience the history of the Inca Empire.

8 **What is NOT true about the Great Wall of China?**

(A) It was built using machines 2,000 years ago.

(B) You are allowed to walk along the wall.

(C) It is one of the wonders of the world.

(D) It is almost 7,000 kilometers in length.

Note

12 Shopping

❗ Key Expressions

1   Fill in each blank with the best word from the word bank.

stop by	special	bargain	discount	impulse
deals	exchange	refund	shopping list	looking for

1   I'm _________________ a Father's Day gift.

2   You can _________________ this sweater for another one.

3   Credit cards can lead to _________________ spending.

4   It is so cheap that it's a real _________________.

5   This place usually has the best _________________.

2   Choose the correct category in the box for each group of words.

groceries	furniture	liquor	toys	clothing

1   shirt, pants, sweater, jacket –

2   chair, sofa, table, desk –

3   milk, eggs, bread, vegetables –

4   doll, blocks, train set, model airplane -

3   Match the sentences with the best corresponding answers.

1   May I help you with anything, sir? •

2   Do you accept credit cards? •

3   How much is this? •

4   Can I get a refund on this? •

5   Does it come with a warranty? •

6   Do you have a cheaper one? •

7   I'm inclined to buy something on impulse. •

• ⓐ Don't forget to make a shopping list.

• ⓑ Yes, if you still have the receipt.

• ⓒ I'm just looking, thank you.

• ⓓ Yes, for the first six months.

• ⓔ Yes, but only Visa and Master Card.

• ⓕ This one is a more reasonable price.

• ⓖ It's 25 dollars due to the 30 percent discount on all items in the store.

 **Listening** Practice

1 **What is the purpose of the talk?**

(A) To complain about the poor service in the mall

(B) To advertise K-Mart

(C) To explain how to find a K-Mart

(D) To introduce a good brand of shoes

Listen again and fill in the blanks.

> I love _____________________ at K−Mart. I can easily find some nice shoes from
> a reputable manufacturer for a _____________________________ there. K−Mart sells
> overstocked and out-of-season shoes, so its prices are generally ________________.
> Come to K−Mart, and get _____________________ on shoes.

2 **What is the topic of the conversation?**

(A) How to overcome a shopping problem

(B) How to buy jewelry

(C) The woman's shopping problem

(D) The place they are shopping at

Listen again and fill in the blanks.

> W Hey, Mike. I can't resist _____________________ beautiful jewelry.
>
> M So do you buy a lot of _____________________?
>
> W Yes. If I see something nice, I always imagine myself wearing it. Then I am not
>   satisfied until I buy it.
>
> M That sounds like an _____________________ habit.
>
> W I know. It is a kind of obsession, but I can't seem to _____________________.

Check Up

Listen and answer the questions.

1 Which question is the speaker likely responding to?

(A) When is a good time to shop in Hong Kong?

(B) What is the best method to shop in Hong Kong?

(C) What is the best place to go shopping overseas?

(D) What kinds of things can we buy in Hong Kong?

🔊 **Listen again.**

2 Check True[T] or False[F].   T   F

1) The old markets in Hong Kong provide excitement.

2) It is not easy to find an old market in Hong Kong.

3) There aren't many brand name stores in Hong Kong.

1 What is the woman trying to tell the man?

(A) She doesn't like shopping.

(B) She has changed.

(C) She doesn't need a new pair of shoes.

(D) She is too honest.

Listening Task *03*

1   **What was the reason the woman said, "No way"?**

(A) Because the man bought his CD player from K-Mart

(B) Because K-Mart doesn't have a wide selection

(C) Because Hi-Mart offers reasonable prices

(D) Because Hi-Mart doesn't have a wide selection

🔊 **Listen again.**

2   **What is true about the conversation?**

(A) The woman thinks it's better to pay more and get good quality.

(B) The woman has the same opinion as the man.

(C) The man regrets going to Hi-Mart.

(D) The man thinks there should be a discount on MP3 players.

Listening Task *04*

1   **Which sentence best shows what the speaker means?**

(A) She thinks Internet shopping is dangerous.

(B) She is trying to warn people against Internet shopping.

(C) She had a bad experience while doing Internet shopping.

(D) She enjoys Internet shopping but thinks people should be cautious.

Listen and answer the questions.

1 How much will the man pay?

(A) 80 dollars

(B) 120 dollars

(C) 108 dollars

(D) 90 dollars

2 Which statement best describes the situation?

(A) They are deciding where to shop today.

(B) The man is telling the woman where to shop.

(C) The woman is helping the man shop around campus.

(D) They are telling a new student how to shop.

3 What will the woman probably say next?

(A) Then, let's go to Lotte.

(B) Any other ideas?

(C) You won't be disappointed.

(D) No problem.

4 How does the man probably feel?

(A) Disappointed

(B) Embarrassed

(C) Angry

(D) Surprised

Note

5 **What will the woman probably do next?**

(A) She will buy the camera at the current store.

(B) She will buy a new handbag.

(C) She will go to the store down the road.

(D) She will start saving.

6 **What sort of computer does the speaker want?**

(A) A $1,000 desktop computer

(B) A $750 laptop computer

(C) A $750 desktop computer

(D) A $1,000 laptop computer

7 **What will Bill probably buy for Emily's birthday?**

(A)

(B)

(C)

(D)

8 **What is NOT recommended by the speaker?**

(A) To shop at places where the prices are clearly marked

(B) To compare prices

(C) To understand what you are buying

(D) To buy goods when the prices are discounted

Note

13 Traveling

! **Key** Expressions

1   **Fill in each blank with the best word from the word bank.**

travel agent	currency	vacation	plane tickets	cruise
documents	paradise	guidebook	destination	backpack

1   Beautiful white, sandy beaches with blue water. Welcome to ________________.

2   Before I go on ________________, I always plan my trip thoroughly.

3   Your adventures might include a ________________ to Antarctica.

4   Any good ________________ can handle your travel arrangements.

5   First, you need to buy a ticket to your ________________.

2   **Circle the things that you need while traveling.**

honeymoon	pants	lantern	business trip	backpack
tent	reservation	map	socks	passport

3   **Match the sentences with the best corresponding answers.**

1   What's your favorite vacation spot? •   • ⓐ How often do you go away?

2   I need to travel a lot for my job. •   • ⓑ Where did you go?

3   The train trip was terrible. •   • ⓒ I like traveling in the spring.

4   I went on a cruise this summer. •   • ⓓ Why? What happened?

5   Have you ever traveled abroad? •   • ⓔ I like Jeju Island the best.

6   What country would you like to visit someday? •   • ⓕ I'd like to visit Spain someday.

7   What's the best season to travel in Korea? •   • ⓖ Yes, I traveled through Europe last summer vacation.

🎧 **Listening** Practice

1 **What is NOT true about the talk?**

(A) She is going on vacation with her husband and kids.

(B) She is at home with her kids every day.

(C) She has not been on vacation with her family in thirteen years.

(D) Her husband likes traveling during his vacations.

Listen again and fill in the blanks.

________________________ is coming. I'm so excited. My family and I are going to Thailand for ________________________. This is our first vacation as a family in thirteen years. My husband is a businessman. He travels ________________________. When he takes a break, he wants to stay at home. But I stay home with the kids every day. It's so boring for me. I plan to go to the beach every day and ________________ with my family.

2 **Where is the conversation taking place?**

(A) A travel agency

(B) An airport

(C) A subway station

(D) A school

Listen again and fill in the blanks.

W How is the ________________ in England in __________?

M During the day, the ________________ is around 31 degrees Celsius, and at night, it's about 18.

W Okay. And what tours do you have?

M We offer trips from London to Liverpool, Manchester, and Oxford.

W What can we see in London?

M The main ________________ are Buckingham Palace and Big Ben.

Check Up

Listen and answer the questions. 

1 **What is the best title for the talk?**

(A) Ways to learn other cultures

(B) Good places to rest

(C) Good things about backpacking

(D) Ways to meet people from other cultures

🔊 Listen again.

2 **Check True[T] or False[F].**   T   F

1) Backpacking is inexpensive.

2) You can learn about backpacking in the classroom.

3) You can learn a new language while backpacking.

4) Backpackers can stay in youth hostels.

1 **Which continent has the man's father NEVER visited?**

(A) Asia

(B) North America

(C) Oceania

(D) Europe

1   Why does the woman say, "I can't believe it"?

(A) She is glad to have finally arrived.

(B) She thinks the hotel is worse than she had thought.

(C) She thinks they have had good luck.

(D) She didn't expect the hotel to have a swimming pool.

🔊 Listen again.

2   What is true about the conversation?

(A) The man and woman are pleased with their hotel.

(B) The man likes the beach view from their hotel.

(C) The woman is not pleased with their hotel.

(D) The man and woman are enjoying a joke together.

1   What is the man concerned about on his trip?

(A) Culture shock

(B) Security problems

(C) Too many tourists

(D) Communication

Listen and answer the questions.

1 What is the speaker talking about?

(A) How to choose a medically safe place

(B) How to make a medically safe trip

(C) How to use the medical facilities in foreign countries

(D) How to treat diseases in foreign countries

2 What will the woman probably do?

(A) Use a travel agency

(B) Plan everything herself

(C) Take a package tour

(D) Go somewhere else

3 What is the topic of the talk?

(A) The best time to travel

(B) How to travel alone conveniently

(C) What to ask your travel agent

(D) How to get lower prices

4 Which sentence best describes the situation?

(A) The woman took a wrong turn and got lost.

(B) The man gave the woman the wrong directions, so she is lost.

(C) The man is giving the woman directions to the information center.

(D) The woman is in trouble and needs to go to the police station.

Note

5 How does the man probably feel after his holiday?

(A) Excited

(B) Anxious

(C) Disappointed

(D) Exhausted

6 Where is the conversation taking place?

(A) At the airport

(B) At City Hall Station

(C) On a bus or subway

(D) At the airport shuttle bus station

7 What will the man and his family probably do for their vacation?

(A) They will find a place that has better weather than Portugal and Spain.

(B) He will ask his parents to choose a place to visit.

(C) They will go to Portugal and Spain for their vacation.

(D) They will visit a travel agency.

8 What was the most important thing for the speaker in choosing a cruise?

(A) Doing various activities

(B) Meeting new people

(C) The price

(D) Not being disturbed by other people

Note

! **Key** Expressions

1 **Fill in each blank with the best word from the word bank.**

separate	charge	includes	bed and breakfast	ocean view
cancel	situated	deposit	accommodation	porter

1 It is _________________ within easy reach of the stores and museums.

2 All rooms have _________________ lounging, sleeping, and dressing areas.

3 Tell me whether there is an extra _________________ for parking a car.

4 I'm afraid my plans have changed, so I have to _________________ my booking.

5 Is this kind of _________________ suitable for children?

2 **Fill in the blanks with the correct questions from the box below.**

ⓐ How are you paying for this?	ⓑ Do you have a reservation?
ⓒ Can I have your name, please?	ⓓ Hello. Can I help you?

A: 1 _________________________ B: Yes, I'd like to check in, please.

A: 2 _________________________ B: Yes, I do.

A: 3 _________________________ B: Certainly. It's Mr. Johnson.

A: That's a single room for two nights? B: Yes, that's right.

A: 4 _________________________ B: Cash, please.

A: Thanks. Here's your key. Room 5. B: Thank you very much.

3 **Match the sentences with the best corresponding answers.**

1 I have a reservation for tonight. •   • ⓐ We'd like a room with twin beds.

2 Is breakfast included? •   • ⓑ Just two nights.

3 The front desk staff was quite rude. •   • ⓒ Yes, it is.

4 What kind of room do you prefer? •   • ⓓ I'll just check our bookings.

5 My room is too small. •   • ⓔ You should tell the manager.

6 How long will you be staying? •   • ⓕ Would you like to move to another room?

🎧 **Listening** Practice

1 **What is the speaker talking about?**

(A) How to make a hotel reservation

(B) New ways to make hotel reservations

(C) The advantages of booking a hotel over the phone

(D) How to choose a good hotel

Listen again and fill in the blanks.

> You can make hotel ________________________ in several ways. The easiest ways are through the phone and over ________________________. These days, the Internet is becoming more and more important for hotel ________________________. There are a number of ________________ to using the Internet, such as reduced costs.

2 **What is the woman doing?**

(A) She is booking a room.

(B) She is complaining about her room.

(C) She is asking for an ocean view.

(D) She is correcting a mistake she made.

Listen again and fill in the blanks.

> W   Excuse me. We ________________________ a double bed, but we only have a single bed in our room.
>
> M   Oh, I'm sorry. ________________________ if we can change that.
>
> W   I made a special request when we booked.
>
> M   I see. Ah, here we are. Room 812. But we'll have to ask you to pay extra as that room has an ________________________.
>
> W   That's not good enough. It wasn't our ________________.

Check Up

Listening Task *01*

1 What is the man's job?

(A) Manager of a five-star hotel

(B) Waiter at the hotel restaurant

(C) Manager of the hotel restaurant and bar

(D) Cook at the hotel restaurant

🔊 Listen again.

2 Check True[T] or False[F].

		T	F
1)	The man has a new job at a busy hotel.	☐	☐
2)	The restaurant serves meals three times a day.	☐	☐
3)	The man doesn't have to make sure that the guests are happy.	☐	☐
4)	The man's job is easy, and he does not work hard.	☐	☐

Listening Task *02*

1 Match each talk with its purpose.

1) To advice:

2) To advertise:

3) To complain:

Listening Task *03*

1   **Which sentence best describes the situation?**

(A) The man is checking in to a hotel.

(B) The man is checking out of a hotel.

(C) The man is asking about a cable charge.

(D) The man is reserving a hotel room.

🔊 **Listen again.**

2   **What mistake did the clerk find?**

(A) The man was charged for something he didn't use.

(B) The clerk forgot to add the insurance to the bill.

(C) The man didn't pay for watching the cable channel.

(D) The clerk forgot to charge extra.

Listening Task *04*

1   **What does the man get nervous about in a new city?**

(A) Staying in a bad hotel

(B) Being overcharged for a taxi ride

(C) Getting lost going to his hotel

(D) Losing his luggage at the airport

Listening Test

Listen and answer the questions.

1 **Why does the man think the hotel will charge them extra for the room?**

(A) The hotel made a mistake with their reservation.

(B) The hotel is not busy.

(C) The hotel upgraded their room.

(D) They have a huge bathtub.

2 **What is true about the conversation?**

(A) There is no discount for the agents.

(B) The man thinks a 10% discount is too low.

(C) The man will not confirm his booking.

(D) The man will check some details before booking.

3 **What are they talking about?**

(A) Famous hotels in New York

(B) Bad hotels in New York

(C) Hotels they have stayed in

(D) How to get to their hotels

4 **What best describes the change in the speaker's emotions?**

(A) Angry → Satisfied

(B) Happy → Angry

(C) Angry → Disappointed

(D) Exciting → Happy

Note

5 **What was the problem with the air conditioner?**

    (A) It was not connected properly.

    (B) The man didn't know how to turn it on.

    (C) The man didn't wait long enough.

    (D) The air was not cold enough.

6 **What is the main topic of the talk?**

    (A) Expensive hotels

    (B) Expensive youth hostels

    (C) The famous youth hostel the man owns

    (D) The small hotel the man wants to own

7 **What will the man probably do next?**

    (A) He will order dinner and wine from room service.

    (B) He will order a snack from room service.

    (C) He will go to the restaurant.

    (D) He will check out of the hotel.

8 **What makes the speaker like the hotel most?**

    (A) Its modern services

    (B) The Roman-style balcony

    (C) The old carpet

    (D) Its historic setting

Note

! **Key** Expressions

1 **Fill in each blank with the best word from the word bank.**

mechanic	stylist	veterinarian	chef	architect
pilot	plumber	flight attendant	lawyer	pharmacist

1 A _______________ cooks food.

2 A _______________ repairs sinks and toilets.

3 A _______________ fixes cars.

4 A _______________ cuts hair.

5 An _______________ designs buildings.

2 **Cross out the word NOT related to each job.**

1 pilot: train / flying / plane

2 journalist : poetry / reporting / newspaper

3 pharmacist : grain / medicine / prescription

4 dentist: toothbrush / sew / drill

5 businessperson : office / client / radio

3 **Match the sentences with the best corresponding answers.**

1 How many hours do you work per week?   •   • ⓐ Congratulations!

2 I'm sorry. You're fired.   •   • ⓑ I am an accountant.

3 What do you do for a living?   •   • ⓒ But why? What did I do wrong?

4 I got promoted!   •   • ⓓ Sure, it's very well-paid.

5 Who will interview me for this job? •   • ⓔ I work at least 50 hours per week.

6 Do you like your job?   •   • ⓕ The manager of the Customer Service Department will interview you.

 Listening Practice

1 **Who is the speaker giving a lecture to?**

(A) College students

(B) High school students

(C) Young kids

(D) Middle school students

Listen again and fill in the blanks.

I am Mr. Peter, and my job is teaching music to _________________ students. I teach the piano and violin. Before this job, I taught music courses at the local ___________. This is my _________________ teaching younger students. I start next week, and I am nervous about this new opportunity! However, I will _________________________.

2 **What is true about the conversation?**

(A) The man wants to know how to dress for the job interview.

(B) The man and woman are planning a date.

(C) The man wants the woman to buy him a suit.

(D) The two of them have to work overtime.

Listen again and fill in the blanks.

M I have a job ____________________________.

W ____________________________ with that.

M Can you give me some tips on how I should _________________?

W Yes, you should dress neatly and look tidy.

M So I should wear a _________________ dress?

W If you want. But a suit will be _________________.

M Okay, thanks!

Check Up

Listen and answer the questions.

1 How does the man feel about his promotion?

(A) Disappointed

(B) Furious

(C) Jubilant

(D) Depressed

🔊 Listen again.

2 Check True[T] or False[F].

		T	F
1)	The man worked for three years.	☐	☐
2)	The woman does not want a promotion.	☐	☐
3)	The man's new office is bigger than his old one.	☐	☐
4)	The man has an old desk.	☐	☐

1 Why does the woman think she can NOT be a good TV news reporter?

(A) She is too nervous to be on television.

(B) She is not glamorous enough.

(C) She is better at accounting.

(D) She is not satisfied with the salary.

1 **Which statement best describes the situation?**

(A) The woman is asking for the man's advice about becoming a veterinarian.

(B) The man does not think the woman should work on weekends.

(C) The man is the woman's professor at university.

(D) The woman wants to work with the man when she graduates.

🔊 **Listen again.**

2 **What is true about the conversation?**

(A) The man doesn't like animals.

(B) The woman loves animals, so she became a veterinarian.

(C) The woman thinks veterinary work is boring.

(D) The man is a veterinarian.

Listening Task 04

1 **What does the speaker think will happen to his son if he does not get a job soon?**

(A) He will never get rich.

(B) His boss will be younger than him.

(C) He will not get enough experience.

(D) He will disappoint his father.

Listening Test

Listen and answer the questions.

1 According to the talk, what is NOT needed to apply for a job?

   (A) To send resumes

   (B) To check the requirements for the position

   (C) To fill out the application forms

   (D) To have confidence

2 Which statement best describes the situation?

   (A) The man is helping the woman prepare for an interview.

   (B) The man is helping the woman start her new job.

   (C) The man is interviewing the woman.

   (D) The man is attending a job interview with the woman.

3 How does the man feel about his new job?

   (A) He doesn't like it.

   (B) He liked his college students more.

   (C) He loves it but misses his old job.

   (D) He wants to change to an elementary school now.

4 Why has the man probably NOT found a part-time job?

   (A) He is desperate.

   (B) He is a student.

   (C) He has no experience.

   (D) He doesn't like to work hard.

Note

5 **What is the main idea of the talk?**

(A) If you are good at writing, you should be a writer.

(B) Making webpages means you have to study graphic designing.

(C) A person should do a job in an enjoyable and interesting field.

(D) Studying what you know will make you the most money in the future.

6 **What is true about the conversation?**

(A) The man does not enjoy his job.

(B) The woman wants to do the same job as the man.

(C) The man is a computer programmer.

(D) The man fixed the computer in three hours.

7 **What is the main idea of the talk?**

(A) You need a lot of luck to find the right job.

(B) It's difficult to find a new job if you already have one.

(C) You can find the right job with luck and hard work.

(D) You need to use your contacts to find a job.

8 **What is the purpose of the talk?**

(A) To warn

(B) To explain

(C) To advertise

(D) To analyze

Note

! **Key** Expressions

1   **Fill in each blank with the best word from the word bank.**

| passport | aisle seat | baggage | peak season | customs |
| flight | boarding pass | return | connecting flights | visa |

1   Please have your ________________ ready at the boarding gate.

2   Is that a one-way or ________________ ticket?

3   Passengers with ________________ should proceed to Gate 11.

4   I'd prefer an ________________ instead of being by the window.

5   I hope I don't get charged for excess ________________. This bag is quite heavy.

2   **Match each activity on the left with the correct place on the right.**

1   board a flight   •   • ⓐ arrival area

2   change money   •   • ⓑ baggage claim

3   meet a friend after arriving   •   • ⓒ newsstand

4   buy a magazine   •   • ⓓ departure gate

5   pick up suitcases after a flight •   • ⓔ currency exchange

3   **Match the sentences with the best corresponding answers.**

1   Hello, I've booked a flight under the   • ⓐ It doesn't matter. Either is okay.
    name of Johnson.

2   Would you like a window or aisle seat? •   • ⓑ Ah, yes. 9 a.m. to Tokyo.

3   Can I see your passport?   •   • ⓒ Yes, here it is.

4   The flight has been delayed 1 hour.   •   • ⓓ Actually, that's the slow season.

5   Isn't that during the peak season?   •   • ⓔ Now we're sure to be late.

6   Which flight would you like?   •   • ⓕ The one at 6:15.

7   When do I have to pay for this ticket? •   • ⓖ Within 2 weeks.

 Listening Practice

1 **What is the best title for the talk?**

(A) The invention of air travel

(B) Travelers and their problems

(C) The challenges and problems of air travel

(D) The fastest way to travel to your destination

Listen again and fill in the blanks.

In the past, people ________________ a lot more of their time getting from place to place. These days, many people choose to fly to their ________________________. But those who fly frequently, such as businesspeople, complain that air travel is not ________________. You have to ________________ your ticket many days or even weeks ________________. There are frequent ________________. Until there is a better alternative, however, air travel still offers the most benefits.

2 **Which statement best describes the situation?**

(A) The man is going through a gate.

(B) The man is checking his luggage in at the airport.

(C) The man is going through a customs check at the airport.

(D) The man has lost his ticket and passport.

Listen again and fill in the blanks.

w May I see your ________________________________ please?

B ________________________.

w Only one bag? Just ________________________ there. Thanks.

B Will this bag be okay for carry-on luggage?

w That should be no problem, sir. And would you prefer a window or aisle seat?

B I'd like a ________________________, thanks.

Check Up

Listening Task 01

1 What will the man probably say at the end?

(A) It was disappointing.

(B) It started to get annoying.

(C) It couldn't have been better.

(D) It made me very angry.

🔊 **Listen again.**

2 Check True[T] or False[F].   T   F

1) He is in France.

2) He's waiting for his friend.

3) He always flies business class.

4) He has come from Beijing.

Listening Task 02

1 On which day is the woman's return flight?

(A) Saturday

(B) Sunday

(C) Monday

(D) Wednesday

Listening Task *03*

1 **Where is this conversation taking place?**

(A) At baggage check-in

(B) At the security check

(C) At the boarding gate

(D) On the airplane

🔊 **Listen again.**

2 **What is true about the conversation?**

(A) The balls are tennis balls.

(B) The balls are grain balls.

(C) The woman bought the balls in Mexico.

(D) The woman doesn't know what the balls are.

Listening Task *04*

1 **Why was the man annoyed?**

(A) The airport was so big that he got lost.

(B) There were many delays in his flight.

(C) He had to transfer to a different airline.

(D) The airline made a mistake about his boarding gate.

Listening Test

1 **What is NOT true about the conversation?**

(A) The man has come alone.

(B) The man will have a couple of business meetings during his stay.

(C) The man will stay at the Lotte Hotel.

(D) The man will spend most of his time vacationing.

2 **What will the woman do after the conversation?**

(A) Visit her hotel

(B) Go to baggage claim

(C) Have dinner with the man

(D) Get on another flight

3 **According to the talk, which safety tip is correct?**

(A) You are allowed to use cell phones during the flight.

(B) Sharp objects can be carried in your luggage.

(C) You may not smoke at all during the flight.

(D) You are allowed to use your computer during take off and landing.

4 **What is true about the conversation?**

(A) The man doesn't know where to get his flight.

(B) The man is taking Flight 345.

(C) Many people are waiting around belt 12.

(D) The woman can't help him.

Note

5 **What will the man do after the conversation?**

(A) He will pay a duty on his luggage.

(B) He will fill in the form.

(C) He will board his flight.

(D) He will arrive at the airport.

6 **What word best describes the speaker's feelings?**

(A) Excited

(B) Depressed

(C) Embarrassed

(D) Satisfied

7 **What will the speaker do the next time?**

(A) Arrive earlier

(B) Fly economy class

(C) Fly business class

(D) Take the train

8 **Which is true about the speaker?**

(A) He was tired because he had to stay in the airport.

(B) He was angry because the airline cancelled the flights.

(C) He was angry because the staff at the desk could not help him.

(D) He was disappointed because he could not go home for his son's birthday.

Note

Dictation Test

Dictation Test

Listen and Fill in the blanks.

1 **Which statement best describes the situation?**

W Hi, James. Do you ___________ me? We met last year.

M Julie! What a ___________. You used to work at McDonald's, right?

W Yes, I still work there.

M Cool. I haven't been there for a long time. ___________ ___________ ___________?

W Okay. So how are you enjoying the party?

M It's good. There are ___________ ___________ ___________ people here. Let's go and get a soda.

2 **What quality is UNLIKELY to describe the man?**

W How would you ___________ yourself, Mr. Pitt?

M I'm a pretty ___________ ___________ who wants to do great things.

W What do you think is most important for you to ___________ ___________ ___________?

M It's important to work hard and be a good person if you want to reach your goals. I think I have these ___________.

3 **What is the best answer to the woman's question?**

M ___________ ___________, but are you Carol?

W Yes, that's right, I just started working here. And what's your name?

M Ben. It's ___________ ___________ ___________ you, Carol.

W It's nice to meet you too, Ben.

M May I ask where ___________ ___________?

W I just moved here from Georgia. How about you?

4 Which question is the speaker likely responding to?

I've always been ___________ ___________ art. When I was young, I spent all my free time drawing. Sometimes it drove my parents crazy. It is natural that I always did well in ___________ ___________ and then studied art at university. I really cannot imagine my life ___________ ___________.

5 Where is the conversation taking place?

M Hi. I see I'm not the only one outside getting some fresh air.

W Yeah, I thought I'd stretch my legs a little during ___________ ___________.

M So, what do you think of ___________ ___________ so far?

W I think it's good. It was worth every penny for the ticket.

M Yeah, I think so, too. Do you come here often?

W Yes, when I'm not bowling.

M Oh, cool. ___________ ___________ do you play?

W My friends and I go ___________ Friday night.

M Awesome. My name is Arthur, by the way, but my friends call me Art.

W I'm Marilyn. Nice to meet you, Art.

6 Why has the woman NOT played chess lately?

W Excuse me. Are you ___________ ___________ someone to play a game of chess with?

M Actually, I am. I'm just a ___________, though.

W That's OK. So am I. I'm Lisa. Nice to meet you.

M Good to meet you. I'm Alan. I haven't seen you around before.

W I ___________ ___________ ___________ when I was younger, but I got busy studying and haven't played for years. I'm sort of rediscovering it. How about you?

M I wanted to get a hobby which could help me meet ___________ ___________.

<u>**7**</u> **What is NOT true about the man?**

My name is William Brightman, and I'm an ____________. I live in Berlin, Germany, but I was born and ____________ ____________ Australia. I'm ____________ and have three children, two boys and one girl. All of my children go to a bilingual school here in Berlin, so they can speak English and German ____________. We like it here and plan to stay here for a few more years, and then we'll ____________ ____________ to Australia.

<u>**8**</u> **Which word best describes the man?**

People say that I ____________ ____________ really smart because I study a lot. It's true that I spend ____________ ____________ ____________ time on my own studying, but the truth is that I am ____________ ____________ and don't go out very often. I would like to meet more people, but I'm not very confident ____________ ____________. It's easier for me to stay home and read.

Dictation Test

Sports

Listen and Fill in the blanks.

1 What is true about the speaker?

I'm only fifteen years old, but I'm very ____________. Everyone told me I should play ____________. So I joined my school's basketball team, and I am ____________ about it. Now they say I'm one of their best players. It's really ____________ ____________ ____________ to jump high and put the ball into the net. I'm not a ____________ ____________, though. I'm just tall.

2 What is true about the conversation?

W I am not sure how it is in Korea, but, here in the UK, ____________ is still a very healthy sport. Soccer is definitely the ____________ ____________ sport here while boxing is not as popular. Is it the same in your country?

M It's kind of ____________ ____________ here. Most people in Korea prefer to watch a ____________ game or maybe a ____________ game rather than a boxing match.

3 What does the speaker think will happen?

The Samsung Lions are playing very well tonight. If they ____________ ____________, they might ____________ this game. If they do, they may win the ____________ for being the best team this season. This team is so ____________, and their hard work is finally showing results. The fans here at the game tonight are ____________ ____________.

4 How did the man feel about the game?

W Did you ____________ the FC Seoul game?

M Yeah. It was ____________.

W So who won?

M It was pretty ____________ until the very end, but FC Seoul ____________ ____________.

W I wish I had been able to see it.

M It's a shame you ____________ it. Definitely soccer at its finest.

5 What is the speaker talking about?

It is hard to understand my ____________. I think he watches the sports ____________
at least 15 hours a day. He doesn't do anything else, like ____________ ____________
with his friends. I don't understand how people live like that. I think it's more fun to
go out and play sports with your friends rather than watching them ____________
____________.

6 How many goals did their team score during the second half of the match?

M How did the ____________ go yesterday afternoon?

W It went very badly.

M Did our team play badly?

W At the end of the ____________ ____________, we were doing well. The
____________ was 1:1. Then our best player got injured.

M How badly did we ____________?

W Very badly. The final score was 6:1.

7 What is true about the talk?

His name is Choi Hong Man, but the world knows him as 'Techno Goliath.' He is
perhaps the ____________ ____________ in Korea today. He used to be a wrestler in
ssireum, which is Korean ____________ wrestling. But now he is a tough fighter in K–1.
He ____________ his fans to stay healthy, take vitamins, and believe in themselves.

8 Why does the man say that he had better start playing properly?

M Whose turn is it to ____________?

W It's yours.

M Hey, you're playing really well today.

W I've been ____________ all week.

M Are you keeping score?

W   Yes, I am. You aren't doing too badly. But I might _____________ _____________.

M   I'd better start playing properly. Throw me the ball.

W   _____________ _____________. Here it comes.

Dictation Test

Phone Calls

Listen and Fill in the blanks.

1 **What will the woman probably say next?**

M   Hello, this is Tom ______________.

W   Hi, Tom. It's Peggy. What are you doing this Sunday?

M   Not much. Homework mostly. ______________ ______________ ______________?

W   I was thinking of watching a baseball game. Want to go with me?

M   That would be fun, but I have a ______________ ______________ next Monday.
I should probably stay home and study.

W   ______________ to hear that.

2 **What is the correct information according to the conversation?**

W   T.G.I Friday's, how may I help you?

M   I would like to ______________ a table for dinner tonight.

W   How many people are in your ______________?

M   Six.

W   OK, and what time will you be ______________?

M   Around 7 p.m.

W   Can I have your name, please?

M   James Kipper.

W   All right. We'll have your table ______________ for you, Mr. Kipper.

M   Thank you. Goodbye.

3 **Why does the man ask the woman where Marvin is?**

W   Good morning, may I help you?

M   Yes, is Marvin there?

W   I'm sorry. He's not in ______________ ______________. May I take a ______________?

M   Do you know where he is?

W   I'm ______________ he didn't leave that information.

M   OK, then. My name is Jason. Please tell him to call me as soon as ______________.
It's really ______________ that I talk to him.

W   Yes, sir.

4   How many calls did she make today?

What a day! I've been on the ______________ all afternoon. First, I called ______________
______________ to remind them of their appointments. I spoke with one but had to
leave a message for the other. Then, a friend of mine called just to ______________
______________. Finally, I had to call three people back to answer some questions and
give them ______________.

5   Why is the man calling?

W   Hello. Anna speaking.

M   Hi, Anna. ______________ ______________ John. I haven't seen you lately.

W   I am just so busy.

M   Do you remember the book I lent you? Have you ______________ reading it?

W   Yes, I finished reading it weeks ago. I've been meaning to return it to you.

M   Good, I need it for my ______________.

W   I'll bring it to your house later.

M   I have to go out this afternoon. Will you ______________ ______________ before you
come over?

W   Sure, I'll call you on your mobile phone.

6   Which question does the talk try to answer?

People don't see ______________ ______________ when they speak on the phone. That
means you don't have to be ______________ very well when you call an old friend. In fact,
you could be lying on the couch in your ______________ ______________. If you meet your
old friend in a coffee shop, it's different. On the telephone, you can also ______________
and catch up with your friend for hours.

7 What is a reason for having voicemail?

The reason most people get voicemail is to ______________ ____________ directly to
other people. They can listen to callers' messages and ____________ who to talk to.
This way, they can avoid talking to annoying friends or a boyfriend/girlfriend they
"____________" to call!

8 Which statement agrees with the man's advice?

W: I have a ____________. My best friend and I talk on the phone a lot. But when
someone else calls on the other line, she ______________ ____________ with me to talk to
them. Then, she never calls me ____________! What should I do?

M: You should tell her how you feel! However, if she's really your best friend, would
she choose her other friends ______________ ____________?

Listen and Fill in the blanks.

1 Why does the boy NOT like the shirt?

M   Thank you for my _____________ gift, Mom.

W   Do you like the shirt I bought you?

M   I don't really like the _____________.

W   Why? Everyone is wearing pink these days.

M   I know, but it's _____________ _____________ for me.

W   Dark colors are so boring.

M   But I don't _____________ _____________ in such bright colors.

2 What is the woman likely to buy?

M   How can I help you today?

W   I really like this dress. But you don't have _____________ _____________.

M   Let me see. We have the dress in your size but in a _____________ _____________.

W   That's too bad. I tried that on earlier. I don't like the striped _____________.

M   What do you think of this dress? This one with dots will be very _____________ during summer.

W   Long dresses are not really my style, but it's a pretty color. OK, I'll take it.

3 What will the boy probably do after this conversation?

M   Mom, I like this shirt.

W   It's too _____________. How about this shirt?

M   I don't like the color.

W   There are many _____________ colors.

M   But I want it in black.

W   Here's one. _____________ _____________ _____________.

M   Hmm... Actually, I might try the _____________ one.

W   The color looks great on you.

M   Thanks, Mom. Let's take it.

4   **What is NOT true about Sally?**

My friend Sally wants to own her own clothing store when she is grown up. She knows
everything about women's _____________. She's always _____________ magazines or
_____________ television shows about clothing and makeup. When we go out together,
she lets me wear some of her clothing. She has a lot of great clothes. The problem is
that all her clothes are _____________ _____________ for me!

5   **Which question does the talk try to answer?**

Young people love to look good and _____________ _____________. They learn about
fashion by watching TV programs and movies. But they also watch how their friends
dress. They don't really want to _____________ _____________ in case their clothes
are not in style. As a result, young people dress like each other in _____________
_____________.

6   **What is true about the conversation?**

W   I love nice clothes. I just wish I had _____________ _____________ to spend.

M   Clothes are very expensive.

W   Especially the clothes that are _____________ _____________.

M   It's not important to wear expensive clothes.

W   Yes, it is. But all my friends wear the _____________ clothing. I wish I could do the
same.

7   **What does the woman NOT want?**

Sometimes a little makeup, but not too much, looks _____________. I like to wear a
little bit of makeup when I go out. I want to look like my favorite pop star. My mom
lets me wear her makeup sometimes. I like to play around and try different shades of
lipstick.But I think many girls wear too much makeup. They look like circus clowns!
When they _____________ _____________ their makeup, they look like different people.

8 Who is the woman they are talking about?

M   Look at that girl! She looks so cool.

W   The girl with the ______________ ______________?

M   No, the one with the skinny ______________.

W   Is she wearing a leather ______________?

M   No, she's wearing a really ______________ T-shirt.

W   I think I see her. She's the best dressed person at the party.

M   She is. That look is so hot right now.

W   Yes, skinny jeans and bright T-shirts are very ______________.

Dictation Test

Listen and Fill in the blanks.

1 **Which word best describes Bill?**

My friend Bill dislikes being ______________. He sees it as an insult. He ______________ ______________ himself very strongly. He doesn't think anyone else's opinion matters. He is too ______________ and never admits when he is wrong. He never ______________ help from anyone at work. He even shouts at his boss. Bill is a very difficult person.

2 **Who is the speaker talking about?**

I may be too picky, but this guy is just full of himself. We have similar interests and ______________, but I found him to be conceited. I'm really ______________. My ex-boyfriend was a man like that. I know how difficult it is for people to change their ______________. I may have to find a ______________ ______________.

3 **Which word best describes Tom?**

I've tried to be ______________, but I have to say this. One night a few weeks ago, after Tom had gone out, I was startled by the doorbell. It was Mr. Salvador, the landlord. He looked angry. "Your roommate ______________ to have the rent money three days ago," he said. It ______________ ______________ that Tom had not paid him for two months.

4 **Which word does NOT describe Dan?**

Dan is my son's teacher. The kids really love him. Not only is he ______________ and ______________, but he also really makes time to help the kids with their ______________. Sometimes he'll play with them on the basketball court for hours. Or he'll tell them a story and explain it to them until they ______________ it. I think they're really lucky to have a teacher like him.

5   **What does the speaker feel for the coach?**

James is probably one of the top tennis ____________. Only a few players get to be coached by a guy like him. He understands the game very well. When he's on the court, he ____________ hard on the game. But ____________ ____________ ____________ he's off the court, he's a friend. He knows how to treat his players ____________ ____________ ____________ the court.

6   **Why was the man surprised?**

W   When Steve comes home late at night, he's always very ____________ ____________ his sleeping neighbors and doesn't make any noise.

M   That's very ____________ of him.

W   When people first meet him, they think he's a ____________ person. Most are surprised to hear that he's so ____________.

M   I'm very surprised. I always imagined he wouldn't care about other people at all.

7   **What is true about the conversation?**

W   That was such an amazing movie. I loved the ____________.

M   Are you ____________ because of that movie?

W   Of course. It really ____________ me.

M   Not me. I thought it was rather boring.

W   I'm surprised. I thought you were more ____________ than that.

8   **According to the speaker, what kind of person is Ben?**

Ben is such a clever guy. He knows a lot about ____________ and ____________. He's also very sophisticated. He goes to the opera at least once a month and knows all of Shakespeare's plays. But he's so easy to ____________ ____________ ____________. He never makes me feel that I am less clever than he is nor ____________ ____________ his intelligence in front of people.

Dictation Test

Parties

Listen and Fill in the blanks.

1 Why will the woman NOT be able to go to the party?

M Did you get ______________ to Jane's birthday party next week?

W Yes, I did. Looks like it will be a cool party.

M Great. Let's go together. I'll ______________ you ______________ at 7.

W I won't make it to the party. I'm working until 10 p. m. that evening.

M Oh, that's terrible. Can you take the evening ______________?

W No, my boss is very ______________.

M Everyone will be at the party. Why don't you come later?

2 What will the man wear at the event?

M Hi, Kim. I'm going to a ______________ event in San Francisco next week. Can you tell me what I should ______________?

W I think it's the same everywhere.

M I know a tuxedo will be ______________. But I'm wondering if I could I get away with that ______________ ______________.

W Yes, I think so. But don't forget the ______________ ______________.

M Thanks for your advice.

3 What is the purpose of the talk?

Hello, Irene. How are you? Thank you so much for ______________ us to John's birthday party last week. We had a ______________ ______________. You went to so much trouble. The birthday cake was really delicious. You know how much I love sweet things. I hope that you can come to ______________ with us soon. Thanks again.

4 When did the speaker eat?

My girlfriend and I went to a party last night, but we ______________ ______________ it.
First, the music was too ______________, so we couldn't talk to anyone without yelling.
Also, there wasn't ______________ ______________ to eat. The food ran out quickly, so
we didn't even get to eat. And we didn't see any of our friends either. We stayed for a
short time and then went home ______________.

5 Why does the man say, "Be careful when living in a house on the coast"?

M   Hey, Peggy. Great party, isn't it?

W   Yeah, pretty good.

M   By the way, did you read about ______________ ______________? Scientists now have
clear evidence.

W   Yeah, I have heard that. The sea level is rising! Isn't it ______________?

M   Just be ______________ when living in a house on the coast.

6 What are the two things the women need before the prom?

W1 We have two weeks to ______________ ______________ for the prom, Michelle.

W2 What are you going to do? I'm going to ask your brother.

W1 My brother? But he can't dance.

W2 It doesn't matter. I don't know who else to ask.

W1 What about the guy who sits next to you on the school bus everyday?

W2 I'll ask him if he'll go with you.

W1 ______________ ______________. Then we'll both have partners.

W2 Then we'll have to find ______________ ______________ to wear to the prom!

7 Which sentence can at the end of the talk?

An office party may seem like a ______________ ______________ to get friendly with
your employer, but your ______________ can affect your career directly. According to
Etiquette International, a company specializing in business etiquette, no matter how
festive the party is, it's still about ______________.

  Which food will NOT be eaten at the party?

Dear friends, please join us for a ______________ ______________ tomorrow evening. The theme is "Foods from around the world." Please ______________ your favorite dish from ______________ ______________, not your traditional food. Snacks and drinks will be provided. But please bring a salad. After dinner, we'll serve your favorite ______________ from around the world.

Dictation Test

Listen and Fill in the blanks.

1 **Which question is the speaker likely responding to?**

I have ____________ my restaurant for the past five years. In that time, it has become more and more ____________. I've learned what my customers like. I use only the freshest food and vegetables. I ____________ ____________ that the food is tasty. The tables and dishes are always clean. Lastly, we always serve the customers in a ____________ ____________ to make them happy.

2 **What best describes the situation in the picture?**

(A)

Bill and his friends are at Pizza Hut. They have decided to order ____________ ____________ of pizza. They get the cheese pizza and kimchi pizza. They ____________ ____________ ____________ eat the pizzas.

(B)

Bill and his friends are sitting around at Pizza Hut. They are ____________, so they ordered two large pizzas, but they have been waiting for the pizza for ____________ 40 ____________. They are ____________ now.

(C)

Bill and his girlfriend are at Pizza Hut. They ordered a pizza and some spaghetti, but the waiter brought them two pizzas. Bill is ____________ to the manager about the waiter's ____________.

3 **What is the right order of the situation?**

ⓐ

Peter and Samantha are at a fancy ____________. They are sitting at a table with red roses and candles. Romantic music is playing softly. They are ____________ ____________ across the table while drinking their glasses of ____________.

(b)

Samantha is waiting for Peter to ________________ ________________ at the restaurant. When he finally does, she scolds him for ____________ ____________.

(c)

The waiter is taking Peter and Samantha's order. He brings them a ____________ ____________ ____________ ____________ and some glasses. He pours them some.

4   What is true about the conversation?

W   You know, they have excellent ____________ here.

M   But I'm allergic to ____________.

W   Really? That's a shame. Then, how about this chicken steak?

M   That does sound delicious. And I know you have ____________ ____________ in food.

W   Okay, then I'll have the shrimp special while you have the steak.

M   Yes, and ____________ and soup for appetizers.

5   What does the woman probably say next?

M   Here's your chicken pot pie.

W   But this is not what I ____________.

M   Oh! I ____________. I made a mistake on your order. We'll correct it ____________ ____________.

---------------------- pause ----------------------

M   Here is your sweet and sour pork. I hope you ____________ ____________.

W   Thank you. I'm starving. It looks delicious.

M   I apologize for the mix up, ma'am.

6   What is the main idea of the talk?

M   I'm Max, and I work at my parent's restaurant. My job is to ____________ ____________ from the customers and ____________ ____________ tables. I've worked here for over a year now. At first, I hated the job, but now I like it since it changed my life by teaching me to be ____________.

7 **What was the reason she mentioned fish in her talk?**

I'm Jane, and I am a ______________. I do not like to eat meat. I don't think that it tastes good at all. I love tofu, bean sprouts, broccoli, and other vegetables. I don't even like to eat ______________. Sometimes it's hard for me to eat when I go out to restaurants. Lots of places don't offer dishes that have no meat. To be a vegetarian is a ______________, but I like it.

8 **What does the woman NOT ask about the restaurant?**

M Cindy, I know of a good restaurant for you.

W Really? Where is it?

M About two miles ______________ ______________ our office.

W How are the prices there?

M ______________. Not that expensive.

W How about the food and the service?

M The food is great, and they have ______________ ______________. I highly ______________ it.

W All right. Thanks!

Dictation Test

Entertainment

Listen and Fill in the blanks.

<u>1</u> What will the speakers probably do after the conversation?

M This ______________ ______________ is amazing!

W It sure is. I don't think we have enough time to go on all the ______________.

M Probably not. So what ride should we go on first?

W How about the ______________ ______________? I love them.

M Uh, no thanks. I'm afraid of ______________. How about doing something else?

W Well, the bumper cars are nearby. Or we could go on the flume.

M Hmm… How about the bumper cars?

W Great. Let's ______________ ______________ line.

<u>2</u> Why will the man see the show at 8:30 p.m.?

M I'd like to ______________ two tickets for the comedy show ______________, please.

W There are two shows, one at 6 p.m. and one at 8:30 p.m.

M I'd like tickets for the six o'clock show.

W There are only a couple of seats ______________. I'm afraid they are right ______________ ______________ ______________.

M That's no good. What about the show at 8:30?

W We have some seats left in the middle and near the back.

M This must be a ______________ show.

W Yes, ______________ love the comedian.

<u>3</u> How did the woman feel about the movie?

M Hey, Jane. Chris told me he watched *Star Wars* with you ______________ ______________.

W Yeah, we did.

M How was it? I plan to watch it with my family this Saturday.

W Please, don't ask about it. Chris and I just ______________ ______________ ______________

M I don't believe it. Everyone says it's a great movie.

W I ______________ ______________ during the movie. It was so bad. There was ______________ ______________ in the movie.

4 What is the woman talking about?

I went to see a ______________ with Sally. We had a great time, so maybe you would like to see it. It's called *Night and Day*; it's a new English play. The ______________ is very sad. The actors are so good that I nearly cried. It's not very ______________. Just remember to buy your ticket at the ______________ half an hour before the play begins.

5 What will they do together on Saturday?

M The weather's going to be great this weekend. Let's do ______________ ______________.

W Yes, let's go away to a place near the ______________ for the weekend.

M Oh, there's a company picnic on Saturday. That might be great.

W Oh, that sounds boring. Let's go to the ______________ ______________ in the park in the evening.

M Okay, then I can catch the baseball game in the afternoon. What will we do on Sunday?

W We'll ______________ ______________ in the park and then see a movie.

M That sounds good.

6 How does the man feel about the program?

M Are you watching that TV ______________ again?

W Yes. I like it. Don't you?

M It's been on about twenty times already.

W Twenty times? That's not true. Anyway, it's still funny.

M Why don't you ______________ ______________ ______________? I'm sure there's something better on.

W Why don't you sit down and watch the program with me? You might enjoy it.

M I have better things to do with my time. I'd ______________ wash the car.

7 **What does the woman NOT want?**

W Hey, Chris, can you go out to the snack bar and get me a ______________ before the

movie starts? I'm really ____________.

M Yeah, I can do that for you. What do you want? Coke or juice?

W Coke. Can you me get some popcorn, too?

M Great, and I'll get some popcorn ____________ ____________ as well. Oh, do you

want an ice cream?

W You can get one for yourself, and I'll ____________ ____________ ____________ it.

8 **How much does the woman have to pay?**

M Hi, may I help you?

W I would like to ____________ some DVDs. How much does it ____________ to rent

them?

M The price ____________ ____________ the DVD itself. ____________ ____________

are three dollars, and others are two dollars.

W I want to rent these three DVDs. Are they new releases?

M Let me take a look at them. Only one of them is new. The others are not.

Dictation Test

Transportation

Listen and Fill in the blanks.

1 **What is the main idea of the talk?**

I'm George, and I'm twenty years old. I'll be getting my ____________ ____________ soon. I drive well, but I still have ____________ with a few things. I'm glad that my ____________ is nearly perfect. It's worth twenty-five percent of the test. I'm sure I can pass that part easily. But I still need to work on it. I also need to work on ____________ ____________.

2 **What is the total cost of the tickets to Seoul Land?**

M   What is the ____________ for two people to Seoul Land?

W   Do you have a student card?

M   No, I'm not a student. But my brother is only ten years old.

W   Children only pay ____________ ____________.

M   That's good. How much is the adult fare?

W   It's ____________ ____________ won.

3 **What did the woman NOT do on the airplane?**

I just flew on an airplane for the first time ever. It was such an ____________ event. First, I got to sit next to the ____________, so I could see everything really clearly. When we ____________ ____________, we were going down the runway so quickly. Suddenly, we ____________ ____________ in the air. The flight was so nice and smooth. We watched a movie. And then I got to have dinner — it was really delicious. Finally, after a few hours, we ____________. I couldn't believe how quickly we traveled across the country. I can't wait to fly again soon.

4 **Where is the conversation taking place?**

M   Hello, I'd like a ticket for Chicago, please.

W   Sure. There is a train ____________ in one hour.

M   Great. I'll take that. How much does the ticket ____________?

W   It will cost ____________ dollars. Will you be paying with ____________ or a
____________ ____________?

M   Cash. Oh, one more question. ____________ ____________ is it leaving from?

W   Go to gate seven. It's right behind us.

5   **Why does the woman think cards are better?**

W   Alex, you should really purchase a ____________ card.

M   Why? These tickets are more ____________.

W   But the cards are cheaper than the tickets.

M   Really?

W   Yes, and you can also use the cards on public buses!

M   You're right. It's also easier to ____________ ____________ ____________ when you
go through the gate.

W   Let's go to the counter and get one for you then!

6   **Which is NOT true about the conversation?**

M   So we're going to the Coex Mall?

w   Yes.

M   What subway stop is that at?

W   It's on line number two, the ____________ ____________, at Samsung Station.

M   ____________ ____________ is that from here at Sadang ____________ station?

W   It's ____________ ____________ away, so it will take us about ____________
____________ to get there.

M   Then let's go!

7   **Which question is the talk responding to?**

The subway is a very convenient form of ____________. It's a lot quicker than buses
or sometimes even taxis. It's cheaper than driving your car everywhere and then
looking for a parking space. Most major cities have a subway system. It's probably the
best way to ____________ ____________ in a big city, which is usually ____________

____________ ____________ and people.

8   How many flights will the man take before he arrives in Boston?

W   Are you going on a long plane trip?

M   Yes, I'm going to Boston, Massachusetts, my hometown.

W   That will be a ____________ ____________.

M   I know, and I have three ____________.

W   Where are they?

M   They're at Narita, Los Angeles, and Chicago.

W   Well, I hope you have a ____________ ____________.

M   Thank you.

Dictation Test

Hobbies

Listen and Fill in the blanks.

1 **Which of the following talks about how to enjoy one's hobby with others?**

ⓐ

If you have a lot of ______________, then consider miniatures. It is an interesting hobby. Making miniature trains, cars, or toy soldiers will include painting, ______________ work, crafts, and more.

ⓑ

Anyone can enjoy drawing or painting as a hobby even if that person doesn't have any ______________ ______________. There are no rules for art. You can draw or paint ______________ you like. It is an activity that allows you to ______________.

ⓒ

Make sure your hobby will not take away from the time you need to spend with ______________ ______________. Ask them to come and watch you play sports. They can even play with you. It will be more ______________.

2 **Which statement best describes the situation?**

W Why does Laurie ______________ ______________? It seems pretty boring to me.

M She has always been fascinated with ______________ money.

W I'm more fascinated with ______________ money. I can ______________ it.

M Some of that old money could bring you a lot of new money.

W If you're lucky, then it could. But I'd rather just spend my money instead of ______________ it.

3 **According to the talk, how can you make money from your hobby?**

Are you ______________ ______________ spending money on your hobby? You could try turning your hobby into a ______________! Maybe you have a hobby that other people find interesting. If you are really ______________ ______________ it, people might want to learn more about this hobby from you. You might be able to earn some money teaching your hobby to others _____________ still doing something you enjoy.

4 **Why will the man NOT give the woman flowers this year?**

M   I became interested in _____________ after my mother told me about my grandmother.

W   Oh really? Was your grandmother a gardener?

M   Yes, that's why we always had flowers in the house.

W   I see. So can I _____________ to receive flowers from you soon?

M   I only started my garden _____________ _____________ _____________. Maybe I'll have flowers next year.

W   I suppose it's a lot of work.

M   Yes, this is the kind of hobby that keeps you _____________ _____________.

5 **What can help you become good at DIY furniture making?**

Building your own simple _____________ items can be an easy weekend activity. It's best to begin with small projects, such as a bookcase or a table. "_____________ _____________ _____________," or DIY, is not as hard as it may seem. There is information on the Internet or in books on the subject of DIY. It will tell you what materials to buy and then guide you as to how to use the materials. After a few tries, DIY furniture making will become a _____________ _____________.

6 **What will they do this weekend?**

M   Rose, what are you doing this weekend?

W   How about a movie?

M   We saw *Star Wars* last week. How about _____________ _____________ _____________?

W   Biking? That's boring.

M   Then, what do you want to do?

W   I'd like to go _____________.

M   I don't think that will be fun for me. How about a _____________?

W   Okay.

<u>**7**</u> **How much will the woman pay?**

M Hi, may I help you?

W Yes, please. I'm ________________ ______________ a baseball glove.

M I see. How about this one?

W That looks good. __________ ____________ ____________ ____________?

M It's ___________ dollars.

W Great. Come to think of it, I need a bat, too.

M This one is ___________ dollars.

W Perfect. I'll take both.

<u>**8**</u> **What is one topic the workshop probably will NOT talk about?**

What's the difference between a ____________, a ____________, and an ____________? What are some common hobbies from around the world? Do males and females have different hobbies? All these questions and more will be answered in our class "Hobbies and Leisure." If you take this class, you'll get hands-on experience in many different ____________. You'll learn lots of different things. So be sure to ____________ ____________ now.

Dictation Test

Listen and Fill in the blanks.

1 **When will the speakers go to Seoul Tower?**

W _____________ _____________ have you been in Korea?

M About a week.

W I have to take you to Seoul Tower ____________ you're here.

M It's the place at the top of Namsan, isn't it?

W Yes, you can see _____________ _____________ of Seoul from the tower.

M Let's go in the ____________. I'd like to take some photographs of the city.

2 **Why does the speaker mention pizza delivery cars?**

For surfers, the only interesting places are those with ____________ ____________.
And, as we all know, the best surf is in ____________. All waves lead to Hawaii, and
Hawaii's north shore especially is a surfer's ____________. Even many pizza delivery
cars have surfboard pictures on their doors and roofs.

3 **Jane is going to visit the Seoul Metro Museum this Friday with her parents
and her three younger brothers. Two of her brothers are younger than 10 years
old. How much will they pay altogether?**

Welcome to the Seoul Metro Museum. Our museum lets you ____________ how
ancient Koreans lived. We are open from 10 a.m. to 6 p.m., Monday to Friday.
____________ is ____________ dollars for adults and ____________ dollars for kids
younger than 10 years old. You can get a 10% ____________ for groups of more than
5 people and 30% for groups of more than 10 people.

4 **Why is it difficult to get a ticket for a game?**

Students at the University of Michigan ____________ ____________ of the famous
football stadium on their campus. It is one of the largest college football stadiums,
with seats for more than 110,000 fans. Most fans have ____________ ____________.

This makes it really _____________ to get tickets to see the games, most of which have been sold out for more than 30 years.

5   **What does the man want the woman to take pictures of?**

M   Hey, Jane. I heard you are visiting Cape Town during vacation.

W   Yes, it will be my _____________ _____________ in South Africa.

M   There's a famous mountain in Cape Town, isn't there?

W   Yes, it's called Table Mountain because its top is _____________ _____________ _____________ a table.

M   I hope you take pictures. I've never seen anything like that before.

W   I know. It's the only mountain in the world with a flat top.

M   I'm sure you'll see _____________ _____________ there, too.

6   **Why does the speaker say that this show isn't for those who get nervous very easily?**

The Museum of Magic is a good place to see special magic shows. The best magicians will show their audiences some of their most _____________ _____________. Not only it is great fun, but it is also educational and motivational for young people. Many young people leave here wanting to study magic. The magicians are very _____________. Their shows are not for those who get nervous very easily or who have weak hearts! The shows are often _____________ _____________. You should _____________ your seat early so that you are not disappointed.

7   **What is NOT true about the Inca Trail Trek?**

The Inca Trail trek is known as probably the most _____________ short hiking trail in the world. Many people around the world visit here _____________. You can walk along a path _____________ _____________ built more than 500 years ago. You can also see the remarkable city of Cusco, which was the capital of the Inca Empire, and the unique _____________ _____________ at Chinchero.

8   **What is NOT true about the Great Wall of China?**

The Great Wall of China was built over 2,000 years ago. It is almost 7,000 kilometers
______________. Can you imagine walking along the entire wall? It would take you a
long time. Thousands of people visit the wall every year. It is difficult to walk there,
and a few people have even been ____________. But everyone agrees that it is one of
the most ____________ manmade wonders of the ____________ ____________.

Listen and Fill in the blanks.

1   How much will the man pay?

W   Hi, can I help you?

M   Yes, please. I am looking for a gift for my girlfriend.

W   How about this ____________?

M   How much is it?

W   At the ____________ ____________, it is 80 dollars, but we are having a special today. If you spend more than ____________ dollars, you get a ____________ ____________ ____________.

M   How much is this hat?

W   It is 40 dollars.

M   Then, I'll take ____________.

2   Which statement best describes the situation?

W   The final thing we want to tell you about is the ____________ ____________. You can go whenever you're out of something. There are several around ____________.

M   That's right. And they have everything you need.

W   They don't usually have milk, though, so you need to walk down to the convenience store close by the ____________.

M   Yeah, she said everything I wanted to say to you.

3   What will the woman probably say next?

W   Here we are. I'm going to stop by Hyundai Department Store first. I might just get lucky today. Who knows, some of their dresses might be ____________ ____________.

M   Hyundai?

W   It's a fairly ____________ department store. Sort of like Lotte. They've got some quality stuff. Do you want to check it out?

M   Why not?

W   You won't be _____________.

4   How does the man probably feel?

M   Excuse me. I _____________ these earrings last week. I'd like to _____________ them for another pair.

W   Do you have the _____________?

M   Unfortunately not. But I only purchased these last week. They're still in the _____________.

W   Our store policy requires a receipt in order for you to exchange them.

M   But that's ridiculous. They are in perfect condition. May I speak to your _____________?

5   What will the woman probably do next?

Look, I just saw _____________ _____________ _____________ at the store down the road. It's on sale, and it's about _____________ the price of this one. It's exactly the same. It would be silly to buy that camera here when you could save so much elsewhere. I hope they have not all sold out. I'll be so happy if I could _____________ _____________ _____________. I can buy myself a new handbag with the money.

6   What sort of computer does the speaker want?

I need a new computer. I am not looking for a desktop PC because I don't do much on my _____________ _____________ except play games and watch movies. I don't really want to spend more than _____________. I know that is cheap, but that is all I think I can _____________. So call me back if you think you have something for me.

7   What will Bill probably buy for Emily's birthday?

Hey, Bill, you want my _____________ on what to get Emily for her birthday? Well, a handbag or a T-shirt might be nice. Designer _____________ is another option. Wait a minute! I have a 15% _____________ _____________ for Penny's Jewelry. I _____________ ever shop there, so go ahead and use the coupon if you can. Here it is.

  What is NOT recommended by the speaker?

Sometimes you may pay more than the ______________ ______________ for a product. In order to ______________ this problem, be sure to shop at places where the products' prices are ______________ ______________. You should also compare prices to get a better idea of a product's price and features before ______________ it. You should also make sure you understand exactly what you are buying.

Dictation Test

Traveling

Listen and Fill in the blanks.

1 What is the speaker talking about?

Some parts of the world are medically ____________ than others. This is partly because of diseases but mainly due to the gap between countries' ____________ ____________. These two things could influence your choice of ____________. When planning a trip, you should ask an expert to find out of what you must be careful. This will make your trip safe and ____________.

2 What will the woman probably do?

W I'd like to go to Peru this year. I heard you have ____________ there.

M Yeah, I was there last year.

W Did you use a travel agency or plan everything ____________ ____________ ____________?

M I just did it ____________ ____________. All the package tours were so expensive, but, if you do it yourself, it's much cheaper.

W Okay, that sounds like good advice.

3 What is the topic of the talk?

It's best to travel when others are not traveling. Just ask your travel agent. An airline can tell you which times of year are ____________ and therefore offer ____________ ____________ and better seats. Hotels and resorts also know when they will have fewer guests. Sometimes, the ____________ is only a week. If you travel just a week earlier or later, you could enjoy a much ____________ ____________.

4 Which sentence best describes the situation?

W Excuse me. Can you help me? Can you tell me where the ____________ ____________ ____________ is?

M It's not far. ____________ ____________ on this road for about five minutes. Then

_____________ _____________, and walk straight for another minute. The information center is _____________ _____________ the bookshop.

W Thank you so much.

M Don't worry. You _____________ _____________ it.

W It sounds simple, but I don't know the city.

5 How does the man probably feel after his holiday?

I was on holiday in Mongolia last month. _____________ _____________, I had a great time. I thought it would be the best experience of my life. But, on the third day, my tour guide _____________ that I pay him more money. I had already paid for a guided tour and didn't have enough money. He _____________ _____________ in my hotel, and I was stuck there for a week because I didn't know how to get around. All I could do was _____________ _____________ the city where the hotel was.

6 Where is the conversation taking place?

W Excuse me. Do you need any help?

M Oh, thanks. I'm trying to get to the _____________.

W You have to go to City Hall Station and _____________ to the airport shuttle bus. It costs about five dollars.

M _____________ _____________ at City Hall Station?

W Yeah. It's only _____________ _____________ from here.

M Great, thanks a lot.

7 What will the man and his family probably do for their vacation?

M Where should we go for our family vacation this year? I hear that Portugal and Spain are very nice. But in March there could be _____________ _____________.

W Last year in March, my family spent a long weekend there. The weather was _____________. We spent the whole weekend _____________ _____________ _____________.

M Well, I hope the weather will be the same as it was last year.

W You never know, but I _____________ that you go there.

8   What was the most important thing for the speaker in choosing a cruise?

W   The travel agent told us that cruises serve different travelers, including ______________, honeymooners, and ______________. Therefore, each cruise has different activities and services onboard the ship. Since we were going on our ______________, we did not want a family cruise. We chose a cruise for people like ourselves so that we could have time ______________ ______________.

Dictation Test

Hotel

Listen and Fill in the blanks.

1 **Why does the man think the hotel will charge them extra for the room?**

M Are you sure they didn't make a ____________ with our ____________? This room is great.

W There's no mistake. The hotel isn't busy, so they ____________ our room.

M Well, this is fantastic. We have a ____________ ____________ from the balcony.

W The bath is huge. We're so lucky.

M Are you sure they won't charge us ____________?

W I don't think so. But why don't you ask the manager?

2 **What is true about the conversation?**

W Hi, may I help you?

M Yes, I would like to know if there is a ____________ ____________ for agents.

W Yes, there is. I think it's 10%, but I can check that for you.

M Okay, ____________ ____________ ____________ if I book it for now and call you back later to confirm? I just need to check one or two ____________.

W That's fine, sir.

3 **What are they talking about?**

W Hey, Chris. I'm going to be visiting New York City soon. ____________ ____________ have you stayed at there?

M I always look for something ____________. I like the Four Seasons on 51st. It used to have a shared bathroom between two rooms.

W I've never been there. But I stayed at the Holiday Inn ____________ ____________, and I really liked it. Maybe I'll just stay there again.

4   What best describes the change in the speaker's emotions?

We arrived at the hotel late last night. The ______________ ______________ made a terrible mistake with my ______________ and didn't have a room for me. Lenny and Sam had to ______________ a room, and I took Lenny's room. To ______________ for the mistake, the hotel manager ______________ us to drinks and dinner. This morning, they moved my luggage to the new room they had arranged for me.

5   What was the problem with the air conditioner?

W   Front Desk. How can I help you?

M   The ______________ ______________ in my room isn't working. Cold air doesn't come out when I ______________ it ______________.

W   How long did you wait after you turned it on?

M   I'm not sure. Maybe a minute.

W   You have to wait more than ______________ ______________ to get cold air after you turn it on.

M   I'm sorry. Aha, there's cold air coming out now. Thank you.

W   ______________ ______________.

6   What is the main topic of the talk?

I've been the owner of my little youth hostel for about eight years now. It's ______________ and ______________. But it's already famous among backpackers ______________ ______________ ______________. They know that it's very cheap but also ______________ and ______________. It's in the city's center, which is a great location for travelers. Some people prefer hotels, but I think they are too ______________ and unnecessary.

7   What will the man probably do next?

M   Excuse me. I checked in late, and I'm really ______________.

W   Would you like dinner or just a snack?

M   I'd like a ______________ and something to ______________. Is that possible?

W   Of course. This is the number for ______________ ______________. They will help you.

M   Is room service still ______________?

W   Yes, it's a 24-hour service.

M   Oh, I'm so glad to hear that. Thanks.

  What makes the speaker like the hotel most?

I wasn't sure what to expect, but I do really like my room. The carpet is old and worn, but you can really sense the _____________ of the place. I like the fact that I have a Roman-style balcony that I can go out on. The staff here even wears medieval-style _____________. It makes me feel like I'm in a _____________ _____________ period. Of course, all of the services are _____________. That's what I liked most. After all, I don't think I would really want to stay in a real Roman-style hotel.

Listen and Fill in the blanks.

1 According to the talk, what is NOT needed to apply for a job?

______________ for a job is never easy. It requires time and patience. First, you should look at the ______________ for the position you want. Don't bother applying if you don't ______________ for the job. You will just be wasting your time. However, if you ______________ the requirements, fill out the ______________ ______________, send your ______________, and be prepared to be rejected just in case. You may have to apply to a lot of jobs, but, if you don't give up, you will find something eventually.

2 Which statement best describes the situation?

M   Your resume is very good.

W   Thank you. I really think I am perfect for the ______________.

M   Why?

W   My qualifications are ______________, and I am a ______________ person.

M   I'm sure you are. But we are looking for someone with more experience.

W   I don't have a lot of experience, but I ______________ ______________ ______________.

3 How does the man feel about his new job?

W   How do you like this job ______________ ______________, Mr. Peter?

M   I love it. The students are wonderful and eager to learn music.

W   I am glad to hear that!

M   I do ______________ my ______________ students though. Sometimes the younger students here are ______________ ______________ with each other.

W   Yes, but that's how younger people are.

4 **Why has the man probably NOT found a part-time job?**

M   I need a _________________ _________________. I have to buy some textbooks.

W   It's difficult to find a good job. Most part-time jobs are hard work, and they don't pay very well.

M   I know that, but it doesn't matter. I'm a little _____________, but I don't have any _____________.

W   I'll ask my boss whether he needs another waiter.

M   That would be great. I'm available to start this weekend if _____________ _____________.

W   I will let you know if he wants to _____________ you.

5 **What is the main idea of the talk?**

When applying for a job, it should be something you _____________ and _____________ _____________ _____________. If you are good at writing, you should look for a job where you will do a lot of writing. Perhaps you have an interesting hobby, _____________ _____________ creating webpages. Then try to become a website and graphic designer. It is better to choose a job doing something you enjoy since you will be spending a lot of time _____________ _____________.

6 **Which is true about the conversation?**

W   So the computer is working now?

M   Yes, I _____________ it.

W   How long did it take?

M   Only about _____________ _____________.

W   It was probably very _____________.

M   Not really. I had fun.

W   You must be good at your job.

M   I do enjoy it. Besides, I _____________ really hard to do this well.

7 **What is the main idea of the talk?**

It could take months of ______________ ______________ to find the job that you really want. If you already have a job, it may be easier to find information about job ______________. You could speak to your co-workers in your company, for example. But it also means that you have ______________ ______________ time to search. If you are unemployed, you can treat your search like a full-time job. You can use newspapers, the Internet, or an employment service. With luck and hard work, you can soon find your ______________ ______________.

8 **What is the purpose the talk?**

These days, it is ______________, when looking for a job, to get professional help. There are many companies offering to help people find ______________ ______________. They are called employment agencies or personnel placement services. If you are looking for a job though, be careful. While most of these companies will ______________ ______________ offer good services, the costs of getting their assistance are ______________. Often the company doesn't provide a guarantee that they will find you a job. You should be ______________ about what they are offering you before paying for their services.

Listen and Fill in the blanks.

1   What is NOT true about the conversation?

W   Could I see your ____________, please?

M   Yes. Here is my passport.

W   Are you coming here on ____________ or on ____________?

M   I have a short business meeting tomorrow, but I'm actually here on vacation.

W   You have a tourist visa, but you're here on business? Please show me your ____________ ____________.

M   Here it is. I only have one business meeting, and the rest of my time will be vacationing.

W   I see. Where are you staying?

M   The Lotte Hotel.

W   Do you have ____________ ____________?

M   No.

W   Okay. ____________ ____________ ____________ ____________.

2   What will the woman do after the conversation?

M   Hi, how was your ____________?

W   It was a little bumpy, but I guess that it wasn't too bad.

M   Yeah, and your plane arrived ____________ ____________ as well. That's always nice.

W   Totally. The last time I came here, I got ____________ by a couple of hours. Do you remember that?

M   Yes, I do. So, did you check any bags for this flight?

W   Yeah, so I guess that we should go ____________ ____________ ____________ now.

3　According to the talk, which safety tip is correct?

Most of us ＿＿＿＿＿＿ the safety video that is played to passengers before the flight takes off. But, actually, we should take careful note of this video. It may be boring, but it is for our own safety. These are some of the ＿＿＿＿＿＿ ＿＿＿＿＿＿. We are reminded to ＿＿＿＿＿＿ our seat belts. All electronic equipments must be ＿＿＿＿＿＿ ＿＿＿＿＿＿ during takeoff and landing. No one is allowed to ＿＿＿＿＿＿ on the flight. Cell phones should remain ＿＿＿＿＿＿ at all times. No sharp objects may be brought on board.

4　What is true about the conversation?

W　Can I help you, sir?

M　I've just come in on KLM Flight 345. Do you know where I can ＿＿＿＿＿＿ ＿＿＿＿＿＿ ＿＿＿＿＿＿?

W　That's over on belt 12, sir.

M　Oh, I see. Where everyone's waiting. I guess I should have ＿＿＿＿＿＿. Thanks.

5　What will the man do after the conversation?

W　Do you have anything to ＿＿＿＿＿＿?

M　What do you mean?

W　Are you carrying any plants or animals? Do you have items, such as alcohol or cigarettes, on which you must ＿＿＿＿＿＿ ＿＿＿＿＿＿ ＿＿＿＿＿＿?

M　No, I don't have any of those items. I was only on a business trip.

W　Very well. Please ＿＿＿＿＿＿ ＿＿＿＿＿＿ this form, and walk through that gate.

M　Which gate is that?

W　The gate with the ＿＿＿＿＿＿ which reads, "＿＿＿＿＿＿ ＿＿＿＿＿＿ ＿＿＿＿＿＿."

6　What word best describes the speaker's feelings?

I had a very ＿＿＿＿＿＿ ＿＿＿＿＿＿ at the airport recently. I walked through the metal detector, and it ＿＿＿＿＿＿ ＿＿＿＿＿＿. The security officer asked me to walk through the machine again after taking off my jacket. But he spoke very ＿＿＿＿＿＿, so many people turned to stare at me. I walked through the machine three times, and it still went off. More and more people stopped to see what was happening. Finally I ___________ my ___________ ___________ and walked through. Everyone ___________ ___________ me.

 What will the speaker do the next time?

I usually arrive at the airport two and a half hours early for my flight. But I still have to wait over an hour to check my bags in. It's very ___________ flying ___________ ___________. The business class counter is never busy. ___________ ___________ passengers who turn up can just go straight there and check in while all of us have to wait. I'm not flying economy class any more if I can ___________ ___________.

8 **Which is true about the speaker?**

I was in the airport last year when I heard this ___________: "We ___________ to inform you that all scheduled flights to Seoul have been cancelled due to bad ___________ ___________." My son's birthday was the following day, and I had promised him I would be home. I went to the desk, but they could not help me. I ___________ ___________ spending the next day in the airport wishing I was at home.

LISTEN to the MAX

The Best Preparation and Practice

for improving your Listening Skills

1

K&Y English Lab

ANSWERS & SCRIPTS

DARAKWON

LISTEN to the MAX

K&Y English Lab

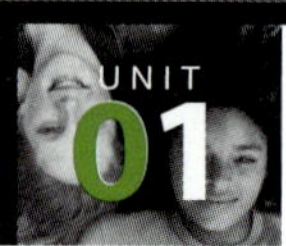

UNIT 01 Getting to Know You

정답 answer

Key Expressions
1 1 shake hands 2 meet 3 alone 4 smile
5 introduce
2 2, 4, 7
3 1 ⓐ 2 ⓒ 3 ⓔ 4 ⓑ 5 ⓖ 6 ⓕ 7 ⓓ

Listening Practice
1 (C)   **2** (B)

Check Up
Listening Task *01* 1 (B)   2 1) T   2) T   3) F
Listening Task *02* 1 1) ⓑ   2) ⓒ   3) ⓐ
Listening Task *03* 1 (C)   2 (B)
Listening Task *04* 1 (D)

Listening Test
1 (D)   **2** (D)   **3** (C)   **4** (C)   **5** (D)   **6** (C)
7 (C)   **8** (B)

스크립트 & 해석 script & translation

Key Expressions

1 표에서 가장 적절한 단어를 골라 빈칸을 채우시오.
1 새로운 사람을 만났을 때, 그들과 악수해야 한다.
2 로빈을 언제 처음 만났니?
3 나는 지금 다른 사람과 함께 살지 않는다. 나는 혼자 산다.
4 만약에 당신이 다른 사람들을 만날 때 웃는다면, 그들은 편안하게 느낄 것이다.
5 앨리스는 내일 진을 폴에게 소개할 것이다.

2 새로운 사람을 만났을 때 사용할 수 있는 표현들을 고르시오.

1 오래만이야.   2 만나서 반갑습니다.
3 잘 지내?   4 처음 뵙겠습니다.
5 나중에 보자.   6 오래만이야.
7 안녕, 내 이름은 김 폴이야.
8 가족에게 안부 전해줘.

3 다음 문장들을 가장 잘 어울리는 대답과 연결하시오.
1 좋아하는 음식이 뭐야?
　ⓐ 나는 일본 음식을 좋아해.
2 안녕, 난 제인이야.
　ⓒ 안녕, 제인. 난 제이슨이야.
3 이봐, 어떻게 지내?
　ⓔ 그럭저럭.
4 안녕, 난 히데오야.
　ⓑ 만나서 반가워. 난 제인이야.
5 어디 출신입니까?
　ⓖ 사실, 전 보스톤 출신이에요.
6 앨런을 어떻게 알아?
　ⓕ 같은 대학교 다녔어.
7 팀, 폴 만난 적 있어? 폴, 이쪽은 팀이야.
　ⓓ 응, 만난 적 있어. 잘 지내니?

Listening Practice

1

Hi, I'm Mary. I'm 14 years old. I go to a school in Boston where I am in grade 9. I was born in America and have lived there all my life. I like playing tennis and basketball as well as some other games. I have two brothers, John and Paul. I have lots of good friends, but my parents say I'm still too young to date.

▶ **be born** 태어나다 **as well as** ~와 마찬가지로, ~도
too ~ to... ~하기엔 너무 ...하다

안녕, 나는 메리야. 14살이지. 보스턴에 있는 학교를 다니고 9학년이야. 난 미국에서 태어났고 거기서 계속 살았어. 난 테니스와 농구, 그리고 다른 운동을 하는 것을 좋아해. 난 존과 폴, 두 명의 남자 형제가 있어. 좋은 친구들이 많이 있지만, 부모님은 내가 데이트 하기에는 아직 어리다고 하셔.

화자에 대해 사실이 아닌 것은?
(A) 몇몇 운동을 하는 것을 좋아한다.
(B) 남자 친구가 없다.
(C) 남자 형제와 여자 형제가 있다.
(D) 다른 나라에서 산 적이 없다.

2

W1　Sally, this is my friend Pete. We are in the English club together.

W2　Hi, Pete. Are you waiting for a table, too?

M　Actually, I'm waiting for my friends. We're supposed to meet here.

W2　Really? Well, I hope they'll get here soon.

M　I hope so, too. I haven't eaten all day.

▶ wait for 기다리다　be supposed to ~하기로 되어 있다
get 도착하다

여1　샐리, 이쪽은 내 친구 피트야. 우린 같은 영어 클럽에 속해 있어.
여2　안녕, 피트. 너도 좌석 기다리고 있는 거야?
남　사실, 난 내 친구들을 기다리고 있어. 여기서 만나기로 했거든.
여2　정말? 그들이 곧 여기 오기를 바래.
남　나도 그러길 바래. 하루 종일 아무것도 못 먹었거든.

남자는 어떻게 느끼고 있을까?

(A) 흥분된
(B) 배고픈
(C) 슬픈
(D) 실망한

Check Up

Listening Task *01*

M　Do you like classical music?

W　Yeah, I like it a lot.

M　Me, too. So how often do you go to concerts?

W　About once a month if I'm not too busy.

M　I see. Did you hear Beethoven's *9th Symphony* in Seoul last month?

W　No, I missed that. How was it?

M　It was great. Anyway, I'm Rod.

W　Hi, Rod. I'm Rachel.

M　Hi, Rachel. So, are you going to go in now?

▶ classical music 클래식 음악　how often...? 얼마나 자주 ~?
Symphony 교향곡　miss 놓치다

남　클래식 음악 좋아해요?
여　예, 굉장히 좋아해요.
남　저도 그래요. 콘서트에는 얼마나 자주 오세요?
여　바쁘지 않으면 한 달에 한 번 정도요.
남　그렇군요. 지난달에 서울에서 연주된 베토벤 9번 교향곡 들었어요?
여　아니요, 못 갔어요. 어땠어요?
남　대단했어요. 아, 전 로드라고 합니다.
여　안녕하세요, 로드. 전 레이첼이에요.
남　안녕하세요, 레이첼. 지금 입장할 건가요?

1　상황을 가장 잘 설명하고 있는 문장은?

(A) 그들은 둘 다 콘서트를 위해 대기하고 있는 음악 가들이다.
(B) 그들은 콘서트 전에 만난 서로 모르는 사이이다.
(C) 그들은 서울에서 하는 베토벤 9번 교향곡을 들으려고 한다.
(D) 그들은 미래의 음악 공연에 대해 얘기하고 있다.

2　맞으면 T, 틀리면 F에 체크하시오.

1) 남자는 베토벤 9번 교향곡을 들으러 갔다.
2) 여자는 대개 한 달에 한 번 콘서트에 간다.
3) 남자는 여자를 잘 안다.

Listening Task *02*

ⓐ

W　Hi, there. My name is Mary.

M　Hi, Mary. I'm Bill. Nice little place, isn't it?

W　Yes, I like coming here on Saturday mornings for coffee. It's nice and quiet, so I can read.

여　안녕하세요, 저는 메리예요.
남　안녕하세요, 메리. 전 빌이에요. 정말 좋은 곳이죠?
여　예, 전 토요일 오전에 커피를 마시러 이곳에 오는 것을 좋아한답니다. 분위기도 좋고 조용해서 책을 읽을 수 있거든요.

ⓑ

M　Excuse me, but can you help me? I can't find my classroom, 22B.

W　Sure. Are you a new student here?

M　Yeah. My name is Jonathan. I just moved here from Toronto.

▶ move 이사하다

남　실례합니다만, 저 좀 도와 주실 수 있나요? 제 교실인 22B를 찾을 수가 없어서요.
여　물론이죠. 여기 새로 온 학생인가 봐요?
남　예. 제 이름은 조나단입니다. 토론토에서 여기로 막 이사 왔어요.

ⓒ

W　Sorry to bother you, but is this the line for section C?

M　Yes, it is. Have you seen this film before?

W　No, but I heard it's good. I love SF movies.

M　Me, too. I'm Robert, by the way.

W　Nice to meet you. I'm Emily.

▶ bother 귀찮게 하다, 번거롭게 하다　section 부분, 구역
SF movie 공상과학 영화

여 방해해서 죄송합니다만, 이 줄이 섹션 C인가요?
남 맞아요. 전에도 이 영화 본 적 있나요?
여 아뇨, 하지만 좋다는 얘기는 들었어요. 전 SF 영화를 좋아해요.
남 저도요. 아, 전 로버트입니다.
여 만나서 반가워요. 전 에밀리입니다.

1 각 그림과 어울리는 대화의 번호를 쓰시오.

1)  2)  3) 

Listening Task 03

M Hi there. I don't think we've met. My name is James.

W Nice to meet you. I'm Alice.

M This is really fun tonight, isn't it?

W It sure is. There are lots of people here. Have you known Mary long?

M Actually, we're cousins. I'm visiting from Seattle just for this birthday party.

W Really? I've never been there before. What's it like?

M It's nice. How do you know Mary?

W We've been friends since I moved here three years ago.

▶ **actually** 사실, 실제로

남 안녕하세요. 우리 초면인 것 같네요. 제 이름은 제임스입니다.
여 만나서 반가워요. 전 앨리스에요.
남 오늘밤 정말 재미있죠?
여 예. 여기는 사람들이 정말 많네요. 메리랑은 얼마나 오랫동안 알고 지냈죠?
남 사실 우린 사촌이에요. 전 이 생일 파티 때문에 시애틀에서 왔어요.
여 정말요? 전 거기 한 번도 가 본 적이 없어요. 어때요?
남 좋은 곳이죠. 메리는 어떻게 알아요?
여 제가 3년 전에 여기로 이사온 이후로 계속 친구로 지내왔어요.

1 이 대화가 이루어지고 있는 곳은 어디인가?

(A)  (B) 

(C)  (D) 

2 남자는 메리를 어떻게 알고 있나?

(A) 그들은 시애틀에서 만났다.
(B) 그들은 사촌 지간이다.
(C) 그들은 3년 동안 친구로 지내왔다.
(D) 그들은 파티에서 만났다.

Listening Task 04

My name is Robert Kim. I was born in Korea, but my family moved to Hawaii when I was very young. I lived there for five years, and then we moved back to Korea. I really miss Hawaii. I used to go to the beach with my friends every weekend. We would go surfing or swimming. My mom and sisters like shopping, so we often went to Waikiki. It's famous for shopping and beaches, so we all had fun.

▶ **move back** 다시 ~로 이사하다 **miss** 그리워하다
used to (과거에) ~하곤 했다 **would** (과거에) ~하곤 했다
have fun 즐겁게 지내다

제 이름은 로버트 김입니다. 전 한국에서 태어났지만, 어렸을 때 저희 가족은 하와이로 이주했습니다. 전 거기서 5년 동안 살았고, 다시 한국으로 돌아왔습니다. 전 정말로 하와이가 그립습니다. 전 매주말마다 친구들과 함께 해변에 가곤 했습니다. 우리는 서핑과 수영을 하곤 했죠. 어머니와 여동생들은 쇼핑을 좋아해서, 종종 와이키키에 갔습니다. 그곳은 쇼핑과 해변으로 유명하기 때문에 우리 모두가 즐거운 시간을 보냈습니다.

1 남자가 하와이에서 즐기지 <u>않았던</u> 것은 무엇인가?

(A) 친구들과 어울려 다니기
(B) 해변에서 수영하기
(C) 해변에서 서핑하기
(D) 와이키키에서 쇼핑하기

Listening Test

1

W Hi, James. Do you remember me? We met last year.

M Julie! What a surprise. You used to work at McDonald's, right?

W Yeah, I still work there.

M Cool. I haven't been there for a long time. How's it going?

W Okay. So how are you enjoying the party?

M It's good. There are a lot of people here. Let's go and get a soda.

▶ **What a surprise!** 이럴수가!! 웬 일이니! **still** 아직도, 여전히
for a long time 오랫동안 **soda** 탄산음료

여　안녕, 제임스, 나 기억해? 우리 작년에 만났는데.
남　줄리! 웬 일이니. 너 맥도날드에서 일했었지, 맞지?
여　응, 아직도 거기서 일해.
남　그렇구나. 난 오랫동안 거기 못 가봤는데. 어떻게 지내?
여　잘 지내. 파티는 어떠니?
남　좋지. 여긴 사람이 너무 많다. 저쪽으로 가서 음료수 마시자.

상황을 가장 잘 설명하고 있는 것은?

(A) 여자는 음료수를 사려 하고 있다.
(B) 그들은 처음으로 만나고 있다.
(C) 두 사람은 맥도날드에서 커피를 사고 있다.
(D) 서로 알고 있는 두 사람이 파티에서 만나고 있다.

2

W　How would you describe yourself, Mr. Pitt?

M　I'm a pretty confident guy who wants to do great things.

W　What do you think is most important for you to achieve your goals?

M　It's important to work hard and be a good person if you want to reach your goals. I think I have these qualities.

▶ **describe** 묘사하다　**pretty** 상당히, 매우　**confident** 자신만만한, 확신 있는　**achieve one's goal** ~의 목표를 성취하다, 이루다 **reach** (손을 뻗어) 잡다　**quality** 자질, 특성

여　당신 자신을 설명한다면 뭐라고 할 수 있나요, 피트 씨?
남　전 훌륭한 일을 하기를 원하는 자신감 있는 남자입니다.
여　당신의 목표를 이루기 위해서 가장 중요한 것이 무엇이라고 생각하나요?
남　목표를 이루기를 원한다면, 열심히 일하고 좋은 사람이 되는 것이 중요합니다. 전 제가 이러한 자질을 가지고 있다고 생각합니다.

남자를 설명하기에 적절하지 못한 자질은 무엇인가?

(A) 자신감 있는
(B) 야심찬
(C) 열심히 일하는
(D) 감상적인

3

M　Excuse me, but are you Carol?

W　Yes, that's right, I just started working here. And what's your name?

M　Ben. It's nice to meet you, Carol.

W　It's nice to meet you too, Ben.

M　May I ask where you're from?

W　I just moved here from Georgia. How about you?

▶ **May I ask ~?** ~을 물어봐도 될까요?(정중히 질문하는 표현)

남　실례하지만, 캐롤 씨인가요?
여　예, 맞아요, 이제 막 여기서 일하기 시작했죠. 성함이 어떻게 되세요?
남　벤이요. 만나서 반가워요, 캐롤.
여　저도 만나서 반가워요, 벤.
남　어디 출신인지 여쭤봐도 될까요?
여　조지아에서 여기로 막 이사 왔어요. 당신은요?

여자의 질문에 대한 남자의 대답으로 가장 알맞은 것은?

(A) 전 조지아를 좋아합니다.
(B) 조지아는 살기 좋은 곳이죠.
(C) 전 뉴욕 출신이에요.
(D) 전 보스턴에 살고 있어요.

4

I've always been interested in art. When I was young, I spent all my free time drawing. Sometimes, it drove my parents crazy. It is natural that I always did well in art classes and then studied art at university. I really cannot imagine my life without art.

▶ **spend A -ing** ~하는 데 A를 쓰다　**drive** 억지로 ~하게 만들다 **natural** 당연한, 타고난

전 항상 미술에 관심이 있었습니다. 어렸을 때는, 모든 여가 시간을 그림 그리면서 보냈습니다. 때때로, 이는 나의 부모님을 화나게 만들었어요. 제가 항상 미술 시간에 잘하고 대학에서 미술을 공부하는 것은 당연한 일입니다. 전 정말로 미술 없는 제 인생을 상상할 수가 없습니다.

화자는 무슨 질문에 답하고 있는가?

(A) 왜 미술을 좋아하나요?
(B) 전공이 무엇이었나요?
(C) 무엇이 당신이 미술가가 되도록 만들었나요?
(D) 당신이 좋아하는 미술가는 누구입니까?

5

M　Hi. I see I'm not the only one outside getting some fresh air.

W　Yeah, I thought I'd stretch my legs a little during the break.

M　So, what do you think of this band so far?

W　I think it's really good. It was worth every penny for the ticket.

M　Yeah, I think so, too. Do you come here often?

W　Yes, when I'm not bowling.

M　Oh, cool. How often do you play?

W　My friends and I go every Friday night.

M Awesome. My name is Arthur, by the way, but my friends call me Art.

W I'm Marilyn. Nice to meet you, Art.

▶ stretch 쭉 펴다, 뻗다 break 휴식 시간 so far 지금까지
worth ~의 가치가 있는 awesome 아주 멋진, 굉장한

남 안녕하세요. 신선한 공기를 마시러 밖에 나온 사람이 저만은 아닌 것 같네요.
여 네, 휴식 시간 동안에 다리 스트레칭 좀 하려고요.
남 이 밴드에 대해 어떻게 생각하세요?
여 정말로 좋아요. 티켓 가격이 전혀 아깝지 않아요.
남 저도 그렇게 생각해요. 여기 자주 오시나요?
여 네, 볼링 치지 않을 때는요.
남 멋지군요. 얼마나 자주 볼링을 치나요?
여 친구들과 저는 매주 금요일 밤에 가요.
남 굉장한데요. 참, 제 이름은 아더에요. 제 친구들은 아트라고 부르죠.
여 전 마릴린이에요. 만나서 반가워요, 아트.

대화가 이루어지고 있는 곳은 어디인가?

(A) 레코드 가게
(B) 볼링 센터
(C) 체육관
(D) 콘서트 홀

6

W Excuse me. Are you looking for someone to play a game of chess with?

M Actually, I am. I'm just a beginner, though.

W That's OK. So am I. I'm Lisa. Nice to meet you.

M Good to meet you. I'm Alan. I haven't seen you around before.

W I used to play when I was younger, but I got busy studying and haven't played for years. I'm sort of rediscovering it. How about you?

M I wanted to get a hobby which could help me meet new people.

▶ play a game of chess 체스 게임을 하다 beginner 초급자
sort of 말하자면 rediscover 재발견하다

여 실례합니다만, 체스 게임을 같이 할 사람을 찾고 있나요?
남 사실, 그렇습니다. 그런데 저는 초보자에요.
여 괜찮아요. 저도 그래요. 전 리사입니다. 만나서 반가워요.
남 만나서 반갑습니다. 전 앨런이에요. 전에 이곳에서 본 적이 없는 것 같아요.
여 어렸을 때는 체스 게임을 하곤 했는데 공부하느라 바빠지면서 몇 년간 못 했어요. 재발견하고 있는 셈이죠. 당신은요?
남 전 새로운 사람을 만날 수 있는 취미를 갖고 싶었어요.

여자는 왜 최근에 체스 게임을 하지 않았나?

(A) 자신감이 부족했다.

(B) 지는 것을 싫어했다.
(C) 너무 바빴다.
(D) 멀리 있었다.

7

My name is William Brightman, and I'm an architect. I live in Berlin, Germany, but I was born and raised in Australia. I'm married and have three children, two boys and one girl. All of my children go to a bilingual school here in Berlin, so they can speak English and German fluently. We like it here and plan to stay for a few more years, and then we'll probably move back to Australia.

▶ architect 건축가 be raised in ~에서 자라다
bilingual 두 나라 말을 하는 fluently 유창하게 probably 아마도

제 이름은 윌리엄 브라이트맨이고, 건축가입니다. 전 독일의 베를린에 살지만 호주에서 태어났고 자랐어요. 전 결혼했고 세 명의 아이들이 있는데, 두 명은 사내 아이들이고 한 명은 여자애에요. 제 아이들은 모두 두 언어를 병용하는 학교에 다녀서 영어와 독일어를 유창하게 말할 수 있답니다. 저희는 이곳을 좋아하고 몇 년 더 이곳에 머무르다가 아마 호주로 다시 돌아갈 것입니다.

남자에 대해 사실이 <u>아닌</u> 것은?

(A) 그는 원래 호주 태생이다.
(B) 그는 베를린에 사는 건축가이다.
(C) 그는 내년에 이사할 계획을 하고 있다.
(D) 그는 두 명의 아들과 한 명의 딸이 있다.

8

People say that I must be really smart because I study a lot. It's true that I spend a lot of time on my own studying, but the truth is that I am quite shy and don't go out very often. I would like to meet more people, but I'm not very confident in public. It's easier for me to stay home and read.

▶ smart 똑똑한 spend time on ~하는 데 시간을 보내다
shy 수줍음을 타는 in public 대중 앞에서

사람들은 내가 공부를 많이 하기 때문에 분명 똑똑할 거라고 말한다. 내가 공부에 많은 시간을 쏟는 것은 사실이지만, 나는 수줍음이 많아 밖에 자주 나가지 못한 것이 사실이다. 나는 더 많은 사람들을 만나고 싶지만, 사람들 앞에서 자신감이 정말 없다. 내게는 집에서 책을 읽는 것이 훨씬 쉬운 일이다.

남자를 가장 잘 설명하는 단어는?

(A) 지적인
(B) 자신이 없는
(C) 불운한
(D) 정열적인

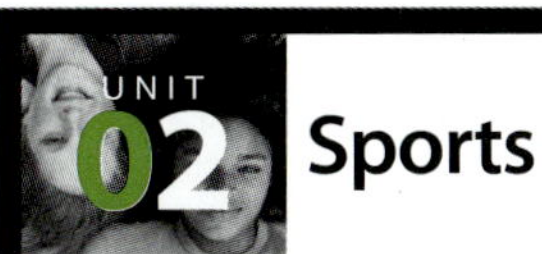

02 Sports

정답 answer

Key Expressions
1　1 umpire　2 score　3 gold medal
　　4 penalty kick　5 dribble
2　1 bat, diamond, strike　2 serve, court, racket
3　1 ⓓ　2 ⓔ　3 ⓑ　4 ⓒ　5 ⓐ　6 ⓕ　7 ⓖ

Listening Practice
1　(C)　　　　**2**　(B)

Check Up
Listening Task *01*　1 (A)　2 (B)
Listening Task *02*　1 1) ⓐ　2) ⓒ　3) ⓑ
Listening Task *03*　1 (C)　2 (C)
Listening Task *04*　1 (B)

Listening Test
1 (C)　**2** (C)　**3** (C)　**4** (A)　**5** (B)　**6** (D)
7 (A)　**8** (B)

스크립트 & 해석 script & translation

Key Expressions

1　표에서 가장 적절한 단어를 골라 빈칸을 채우시오.
　1 주 심판이 "파울볼!"이라고 외쳤다.
　2 점수는 5대 0으로 우리가 앞섰다.
　3 그는 2004년 올림픽 경기에서 금메달을 땄다.
　4 심판은 그들에게 심한 파울에 대한 페널티킥을 주었다.
　5 농구에서는 공을 패스하고 슛을 쏘고 드리블하는 법을 알아야 한다.

2　그림과 관련 있는 단어를 아래에서 찾으시오.

서브하다	그라운드	코트	어시스트	라켓
배트	투수판	스트라이크	전반전	슛하다

3　다음 문장들을 가장 잘 어울리는 대답과 연결하시오.
　1 얼마나 자주 야구 경기장에 가니?
　　ⓓ 한 달에 한 번 정도.
　2 어떤 팀에 소속되어 경기하니?
　　ⓔ 응, 난 야구 팀 멤버야.
　3 좋아하는 축구팀이 어디야?
　　ⓑ 난 맨유 팬이야.
　4 무슨 운동해?
　　ⓒ 매일 아침 조깅을 해.
　5 레슬링 좋아해?
　　ⓐ 아니, 근데 보는 건 좋아해.
　6 스노우보드 타 본 적 있어?
　　ⓕ 응, 정말 재미있었어.
　7 너희 나라에서 가장 인기 있는 스포츠는 뭐야?
　　ⓖ 당연히 축구지.

Listening Practice

1

The basic rules of this game are very simple. There are two teams playing against each other. Each team must try to get control of the ball and kick it into the other team's net. Whoever kicks the most balls into the net wins the game. The players may not touch the ball with their hands.

▶ basic 기본의　simple 간단한　against ~에 대항하여, 반대하여　get control of ~을 조절하다　net 그물

이 게임의 기본 규칙은 아주 간단하다. 두 팀이 대항해서 경기를 한다. 각 팀은 공을 잘 다뤄서 다른 팀의 네트 안으로 그것을 차야 한다. 네트 안에 공을 가장 많이 넣는 팀이 경기에서 이긴다. 선수들은 손으로 공을 만져서는 안 된다.

남자가 설명하고 있는 스포츠는 무엇인가?

(A) 크리켓
(B) 테니스
(C) 축구
(D) 배드민턴

2

W　Hey, Jim. What do you think about tonight's game?

M I think the New York Yankees will lose to the LA Dodgers by three.

W Me, too. I think the Dodgers will finally win the World Series.

M Actually, they should have won last year, but their best pitcher was out with an injury during the playoffs.

W Yeah. That's too bad.

▶ lose to ~에게 지다 should have p.p. ~했어야 했다
pitcher 야구의 투수 injury 부상 playoff 우승 결정전 시리즈

여 안녕, 짐. 오늘밤 경기에 대해 어떻게 생각해?
남 난 뉴욕 양키즈가 LA 다저스에게 3점차로 질 것 같아.
여 나도 그래. 다저스가 결국 월드시리즈에서 우승할 것 같아.
남 사실, 작년에서 우승했어야 했는데 최고 투수가 플레이오프 중 부상으로 빠졌잖아.
여 응. 그것 참 안됐지.

대화에 대해 사실이 <u>아닌</u> 것은?

(A) 그들은 야구 경기에 대해 얘기하고 있다.
(B) 남자는 양키즈가 경기에서 이길 것으로 기대한다.
(C) 남자는 다저스가 작년에 이겼어야 했다고 믿고 있다.
(D) 그들은 경기의 승리팀에 대해 같은 의견을 갖고 있다.

Check Up

Listening Task 01

I started learning how to play golf a few weeks ago, but it's not as easy as it looks. I've been spending a lot of time on the golf course. At first, I could not hit the ball very far, and I was hitting it into the trees. Now I'm hitting it straight and much further. But I still have a long way to go.

▶ straight 똑바로, 일직선으로 further 더 멀리(far의 비교급)

몇 주 전에 골프를 배우기 시작했는데, 보는 것처럼 쉽지 않다. 나는 많은 시간을 골프 코스에서 보내고 있다. 처음에는 공을 멀리 치지도 못했고, 나무에 맞추기도 했다. 지금은 똑바로 치고 훨씬 더 멀리 친다. 하지만 아직도 갈 길이 멀다.

1 **남자는 무엇에 대해 말하고 있나?**

   (A) 그의 새로운 취미
   (B) 골프를 좋아하는 이유
   (C) 골프 공을 치는 방법
   (D) 골프를 치는 이유

2 **골프 능력에 대한 그의 느낌을 보여주는 진술은?**

   (A) 급속히 향상되고 있다.

(B) 향상되고 있지만, 빠른 속도는 아니다.
(C) 그는 결코 좋은 골퍼가 되지 못할 것이다.
(D) 그는 천성적으로 훌륭한 골퍼이다.

Listening Task 02

ⓐ

It's one of those sports that involves cars. This sport is about speed. Some say it's a little dangerous. The cars are built especially for this exciting sport.

▶ involve 관련시키다, 포함하다 especially 특별히

이것은 자동차와 관련된 스포츠들 중 하나이다. 이 스포츠는 스피드와 관계가 있다. 어떤 사람들은 이 스포츠가 다소 위험하다고 말한다. 차들은 이 흥미진진한 스포츠를 위해 특별히 만들어진다.

ⓑ

You need really strong arms for this sport. You also need strong legs and a strong back because you are lifting things which are much heavier than you are.

▶ back 등 lift 들어올리다

이 스포츠를 하기 위해서는 강한 팔이 필요하다. 또한 당신의 몸무게보다도 훨씬 무거운 것들을 들어올려야 하기 때문에 강한 다리와 강한 등도 필요하다.

ⓒ

My kids are taking lessons in this sport. The first thing they learn is how to put their faces under the water and hold their breath for a few seconds.

▶ hold breath 숨을 참다

나의 아이들은 이 스포츠를 위해 수업을 받고 있다. 아이들이 맨 처음 배우는 것은 그들의 얼굴을 물 속에 넣고 몇 초간 숨을 참는 법이다.

1 **각 그림과 어울리는 대화의 번호를 쓰시오.**

1)  2)  3) 

Listening Task 03

M Ms. Rachel Simms, when you are playing tennis, does the fans' cheering give you the extra drive to win?

W Of course, it can make a difference. You can tell what the crowd thinks by the noise they make. But, mostly, you are so focused you don't really hear them.

M Do you have any superstitions for game days?

W Yes, I do. I always listen to the same song before every match.

▶ cheering 응원 extra 여분의, 별도의 drive 욕구, 추진력
crowd 군중, 관중 focus 집중하다 superstition 미신
match 경기, 시합

남 레이첼 심즈 씨, 테니스 경기를 할 때 팬들의 함성이 승리하는 데 도움이 되나요?

여 물론, 차이가 있습니다. 관중들이 내는 소리로 그들이 무엇을 생각하고 있는지 알 수 있죠. 하지만 대부분 경기에 집중하므로 실제로는 관중의 소리를 듣지 못합니다.

남 경기에 대한 어떤 미신을 가지고 있나요?

여 예. 전 항상 경기 전에 같은 노래를 들어요.

1 팬들의 환호는 선수에게 어떠한 영향을 미치나?

(A) 전혀 그 소리를 듣지 못한다.
(B) 너무 시끄럽다고 생각한다.
(C) 때때로 그녀의 기운을 북돋아 준다.
(D) 환호성이 그녀가 집중력을 잃게 한다.

2 대화에 대해 사실이 <u>아닌</u> 것은 무엇인가?

(A) 팬들의 환호성은 그녀의 경기에 영향을 미칠 수 있다.
(B) 여자는 관중들의 소리를 대부분 듣지 못한다.
(C) 여자는 미신을 전혀 믿지 않는다.
(D) 여자는 경기 전에 음악을 듣는다.

Listening Task *04*

I don't enjoy playing team sports such as soccer or baseball. I really dislike the competition in sports. It's not fun. I rather prefer running or cycling. I can do that alone or with a friend. I get up early every morning and then cycle for an hour. My legs usually hurt afterwards, but it's a great way to keep in shape.

▶ competition 경쟁 prefer 선호하다 afterward 그 후에, 나중에
keep in shape 건강을 유지하다, 몸매를 유지하다

나는 축구와 야구와 같은 팀 스포츠를 하는 것을 좋아하지 않는다. 나는 스포츠에서의 경쟁을 아주 싫어한다. 재미가 없다. 나는 달리거나 사이클 타는 것을 더 좋아한다. 혼자서 할 수도 있고 친구들과 함께 할 수도 있다. 나는 매일 아침 일찍 일어나서 한 시간 동안 사이클을 탄다. 운동 후에는 다리가 아프지만, 그것은 건강을 유지하는 좋은 방법이다.

1 남자는 축구나 야구와 같은 스포츠의 어떠한 점을 싫어하나?

(A) 친구와 함께 해야 한다.
(B) 다른 사람들과 경쟁해야 한다.

(C) 아침에 일찍 운동할 수 없다.
(D) 운동 후에 다리가 아프다.

Listening Test

1

I'm only fifteen years old, but I'm very tall. Everyone told me I should play basketball. So I joined my school's basketball team, and I am happy about it. Now they say I'm one of their best players. It's really easy for me to jump high and put the ball into the net. I'm not a great player, though. I'm just tall.

▶ join ~에 가입하다, 참가하다

나는 겨우 15살이지만 키가 굉장히 크다. 모든 사람들이 내가 농구를 해야 한다고 말한다. 그래서 나는 학교 농구팀에 가입했고, 이에 대해 만족하고 있다. 그들은 내가 베스트 선수들 중 한 명이라고 말한다. 높이 뛰고 네트에 공을 집어 넣는 일은 내겐 정말 쉬운 일이다. 하지만 나는 훌륭한 선수는 아니다. 키가 클 뿐이다.

화자에 대해 사실인 것은 무엇인가?

(A) 그는 농구를 싫어하지만 좋은 선수이다.
(B) 그는 농구를 좋아하지만 형편없는 선수이다.
(C) 그는 농구를 좋아하지만 자신이 훌륭한 선수라고 생각하지 않는다.
(D) 그는 농구를 싫어하고 그의 팀은 그가 형편없는 선수라고 생각한다.

2

W I am not sure how it is in Korea, but, here in the UK, boxing is still a very healthy sport. Soccer is definitely the number one sport here while boxing is not as popular. Is it the same in your country?

M It's kind of the same here. Most people in Korea prefer to watch a baseball game or maybe a soccer game rather than a boxing match.

▶ definitely 확실히, 명확히 while 반면에, 그런데
rather than ~보다는

여 여기 영국에서 권투는 여전히 아주 건강한 스포츠인데 한국에서는 어떤지 모르겠습니다. 영국에서 축구는 확실히 최고로 인기 있는 스포츠인 반면 권투는 그 만큼의 인기는 없습니다. 당신의 나라에서도 그런가요?

남 여기도 비슷합니다. 한국에 있는 대부분의 사람들은 권투 시합보다 야구나 축구를 보는 것을 더 좋아합니다.

	영국에서 인기 있는 스포츠	한국에서 인기 있는 스포츠
(A)	권투	야구
(B)	권투	권투
(C)	축구	야구
(D)	축구	권투

3

The Samsung Lions are playing very well tonight. If they defend well, they might win this game. If they do, they may win the prize for being the best team this season. This team is so talented, and their hard work is finally showing results. The fans here at the game tonight are going crazy.

▶ **defend** 방어하다, 수비하다 **prize** 상, 포상 **season** (운동 경기 등의) 시즌 **talented** 재능이 있는, 유능한 **go crazy** 흥분하다

삼성 라이온즈는 오늘밤 매우 선전하고 있습니다. 그들이 수비를 잘 한다면 이 경기를 이길 것입니다. 만약 그렇다면, 그들은 이번 시즌 최고의 팀에게 주는 상을 받게 될 것입니다. 이 팀은 정말로 훌륭하고, 그들의 노력이 마침내 결실을 보여 주고 있습니다. 오늘밤 이곳에서 경기를 관람하는 팬들이 흥분하고 있습니다.

화자는 무슨 일이 일어날 거라고 생각하고 있나?

(A) 라이온즈가 승리하기가 어려울 것이다.
(B) 라이온즈가 이길 수 없을 것이다.
(C) 라이온즈는 경기에서 이길 가능성이 있다.
(D) 라이온즈는 실력이 있지만, 우승하는 것은 어려울 것이다.

4

W Did you watch the FC Seoul game?
M Yeah. It was fantastic.
W So who won?
M It was pretty tense until the very end, but FC Seoul finally won.
W I wish I had been able to see it.
M It's a shame you missed it. Definitely soccer at its finest.

▶ **tense** 팽팽한, 긴장한 **It's a shame (that)...** ~이어서 아쉽다, 유감이다 **definitely** 확실히, 명확하게

여 FC 서울 경기 봤어?
남 응. 굉장했어.
여 그래서 누가 이겼는데?
남 마지막까지 아주 팽팽했지만, 결국에는 FC 서울이 이겼어.
여 나도 봤으면 좋았을 텐데.
남 그걸 놓치다니 아쉽다. 정말 최고 축구 경기였어.

(A) 대단했다.
(B) 끝까지 재미없었다.
(C) 경기 끝은 수치스러웠다.
(D) 어느 누구도 잘하지 못했다.

5

It is hard to understand my roommate. I think he watches the sports channel at least 15 hours a day. He doesn't do anything else, like going out with his friends. I don't understand how people live like that. I think it's more fun to go out and play sports with your friends rather than watching them by yourself.

▶ **It is hard to...** ~하기 어렵다 **at least** 최소한 **by oneself** 혼자서, 혼자 힘으로

내 룸메이트를 이해하기가 어렵다. 내 생각에 그는 하루에 최소한 15시간은 스포츠 채널을 보는 것 같다. 그는 친구들과 밖에 나가지도 않고, 그 밖에 다른 것을 하지도 않는다. 난 어떻게 사람이 그렇게 살 수 있는지 이해할 수가 없다. 난 혼자서 스포츠를 보는 것보다 친구들과 밖에 나가서 스포츠를 하는 게 훨씬 재미있다고 생각한다.

화자는 무엇에 대해 얘기하는가?

(A) 스포츠 경기를 보는 것이 얼마나 지루한 일인가
(B) 스포츠를 너무 많이 보는 사람
(C) 스포츠 채널이 가진 문제점
(D) 화자는 친구들과 무엇을 하는 것을 좋아하는가

6

M How did the match go yesterday afternoon?
W It went very badly.
M Did our team play badly?
W At the end of the first half, we were doing well. The score was 1:1. Then our best player got injured.
M How badly did we lose?
W Very badly. The final score was 6:1.

▶ **the first half** 전반전 **score** 득점, 득점 기록 **get injured** 부상을 당하다

남 어제 오후에 했던 경기 어땠어?
여 형편 없었어.
남 우리 팀이 형편 없었어?
여 전반전 마지막에는 잘했어. 점수가 1대 1이었어. 그리고 나서는 우리 팀 최고 선수가 부상을 당했지.
남 얼마나 형편 없이 졌는데?
여 아주 안 좋아. 최종 점수는 6대 1이었어.

화자들의 팀은 후반전에 몇 골을 넣었나?

(A) 1골

(B) 5골

(C) 7골

(D) 한 골도 못 넣었다.

7

His name is Choi Hong Man, but the world knows him as 'Techno Goliath.' He is perhaps the biggest athlete in Korea today. He used to be a wrestler in ssireum, which is Korean traditional wrestling. But now he is a tough fighter in K−1. He encourages his fans to stay healthy, take vitamins, and believe in themselves.

▶ athlete 운동선수 wrestler 레슬링 선수, 씨름 선수 traditional 전통의, 전통적인 encourage 장려하다, 용기를 북돋우다 stay healthy 건강을 유지하다 vitamin 비타민 believe in ~을 믿다

그의 이름은 최홍만이지만 세상 사람들은 그를 '테크노 골리앗'으로 알고 있다. 아마도 그는 현재 한국에서 가장 덩치 큰 선수이다. 그는 한국의 전통 레슬링인 씨름의 씨름꾼이었다. 그러나 이제 그는 K−1의 강한 파이터이다. 그는 그의 팬들이 항상 건강하고 비타민을 섭취하고 그들 자신을 믿도록 격려하고 있다.

이야기의 내용에 대해 사실인 것은 무엇인가?

(A) 홍만은 원래 그가 하던 스포츠를 하지 않는다.

(B) 홍만은 한국에서 가장 덩치 큰 사람이다.

(C) 홍만은 씨름에서 새로운 재미를 만들어냈다.

(D) 홍만에게는 훈련이 경기보다 훨씬 중요하다.

8

M   Whose turn is it to serve?

W   It's yours.

M   Hey, you're playing really well today.

W   I've been practicing all week.

M   Are you keeping score?

W   Yes, I am. You aren't doing too badly. But I might beat you.

M   I'd better start playing properly. Throw me the ball.

W   Watch out. Here it comes.

▶ turn 차례 serve (공을) 서브하다 practice 연습하다 keep 기입하다, 적다 beat (상대를) 패배시키다, 이기다 properly 올바르게, 정확히 watch out 조심하다

남   누가 서브할 차례지?

여   네 차례야.

남   너 오늘 정말 잘하는데.

여   이번 주 내내 연습했어.

남   점수 기록하고 있어?

여   응. 너도 나쁘진 않아. 하지만 내가 널 이길 거야.

남   좀더 집중해서 해야겠군. 공 던져.

여   조심해. 간다.

왜 남자는 좀 더 집중해서 해야겠다고 말했나?

(A) 그는 그가 잘 못하고 있다고 생각한다.

(B) 그는 여자가 그 경기에서 이기기를 원치 않는다.

(C) 그는 경기를 즐기고 있지 않다.

(D) 그는 연습을 안 했다.

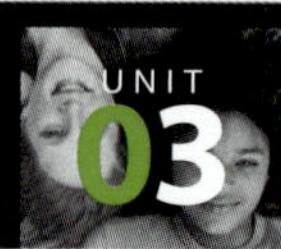

UNIT 03 Phone Calls

정답 answer

Key Expressions

1 1 residence   2 take a message   3 contact
   4 hang up   5 wrong number
2 1 ⓒ   2 ⓐ   3 ⓔ   4 ⓓ   5 ⓑ
3 1 ⓓ   2 ⓰   3 ⓐ   4 ⓒ   5 ⓑ   6 ⓕ   7 ⓔ

Listening Practice

1 (D)   **2** (A)

Check Up

Listening Task *01*   1 (C)   2 (C)
Listening Task *02*   1 1) F   2) F   3) F
Listening Task *03*   1 (C)   2 1) T   2) F   3) T
Listening Task *04*   1 (B)

Listening Test

1 (C)   **2** (C)   **3** (B)   **4** (A)   **5** (B)   **6** (C)
7 (B)   **8** (A)

스크립트 & 해석 script & translation

Key Expressions

1 표에서 가장 적절한 단어를 골라 빈칸을 채우시오.

   1 김 선생님 댁인가요?

   2 안 계시는데요. 메시지 남겨 드릴까요?

   3 비상시 우리가 연락을 취할 수 있는 사람이 있나요?

   4 끊지 마세요. 아직 할 얘기가 있어요.

   5 미안하지만, 전화를 잘못 거셨어요.

2 각각의 상황을 적절한 표현과 연결하시오.

   1 소리가 너무 작다.
      ⓒ "잘 안 들려요!"

   2 다른 사람에게 바꿔 준다.
      ⓐ "잠시만 기다리세요!"

   3 다른 사람과 통화중이다.
      ⓔ "죄송합니다. 통화중입니다."

   4 휴대폰이 통화권 밖이다.
      ⓓ "신호가 너무 약해요."

   5 전화번호가 변경됐다.
      ⓑ "이 번호는 더 이상 사용되지 않습니다."

3 다음 문장들을 가장 잘 어울리는 대답과 연결하시오.

   1 제게 온 메세지 있어요?
      ⓓ 예, 마크에게서 전화왔어요.

   2 다시 거시겠어요?
      ⓰ 예. 언제가 괜찮습니까?

   3 523-6397 아닌가요?
      ⓐ 전화 잘못 거셨는데요.

   4 그가 메시지를 받아볼 수 있게 할게요.
      ⓒ 감사합니다. 아주 중요한 일입니다.

   5 확실히 하기 위해, 다시 불러 드릴게요.
      ⓑ 예. 불러보세요.

   6 누구시지요?
      ⓕ 피터입니다.

   7 죄송한데 전화 거신 분은 지금 안 계세요.
      ⓔ 예, 제가 나중에 다시 걸겠습니다.

Listening Practice

1

Hello, Chris. This is Mark. I just called to ask if you can join us this weekend. My sister and I are going to the amusement park, and we have four tickets. You can bring your little brother if you want. Anyway, give me a phone call as soon as you listen to this message! Bye!

▶ amusement park 유원지, 놀이공원   bring 데리고 가다

안녕, 크리스. 나 마크야. 이번 주말에 우리랑 같이 갈 수 있는지 물어보려고 전화했어. 누나랑 내가 놀이공원에 갈 건데, 티켓이 4장 있어. 원한다면 네 남동생을 데리고 와도 돼. 어쨌든, 이거 듣는대로 전화해줘! 잘 있어!

이야기에 대해 사실이 아닌 것은 무엇인가?

(A) 마크가 크리스에게 전화했다.
(B) 크리스는 전화를 받을 수 없다.
(C) 마크가 크리스를 놀이공원에 초대하고 있다.
(D) 마크는 대답을 듣기 위해 다시 전화할 것이다.

2

W Hello. City Subway Lost and Found. How may I help you?

M Hi, I lost my bag today at City Hall Subway Station. I would like to know if someone found it.

W OK, could you describe it for me?

M _______________________________________

▶ lost and found 분실물 취급소   I would like to know if... ~인지 (아닌지) 알고 싶다   describe 묘사하다, 설명하다

여 여보세요. 지하철 분실물 센터입니다. 무엇을 도와 드릴까요?

남 예, 오늘 시청역에서 가방을 잃어버렸어요. 누군가 그것을 찾았는지 알고 싶어서요.

여 그 가방 모양을 설명해 주시겠습니까?

남 _______________________________________

남자는 뭐라고 대답할까?

(A) 음, 크고 갈색이에요. 제 이름이 안에 있어요.
(B) 제가 생각하기론, 좌석에 그것을 두었어요.
(C) 제 옆에 있는 여자가 말을 걸어서 혼란스러웠어요.
(D) 신경 쓰지 마세요. 제가 찾을게요.

Check Up

Listening Task *01*

M Hello, Jenny. How are you?

W I'm fine, thank you. Will I see you this afternoon for lunch?

M I'm calling to ask if we can change our appointment. Can we meet in the evening?

W I'm not sure if I'm busy this evening. Please hold on.

M OK.

W It looks as if I'm not busy. Are you free at 6 p.m.?

M How about an hour later?

W OK. See you then.

M Thanks. Bye.

▶ appointment (만나기로 한) 약속   hold on (전화를) 끊지 말고 기다려   It looks as if... ~인 듯하다   free 선약이 없는, 비어 있는, 한가한

남 여보세요, 제니. 잘 지내?

여 잘 지내, 고마워. 오늘 오후 점심에 보기로 했지?

남 약속 바꿀 수 있나 물어보려고 전화했어. 저녁에 보면 안 될까?

여 오늘 저녁에 바쁜지 아닌지 잘 모르겠는데. 잠시만.

남 응.

여 바쁘지 않을 것 같아. 저녁 6시 괜찮아?

남 한 시간 늦게는 어때?

여 좋아. 그럼 그때 보자.

남 고마워. 안녕.

1 여자는 왜 남자에게 잠시 기다려 달라고 했을까?

(A) 점심을 먹을 수 없어서 화가 났다.
(B) 점심을 먹고 있어서 바쁘다.
(C) 한가한지 보기 위해 다이어리를 체크하고 있다.
(D) 저녁에 외출할 수 있는지 아버지에게 물어보고 있다.

2 그들은 언제 만날 것인가?

(A) 점심 식사 후에
(B) 저녁 6시에
(C) 저녁 7시에
(D) 다음 날 점심 시간에

Listening Task *02*

M Good evening. Milano's Pizza. May I help you?

W Good evening. May I place an order?

M Sure. Will that be for delivery?

W No, I'll come to collect it.

M I see. What's your order, please?

W I'd like a jumbo-sized pizza with extra cheese and sausage, please.

M A large pizza with extra cheese and sausage, right?

W No, it's a jumbo size.

M I'm sorry. It will be ready in twenty minutes. Thanks for calling.

▶ place an order 주문하다   delivery 배달   collect (수하물을) 가지러 가다, 가져오다

남 안녕하세요. 밀라노 피자입니다. 무엇을 도와 드릴까요?

여 안녕하세요. 주문할 수 있나요?

남 예. 배달이신가요?

여 아뇨, 제가 가지러 갈게요.

남 알겠습니다. 무엇을 주문하시겠습니까?

여 치즈와 소시지가 있는 점보 사이즈 피자요.

남 치즈와 소시지가 있는 라지 피자, 맞으세요?

여 아뇨, 점보 사이즈요.

남 죄송합니다. 20분 후에 준비됩니다. 전화 주셔서 감사합니다.

1 맞으면 T, 틀리면 F에 체크하시오.

1) 여자는 치즈와 소시지가 있는 스몰 피자를 원한다.
2) 여자는 15분 후에 피자를 먹을 것이다.
3) 그들은 피자를 배달할 것이다.

Listening Task *03*

M Good day. How may I help you?

W Hello, operator. I'm trying to call someone in Canada, but I have a problem. Can you help me?

M Do you have the correct number including the international code for Canada as well as the city code?

W Yes, I do, but I can't get through. I've called this number many times before.

M Please read me the number, and I'll try to put your call through.

W Will there be an extra charge if you do that?

M No, you will be charged the same rate for the call. Please hold on.

▶ operator (전화국의) 교환원 include 포함하다
international code 국가 번호 city code 도시 번호
get through (전화를) 연결하다 put through (전화를) 연결하다
extra charge 추가 요금 rate 요금, 대금

남 좋은 하루입니다. 무엇을 도와 드릴까요?

여 안녕하세요, 교환원님. 캐나다로 전화하려고 하는데 문제가 있어요. 도와 주시겠어요?

남 캐나다 국가 번호와 도시 번호를 포함한 정확한 번호를 알고 계십니까?

여 네, 하지만 연결할 수 없었어요. 전에 이 번호로 여러 차례 전화를 걸었었는데요.

남 제게 번호를 알려주시면 연결시켜 드리겠습니다.

여 그러면 별도 비용이 드나요?

남 아뇨, 통화에 대한 요금만 부담하시면 됩니다. 잠시만 기다려 주세요.

1 **왜 여자는 자기가 맞는 번호를 가지고 있다고 생각하나?**

  (A) 그녀는 캐나다 출신이다.
  (B) 직접 번호를 찾아 보았다.
  (C) 전에 그 번호로 전화를 걸었었다.
  (D) 전에 교환원으로 일했었다.

2 **맞으면 T, 틀리면 F에 체크하시오.**

  1) 교환원이 전화를 연결해도 별도의 요금이 부과되지 않는다.
  2) 교환원은 그녀가 잘못된 도시 번호를 가지고 있다고 생각한다.
  3) 교환원은 그녀의 전화를 연결하려고 하고 있다.

Listening Task *04*

W Good morning, sir. How can I help you?

M Yes, I want to ask about my phone bill. It seems a little high. I'd like to see the charges, please.

W Oh, I'm sorry. You have to ask to receive an itemized bill. Would you like that?

M Yes, please.

W Ok. I just updated your file.

M So I will receive an itemized bill next time?

W Yes, so you'll be able to see all of the charges.

M Perfect. Thank you.

W Thank you for calling.

▶ phone bill 전화요금 청구서 charge 청구 금액, 요금
itemize 항목별로 쓰다

여 안녕하십니까, 무엇을 도와 드릴까요?

남 예, 제 전화 요금에 대해 문의 드리려고 합니다. 좀 많이 나온 것 같아요. 청구 금액을 보고 싶습니다.

여 죄송합니다. 항목별로 된 고지서를 받도록 요청하셔야 합니다. 그렇게 하시겠습니까?

남 예, 그렇게 해주세요.

여 예, 파일을 업데이트해 드렸습니다.

남 그럼 다음 번에는 항목별 고지서를 받게 됩니까?

여 예, 그럼 요금의 모든 것을 보실 수 있을 겁니다.

남 예. 감사합니다.

여 전화 주셔서 감사합니다.

1 **남자는 다음 번에 무엇을 받게 되는가?**

  (A) 더 많은 청구 금액
  (B) 항목별로 된 고지서
  (C) 남자의 파일
  (D) 새로운 전화번호

Listening Test

1

M Hello, this is Tom speaking.

W Hi, Tom. It's Peggy. What are you doing this Sunday?

M Not much. Homework mostly. How about you?

W I was thinking of watching a baseball game. Want to go with me?

M That would be fun, but I have a final exam next Monday. I should probably stay home and study.

W ________________________________

▶ mostly 대부분, 주로 final exam 기말고사

남 여보세요, 톰입니다.

여 안녕, 톰. 페기야. 이번 일요일에 뭐할 거야?

남 특별한 일은 없는데. 아마 숙제할 거야. 넌?

여 야구 경기 보려고 하는데. 같이 갈래?

남　그거 재미있겠다. 근데 나 다음 월요일에 기말 고사가 있어. 집에서 공부해야 해.

여　______________________

여자가 다음에 할 말로 적절한 것은?

(A) 좋아. 그때 보자.
(B) 네가 그럴 줄 알았어.
(C) 안타깝다.
(D) 난 시험이 없어.

2

W　T.G.I Friday's, how may I help you?
M　I would like to reserve a table for dinner tonight.
W　How many people are in your party?
M　Six.
W　OK, and what time will you be arriving?
M　Around 7 p.m.
W　Can I have your name, please?
M　James Kipper.
W　All right. We'll have your table ready for you, Mr. Kipper.
M　Thank you. Goodbye.

▶ reserve a table (식당의) 자리를 예약하다　party 일행, 무리

여　T.G.I Fiday's입니다. 무엇을 도와 드릴까요?
남　오늘밤 저녁 식사를 예약하려고 합니다.
여　일행이 몇 분이십니까?
남　6명이요.
여　네, 그럼 몇 시쯤 도착할 예정이신가요?
남　7시쯤요.
여　성함은요?
남　제임스 키퍼요.
여　알겠습니다. 테이블 예약해 두겠습니다, 키퍼 씨.
남　고맙습니다. 그럼.

대화에 따르면 다음 중 올바른 정보는 무엇인가?

	도착 시간	인원수
(A)	6	6
(B)	6	7
(C)	7	6
(D)	7	7

3

W　Good morning, may I help you?
M　Yes, is Marvin there?

W　I'm sorry. He's not in right now. May I take a message?
M　Do you know where he is?
W　I'm afraid he didn't leave that information.
M　OK, then. My name is Jason. Please tell him to call me as soon as possible. It's really important that I talk to him.
W　Yes, sir.

▶ take a message 메시지를 적다　leave 남기다

여　안녕하세요, 무슨 일이신가요?
남　네, 마빈 있습니까?
여　죄송합니다. 지금 부재중인데요. 메시지를 전해 드릴까요?
남　그가 어디 있는지 아십니까?
여　얘기를 안하고 나가서 모르겠어요.
남　네, 그럼. 제 이름은 제이슨입니다. 그에게 가능한 빨리 제게 전화해달라고 전해 주세요. 정말 중요한 일입니다.
여　네, 선생님.

왜 남자는 여자에게 마빈이 어디 있는지 물었나?

(A) 그는 마빈을 방문하기를 원한다.
(B) 그는 마빈과 긴급히 얘기해야 한다.
(C) 그는 마빈이 위험에 처해 있다고 생각한다.
(D) 그는 마빈의 좋은 친구이다.

4

What a day! I've been on the phone all afternoon. First, I called two people to remind them of their appointments. I spoke with one but had to leave a message for the other. Then, a friend of mine called just to say hello. Finally, I had to call three people back to answer some questions and give them information.

▶ remind 생각나게 하다, 상기시키다
　leave a message 메시지를 남기다

힘든 하루였다! 난 오후 내내 전화기를 붙들고 있었다. 먼저, 두 명에게 약속을 상기시켜 주려고 전화했다. 한 명하고는 통화했지만, 다른 한 명에게는 메시지를 남겨야 했다. 그리고 나서 내 친구가 안부를 물으려고 전화했다. 마지막으로, 난 세 명에게 몇 가지 질문에 답하고, 정보를 주기 위해 전화해야만 했다.

여자는 오늘 몇 통의 전화를 걸었나?

(A) 5
(B) 6
(C) 7
(D) 8

5

W   Hello. Anna speaking.

M   Hi, Anna. This is John. I haven't seen you lately.

W   I am just so busy.

M   Do you remember the book I lent you? Have you finished reading it?

W   Yes, I finished reading it weeks ago. I've been meaning to return it to you.

M   Good, I need it for my assignment.

W   I'll bring it to your house later.

M   I have to go out this afternoon. Will you call me before you come over?

W   Sure, I'll call you on your mobile phone.

▶ **lend** 빌려주다　**mean** ~할 작정이다, 의도하다
return 돌려주다, 반환하다　**assignment** 숙제, 연구 과제

여　여보세요. 안나입니다.

남　안녕, 안나. 존이야. 요새 통 못 봤네.

여　너무 바빴어.

남　내가 빌려 줬던 책 기억나? 그거 다 읽었어?

여　응, 몇 주 전에 다 읽었어. 너에게 돌려 주려고 생각하고 있었는데.

남　다행이다. 나 숙제하는 데 필요하거든.

여　나중에 너희 집에 가져다 줄게.

남　오늘 오후에 외출해야 하는데. 오기 전에 전화 줄래?

여　알았어. 휴대폰으로 전화할게.

남자가 전화한 목적은 무엇인가?

(A) 안나를 도와 주기를 원한다.

(B) 그녀로부터 책을 돌려 받기를 원한다.

(C) 숙제에 관해서 도움을 요청하고 있다.

(D) 바빠서 도움을 원한다.

6

People don't see each other when they speak on the phone. That means you don't have to be dressed very well when you call an old friend. In fact, you could be lying on the couch in your old clothes. If you meet your old friend in a coffee shop, it's different. On the telephone, you can also relax and catch up with your friend for hours.

▶ **speak on the phone** 전화통화하다　**couch** 긴 의자, 소파
relax 편하게 쉬다, 긴장을 늦추다

사람들은 전화로 얘기할 때 서로를 보지 못한다. 이것은 옛 친구에게 전화할 때 옷을 잘 갖춰 입을 필요가 없다는 것을 의미한다. 사실, 낡은 옷을 입고 소파에 누워있을 수도 있다. 만약에 커피숍에서 옛 친구를 만난다면, 상황은 다를 것이다. 전화상으로 당신은 친구와 몇 시간이고 편하게 얘기할 수 있다.

이 이야기는 어떤 질문에 대한 답인가?

(A) 옛 친구들을 어떻게 만나는가?

(B) 옛 친구들과 어떻게 휴식을 취하며 얘기하는가?

(C) 왜 친구들을 만나는 것보다 전화하는 것을 좋아하는가?

(D) 왜 친구들을 커피숍에서 만나는가?

7

The reason most people get voicemail is to avoid talking directly to other people. They can listen to callers' messages and choose who to talk to. This way, they can avoid talking to annoying friends or a boyfriend/girlfriend they "promised" to call!

▶ **avoid** 피하다　**directly** 직접, 곧바로　**annoying** 성가신, 귀찮은

대부분의 사람들이 음성 사서함을 갖는 이유는 다른 사람들과 직접적으로 얘기하는 것을 피하기 위해서다. 그들은 전화 건 사람들의 메시지를 듣고 누구와 얘기할지 선택할 수 있다. 이런 식으로 그들은 짜증나는 친구들이나 그들이 전화하기로 약속했던 남자 친구/여자 친구와 얘기하는 것을 피할 수 있는 것이다!

음성 사서함을 갖는 이유는 무엇인가?

(A) 짜증나는 친구에게 메시지를 보내기 위해

(B) 사람들과 직접적으로 얘기하는 것을 피하기 위해

(C) 어머니와 얘기하기 위해

(D) 다른 사람들을 만나는 것을 피하기 위해

8

W   I have a problem. My best friend and I talk on the phone a lot. But when someone else calls on the other line, she hangs up with me to talk to them. Then, she never calls me back! What should I do?

M   You should tell her how you feel! However, if she's really your best friend, would she choose her other friends over you?

▶ **hang up** (전화를) 끊다　**choose A over B** B 말고 A를 선택하다

여　문제가 하나 있어. 나는 내 베스트 프렌드와 전화로 얘기를 많이 해. 그런데 다른 사람이 전화를 걸면 그녀는 그들과 얘기하기 위해 내 전화를 끊어. 그리고서는 내게 다시 전화를 하지 않아! 내가 어떻게 해야 할까?

남　그녀에게 네가 어떤 기분인지 말해야 해. 하지만 만약에 그녀가 정말로 너의 가장 좋은 친구라면, 네가 아닌 다른 친구들을 선택할까?

남자의 충고와 일치하는 것은?

(A) 그녀의 베스트 프렌드는 그녀를 많이 좋아하지 않는다.

(B) 그녀는 다른 베스트 프렌드를 선택해야 한다.

(C) 그녀는 베스트 프렌드와 절교해야 한다.

(D) 그녀는 새로운 친구들을 찾아야 한다.

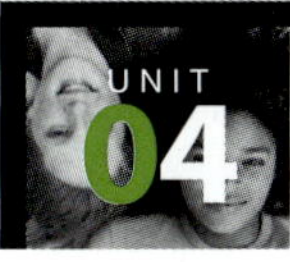

UNIT 04 Fashion

정답 answer

Key Expressions

<u>1</u> 1 hairstyle 2 dress up 3 out of fashion
   4 take off 5 in style
<u>2</u> 1 pajamas 2 suit 3 trousers
   4 undershirt 5 briefs
<u>3</u> 1 ⓖ 2 ⓐ 3 ⓔ 4 ⓑ 5 ⓓ 6 ⓕ 7 ⓒ

Listening Practice

<u>1</u> (A)   <u>2</u> (A)

Check Up

Listening Task *01* 1 (C)   2 1) F   2) T   3) F
Listening Task *02* 1 1) ⓑ   2) ⓐ   3) ⓒ
Listening Task *03* 1 (B)   2 (D)
Listening Task *04* 1 (B)

Listening Test

1 (B)   2 (D)   3 (C)   4 (D)   5 (C)   6 (D)
7 (C)   8 (C)

스크립트 & 해석 script & translation

Key Expressions

1 표에서 가장 적절한 단어를 골라 빈칸을 채우시오.
   1 당신의 새로운 스타일이 마음에 듭니까?
   2 파티에 갈 때는 잘 차려 입어야 합니다.
   3 누구도 더 이상 이런 스타일을 입지 않는다. 그건
     유행이 지났다.
   4 내가 가는 모든 집에 들어가기 전에 신발을 벗어야 한다.
   5 어떤 사람들은 새로운 종류의 옷만 입는다. 그들은
     유행하는 옷을 좋아한다.

2 각 단어들을 그것을 설명하는 그림과 연결하시오.

  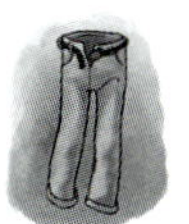 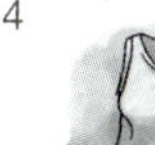 

3 다음 문장들을 가장 잘 어울리는 대답과 연결하시오.
   1 도와 드릴까요?
     ⓖ 네, 전 아이 옷을 찾고 있어요.
   2 그 티셔츠 사이즈가 어떻게 되죠?
     ⓐ 스몰 사이즈요.
   3 세일 중인가요?
     ⓔ 네, 5달러 밖에 안 해요.
   4 이 드레스 맘에 드니?
     ⓑ 좋은데 너무 짧은 것 같아.
   5 이 바지를 반품하고 싶어요.
     ⓓ 무슨 문제가 있나요?
   6 정장 스타일로 입는 거 좋아하니?
     ⓕ 아니, 난 캐주얼 스타일을 좋아해.
   7 보통 옷 어디서 사?
     ⓒ 백화점에서.

Listening Practice

<u>1</u>

My dad always wears funny clothes. Today, he has on a striped suit with a bright pink shirt and a pink tie. He always makes sure that his shirt and tie match. His shoes are very shiny. I think my dad's clothes have too many colors.

▶ striped suit 줄무늬 양복   make sure 확인하다, 확신하다
  match 조화되다, 어울리다   shiny 빛나는, 광택이 나는

우리 아빠는 항상 옷을 재미있게 입으신다. 오늘, 아빠는 줄무늬 정장과 핑크색 셔츠, 핑크색 타이를 매셨다. 아빠는 항상 셔츠와 타이 색을 맞추신다. 신발은 아주 반짝거린다. 난 아빠의 옷이 너무 많은 색깔을 포함하고 있다고 생각한다.

화자의 아버지가 입고 있는 옷은?

(A)    (B)  

  (C)  (D)

2

M Sally, you can't go to school in that skirt.
W Why not, Dad?
M It's too short. It's very cold today.
W But, Dad, my friends can wear skirts like this.
M No, you have to wear pants.
W Okay. I will wear pants today.

▶ wear 입다

남 샐리, 너 그 스커트를 입고 학교에 가면 안 된다.
여 왜요, 아빠?
남 너무 짧잖아. 오늘은 아주 추워.
여 하지만, 아빠, 제 친구들은 다 이렇게 입어요.
남 안 돼, 바지 입고 가거라.
여 알았어요. 오늘은 바지 입을게요.

무엇이 문제인가?

(A) 아버지는 샐리의 스커트가 마음에 들지 않는다.
(B) 샐리의 친구들은 스커트를 입는다.
(C) 아버지는 긴 치마를 좋아한다.
(D) 샐리는 바지를 좋아하지 않는다.

Check Up

Listening Task *01*

Clothing goes out of fashion very quickly. But the same clothing may become accepted again in the future. Fashion trends from the 1970s are popular again. Kids wear the same kinds of clothing their parents wore when they were growing up. They wear the same styles of jeans and the same bright colors. They can now wear their parents' clothing without being embarrassed that it's old-fashioned!

▶ out of fashion 유행에 뒤떨어지다, 한물가다   accept 받아들이다
trend 경향, 유행 스타일   embarrassed 당황한, 부끄러운
old-fashioned 구식의

옷은 금새 유행이 지난다. 하지만 똑같은 옷이 다시 유행할지도 모른다. 1970년대의 패션 트렌드가 다시 유행하고 있다. 아이들은 그들의 부모들이 자랄 때 입었던 것과 같은 옷을 입는다. 그들은 같은 스타일의 청바지와 같은 밝은 색깔의 옷을 입는다. 그들은 구식이라고 창피해 하지 않으면서 그들의 부모님의 옷을 입을 수 있다!

---

1 **이 이야기의 요지는 무엇인가?**

(A) 때때로 옷은 유행이 지난다.
(B) 때때로 아이들은 그들의 어머니의 옷을 입을 수 있다.
(C) 때때로 구식 옷이 나중에 다시 유행한다.
(D) 밝은 색깔이 다시 유행한다.

2 **맞으면 T, 틀리면 F에 체크하시오.**

1) 아이들은 그들의 부모님의 옷을 입을 수 없다.
2) 아이들은 그들의 부모님이 입었던 옷을 입고 있다.
3) 1970년대의 스타일은 유행하지 않는다.

Listening Task *02*

ⓐ

Many people are serious about clothes. I like to have fun. I like colors and designs on my clothes. Flowers, stripes, polka dots – I like them all!

▶ serious 진지한   have fun 즐기다, 재미 보다
polka dots 물방울 무늬

많은 사람들은 옷에 대해 진지하다. 난 재미있는 것이 좋다. 난 내 옷의 색깔과 디자인을 좋아한다. 꽃무늬, 줄무늬, 물방울 무늬 – 이것 모두를 좋아한다!

ⓑ

I'm really tall, so it's difficult to find clothing that is my size. Sometimes jeans are too short for me. Now my mother designs my clothing and then makes it herself. I can wear anything I want now.

▶ size 사이즈, 치수

난 키가 너무 커서 내게 맞는 사이즈의 옷을 찾는 것은 어렵다. 때때로 청바지들은 내게 너무 짧다. 지금은 어머니가 내 옷을 디자인하고 직접 만들어 주신다. 지금은 입고 싶은 옷을 입을 수 있다.

ⓒ

I don't like the clothes my sister wears. She only wears dresses and skirts. I like shorts and sneakers.

▶ shorts 반바지   sneakers 운동화

난 내 여동생이 입는 옷 스타일을 좋아하지 않는다. 그녀는 드레스와 스커트만 입는다. 난 반바지와 스니커즈를 좋아한다.

1 **각 그림과 어울리는 이야기의 번호를 쓰시오.**

1)    2)    3)  

Listening Task 03

M Where are my jeans, Mom?

W I put them in the garbage.

M Oh no! Why did you do that?

W There were holes in them. You can't wear them.

M But they were my favorite jeans.

W I'm sorry, but I want you to look nice.

M They're supposed to have holes in them. It's the fashion.

W Everyone will think you need new jeans.

▶ **jeans** 청바지 **garbage** 쓰레기
be supposed to ~하기로 되어 있는

남 엄마, 제 청바지 어디 있어요?

여 쓰레기통에 넣었는데.

남 오, 이런! 왜 그러셨어요?

여 구멍이 나서. 그런 걸 입을 수는 없잖아.

남 하지만 제가 제일 좋아하는 청바지에요.

여 미안한데, 난 네가 멋지게 입고 다녔으면 한단다.

남 원래부터 구멍이 있는 거에요. 그게 유행이라고요.

여 다른 사람들은 다 네가 새 청바지가 필요하다고 생각할 거야.

1 소년의 감정을 가장 잘 묘사하는 단어는?

 (A) 기쁜

 (B) 속상한

 (C) 피곤한

 (D) 행복한

2 두 화자 사이의 가장 큰 차이점은 무엇인가?

 (A) 청바지에 구멍을 만드는 방식

 (B) 청바지를 쓰레기통에 넣는 방식

 (C) 새 청바지를 고르는 방식

 (D) 패션을 보는 방식

Listening Task 04

M I heard that you're getting married next week.

W Yes, I have so many things to do. My dress is not ready yet.

M Is it a long, white dress?

W No, it's a traditional Korean dress.

M I've never seen a Korean traditional wedding dress before.

W It's very colorful with red and green cloth.

M Will your fiancé also wear traditional wedding clothing?

W Not really. He will wear a black tuxedo.

M That's interesting. I hope that you will show me the photographs.

▶ **get married** 결혼하다 **fiancé** 약혼자 **tuxedo** 턱시도

남 너 다음 주에 결혼한다며.

여 응, 할 일이 너무 많아. 아직 드레스도 준비 안 됐어.

남 길고 하얀 드레스니?

여 아니, 전통적인 한국식 혼례복이야.

남 한국식 전통 혼례복은 본 적 없는데.

여 빨간색과 초록색이 들어간 색채가 풍부한 옷이야.

남 네 약혼자도 전통 혼례복 입어?

여 아니, 그는 검정색 턱시도를 입을 거야.

남 그거 재미있는데. 내게 사진 좀 보여줘.

1 여자의 결혼 사진은 무엇인가?

Listening Test

1

M Thank you for my birthday gift, Mom.

W Do you like the shirt I bought you?

M I don't really like the color.

W Why? Everyone is wearing pink these days.

M I know, but it's too bright for me.

W Dark colors are so boring.

M But I don't look good in such bright colors.

▶ **bright** (색이) 선명한, 산뜻한

남 생일 선물 고마워요, 엄마.

여 내가 사온 셔츠 맘에 드니?

남 색깔이 정말 맘에 안 들어요.

여 왜? 요즘에 다들 핑크색 입잖아.

남 알지만, 핑크색은 제겐 너무 밝아요.

여 어두운 색깔은 너무 따분해.

남 하지만 전 이런 밝은 색깔 옷이 안 어울려요.

왜 소년은 그 셔츠를 좋아하지 않나?

(A) 그는 셔츠의 색깔을 좋아하지 않는다.

(B) 그는 그것이 자기에게 어울리지 않는다고 생각한다.
(C) 어두운 색깔은 너무 따분하다.
(D) 남들과 같은 색의 옷을 입는 것이 싫다.

2

M　How can I help you today?
W　I really like this dress. But you don't have my size.
M　Let me see. We have the dress in your size but in a different color.
W　That's too bad. I tried that on earlier. I don't like the striped pattern.
M　What do you think of this dress? This one with dots will be very popular during summer.
W　Long dresses are not really my style, but it's a pretty color. OK, I'll take it.

▶ try (옷을) 입어보다　striped pattern 줄무늬　dot 물방울 무늬

남　무엇을 도와 드릴까요?
여　전 이 드레스가 굉장히 마음에 들어요. 그런데 제게 맞는 사이즈가 없네요.
남　어디 볼까요. 이 드레스로 고객님에게 맞는 사이즈는 있는데 색깔이 다르네요.
여　이런. 전에 그 옷을 입어봤어요. 전 줄무늬를 안 좋아해요.
남　이 드레스는 어때요? 여름에는 물방울 무늬가 유행할 거예요.
여　긴 드레스는 제 스타일이 아니지만 색깔이 이뻐요. 그걸로 할게요.

여자가 사려고 하는 옷은 무엇인가?

(A) 　(B) 

(C) 　(D) 

3

M　Mom, I like this shirt.
W　It's too expensive. How about this shirt?
M　I don't like the color.
W　There are many different colors.
M　But I want it in black.
W　Here's one. Try it on.
M　Hmm... Actually, I might try the blue one.

W　The color looks great on you.
M　Thanks, Mom. Let's take it.

▶ Try it on. 입어보세요.

남　엄마, 전 이 셔츠가 좋아요.
여　그건 너무 비싸. 이 셔츠는 어떠니?
남　색깔이 맘에 안 들어요.
여　다른 색깔도 있잖니.
남　검정색이었으면 좋겠어요.
여　여기 있네. 한 번 입어봐.
남　흠... 파란색 입어볼래요.
여　그 색깔 너한테 잘 어울리는데.
남　고마워요, 엄마. 그걸로 할게요.

대화 후, 소년은 무엇을 할까?

(A) 비싼 셔츠를 산다.
(B) 검정색 셔츠를 산다.
(C) 파란색 셔츠를 산다.
(D) 다른 가게로 간다.

4

My friend Sally wants to own her own clothing store when she is grown up. She knows everything about women's fashion. She's always reading magazines or watching television shows about clothing and makeup. When we go out together, she lets me wear some of her clothing. She has a lot of great clothes. The problem is that all her clothes are too small for me!

▶ own 소유하다, 갖다　makeup 메이크업, 화장

내 친구 샐리는 크면 자신의 옷가게를 갖기를 원한다. 그녀는 여성 패션에 관한 모든 것을 알고 있다. 그녀는 항상 옷과 메이크업에 관한 잡지를 읽거나 텔레비전 쇼를 본다. 우리가 같이 외출할 때, 그녀는 자기 옷을 내가 입도록 해준다. 그녀는 좋은 옷을 많이 가지고 있다. 문제는 그녀의 옷이 내게는 너무 작다는 거다!

샐리에 대해 사실이 <u>아닌</u> 것은 무엇인가?

(A) 그녀는 가게 주인이 되고 싶어 한다.
(B) 그녀는 TV와 잡지에서 패션에 대해 배운다.
(C) 그녀는 많은 좋은 옷을 많이 가지고 있다.
(D) 그녀는 친구들이 자기 옷을 입는 것을 싫어한다.

5

Young people love to look good and dress well. They learn about fashion by watching TV programs and movies. But they also watch how their friends dress. They don't really want to look different in case their clothes are not in style. As a result, young people dress like each other in similar clothes.

▶ in case ~한 경우 as a result 결과적으로 similar 비슷한

젊은 사람들은 외모를 가꾸고 옷을 잘 입고 싶어 한다. 그들은 TV 프로그램과 영화를 보면서 패션에 대해 배운다. 그러나 그들은 또한 친구들이 옷 입는 법을 본다. 그들은 자신들의 옷차림이 화려하지 않다면 다르게 보이기를 원치 않는다. 결과적으로, 젊은 사람들은 서로 비슷한 옷을 입는다.

이 이야기는 어떤 질문에 대한 대답인가?

(A) 배우와 가수들은 왜 좋은 옷을 입는가?
(B) 젊은이는 패션에 대해 어떻게 배우는가?
(C) 왜 젊은이는 비슷한 옷을 입는가?
(D) 왜 젊은이는 TV 프로그램과 영화에 관심을 갖는가?

6

W I love nice clothes. I just wish I had more money to spend.
M Clothes are very expensive.
W Especially the clothes that are in fashion.
M It's not important to wear expensive clothes.
W Yes, it is. But all my friends wear the best clothing. I wish I could do the same.

▶ in fashion 유행하는

여 난 좋은 옷이 좋아. 쓸 돈이 좀 많이 있으면 좋겠다.
남 옷은 너무 비싸.
여 특히 유행하고 있는 옷들은 더 그래.
남 비싼 옷을 입는 게 중요한 건 아니야.
여 맞아. 하지만 내 친구들은 다 좋은 옷을 입어. 나도 그럴 수 있으면 좋겠어.

대화에 대해 사실인 것은 무엇인가?

(A) 여자는 돈을 많이 가지고 있다.
(B) 남자는 좋은 옷을 좋아한다.
(C) 여자는 좋은 옷을 좋아하지 않는다.
(D) 유행하는 옷은 비싸다.

7

Sometimes a little makeup, but not too much, looks nice. I like to wear a little bit of makeup when I go out. I want to look like my favorite pop star. My mom lets me wear her makeup sometimes. I like to play around and try different shades of lipstick. But I think many girls wear too much makeup. They look like circus clowns!

When they take off their makeup, they look like different people.

▶ shade (색조의) 미미한 차이 circus clown 서커스 광대 take off one's makeup ~의 화장을 지우다

때때로 지나치지 않은 가벼운 화장은 더 예뻐 보인다. 난 외출할 때 화장을 약간 하는 것을 좋아한다. 난 내가 좋아하는 팝 스타처럼 보이기를 원한다. 엄마는 가끔씩 내가 엄마의 화장품을 쓰도록 허락해 주신다. 난 다른 색깔의 립스틱을 칠해 보는 것을 좋아한다. 하지만 난 많은 여자 아이들이 화장을 너무 진하게 한다고 생각한다. 그들은 서커스 광대처럼 보인다! 화장을 지우면 다른 사람처럼 보인다.

여자가 원하지 <u>않는</u> 것은 무엇인가?

(A) 화장하는 것
(B) 팝스타처럼 보이는 것
(C) 서커스 광대처럼 보이는 것
(D) 예뻐 보이는 것

8

M Look at that girl! She looks so cool.
W The girl with the white shirt?
M No, the one with the skinny jeans.
W Is she wearing a leather jacket?
M No, she's wearing a really bright T-shirt.
W I think I see her. She's the best dressed person at the party.
M She is. That look is so hot right now.
W Yes, skinny jeans and bright T-shirts are very modern.

▶ leather jacket 가죽 자켓 modern 최신의, 현대적인

남 저 여자 좀 봐! 멋진데.
여 흰색 셔츠 입고 있는 여자?
남 아니, 스키니진 입고 있는 여자 말이야.
여 그녀가 가죽 재킷을 입고 있니?
남 아니, 밝은 색 셔츠를 입고 있는데.
여 알겠다. 파티에서 제일 옷을 잘 입었네.
남 맞아, 저 스타일이 요즘 유행이지.
여 응, 스키니진과 밝은 색 셔츠가 최신 유행이야.

그들이 얘기하고 있는 여자는 누구인가?

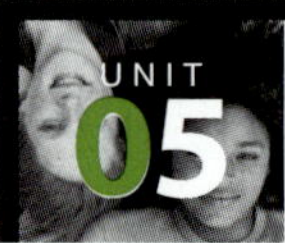

05 Characters

Key Expressions

1 1 shy 2 bossy 3 imaginative 4 generous
5 outgoing

2 patient, honest, polite, enthusiastic, friendly

3 1 ⓔ 2 ⓒ 3 ⓓ 4 ⓑ 5 ⓐ 6 ⓖ 7 ⓕ

Listening Practice

1 (A)   **2** (C)

Check Up

Listening Task 01 1 (D)   2 1) T   2) F   3) T

Listening Task 02 1 (B)

Listening Task 03 1 (B)   2 (A)

Listening Task 04 1 (D)

Listening Test

1 (C)   **2** (C)   **3** (D)   **4** (B)   **5** (C)   **6** (C)

7 (B)   **8** (B)

Key Expressions

1 표에서 가장 적절한 단어를 골라 빈칸을 채우시오.

1 부끄러움을 타면 낯선 사람들에게 말하는 것이 어렵다.

2 만약에 당신이 항상 다른 사람들에게 무엇을 해야 하는지 말한다면, 그들은 당신이 두목 행세한다고 할 것이다.

3 지나는 항상 창조적인 아이디어를 많이 갖고 있다. 그녀는 상상력이 풍부하다.

4 그는 정말로 관대해서 항상 아낌없이 베푼다.

5 에이미는 사람들과 함께 있는 것을 좋아한다. 그녀는 굉장히 사교적이다.

2 긍정적인 성격을 묘사하는 단어에 동그라미 치시오.

참을성 있는	정직한	예의 바른	심술 궂은
공격적인	열정적인	다정한	게으른
비열한	허영적인		

3 다음 문장들을 가장 잘 어울리는 대답과 연결하시오.

1 좀 부정적인거 아니니?
ⓔ 아니, 현실적인 거야.

2 너무 까다롭게 굴지 마.
ⓒ 하지만 난 모든 게 완벽했으면 좋겠어.

3 성미가 너무 급한거 조심해.
ⓓ 알았어, 진정할게.

4 너무 부끄러워 하지 마. 모두가 널 좋아해.
ⓑ 미안, 하지만 난 외향적이지 않아서.

5 그녀는 요즘 너무 멍한 것 같아.
ⓐ 일이 너무 바빠서 그래.

6 당신은 사교적인 사람인가요?
ⓖ 예, 전 나가서 새로운 사람들을 만나는 걸 좋아해요.

7 당신의 아들은 좀 고집이 센 것 같아요.
ⓕ 맞아요, 아주 강한 의지를 가졌지요.

Listening Practice

1

I have an elder brother. I really admire him. He's very hardworking and motivated. He never takes a vacation, but he doesn't complain. Whenever he has free time, he helps his brother with his homework. Sometimes he helps me, too. I study hard so that I can be successful like him.

▶ admire 동경하다, 감탄하다 hardworking 근면한, 열심히 일하는
motivated 의욕을 가진 complain 불평하다

나는 오빠가 한 명 있다. 난 정말로 그를 존경한다. 그는 일을 열심히 하고 의욕적이다. 그는 휴가를 가져 본 적이 없지만 불평하지 않는다. 여유 시간을 가질 때마다 남동생의 숙제를 봐 준다. 때때로 그는 날 도와 주기도 한다. 난 오빠처럼 성공하기 위해 열심히 공부한다.

화자의 오빠를 묘사하는 단어가 아닌 것은?

(A) 보수적인

(B) 열심히 일하는

(C) 성공적인

(D) 도움을 주는

2

M   Carl said he'd be here half an hour ago.

W　It seems like he forgot as usual.

M　Well, he's got a lot on his plate. You know he is preparing for his final exams.

W　Yeah, but this isn't the first time. He always does this. I'll give him a call.

M　I've already tried. He's not answering.

▶ **as usual** 여느 때와 같이, 평소처럼　**on one's plate** 해야 할 일을 잔뜩 안고　**give a call** 전화를 걸다

남　칼은 30분 전에 여기 올 거라고 말했어.

여　평상시와 마찬가지로 잊어버린 것 같네.

남　음, 뭔가 할 일이 많던데. 너도 알다시피 기말 고사 준비하잖아.

여　응, 하지만 이번이 처음이 아니야. 그는 항상 이런 식이야. 전화 해봐야겠어.

남　내가 이미 해봤어. 전화 안 받아.

칼을 가장 잘 설명하는 것은?

(A) 그는 매우 부지런하다.

(B) 그는 사교적이지 않다.

(C) 그는 시간을 지키지 않는다.

(D) 그는 믿을 만하다.

Check Up

Listening Task *01*

Whenever I meet new people or when I see my friends, I have nothing to say to them. My mind goes blank, and I'm very quiet. When I'm alone, I can always think of lots of things to say. I think people see me as boring or a snob.

▶ **whenever** ~할 때면 언제나　**go blank** 텅 비다
snob 속물, 거만한 사람

새로운 사람들을 만나거나 친구들을 만날 때, 나는 그들에게 할 말이 없다. 머리가 멍해져서 아주 조용히 있는다. 혼자 있을 때는 난 항상 많은 말을 생각한다. 사람들은 나를 지루하거나 건방지다고 생각할 것이다.

1　화자의 성격을 가장 잘 설명하는 단어는?

(A) 외향적인

(B) 친절한

(C) 수다스런

(D) 소심한

2　맞으면 T, 틀리면 F에 체크하시오.

1) 그녀는 새로운 사람들을 만나는 것을 좋아하지 않는다.

2) 그녀는 낯선 사람들에게 할 말이 많다.

3) 그녀는 사람들에게 말하는 것이 어렵다고 느낀다.

Listening Task *02*

M　Whenever we're speaking, Jeremy always thinks it's all about him. He's not interested in anyone but himself.

W　Yeah, I know. It always seems like he's just waiting for his turn to talk. He doesn't listen.

M　He's totally self-centered.

W　Has he always been like that?

M　Yes, ever since I met him five years ago.

▶ **self-centered** 자기중심적인, 이기적인

남　우리가 얘기할 때마다, 제레미는 항상 그게 자기에 관한 거라고 생각해. 그는 자신 외에는 다른 사람에게 관심이 없어.

여　응, 나도 알아. 그는 항상 자기가 말할 차례를 기다리는 것 같아. 다른 사람 말을 안 들어.

남　완전히 자기 중심적이야.

여　항상 그랬어?

남　응, 5년 전에 그를 만난 이후로 계속 그랬어.

1　그들은 제레미가 어떻게 바뀌어야 한다고 생각하나?

(A) 좀 더 말을 많이 해야 한다.

(B) 덜 자기 중심적이 되어야 한다.

(C) 모두와 대화해야 한다.

(D) 더 자기 중심적이 되어야 한다.

Listening Task *03*

W　I'm worried about Chris. He's so irresponsible.

M　Hey, our son is only eleven. He's still a child.

W　Whenever I ask him to do something for me, he forgets.

M　That's natural. When I was his age, I was the same.

W　No, it's not natural. Today, I asked him to fetch my letters, but he forgot.

M　I'll talk to him later this evening.

W　If he wants to become an important person, he must learn to be more responsible.

▶ **irresponsible** 무책임한, 책임감이 없는　**fetch** 가지고 오다
responsible 책임감 있는

여　난 크리스가 걱정이야. 책임감이 너무 없어.

남　우리 애는 이제 겨우 11살이야. 아직 애라고.

여　내가 뭔가를 해달라고 부탁할 때마다, 그 앤 잊어버려.

남　자연스러운 일이야. 나도 그 나이에는 그랬어.

여　아냐, 자연스러운 일이 아니야. 오늘 내 편지를 갖다 달라고 얘기했는데 잊어버렸어.

남　오늘밤에 내가 얘기해 볼게.

여　훌륭한 사람이 되려면, 더 책임감 있게 행동하는 법을 배워야 해.

1 화자들은 무엇에 대해 얘기하고 있는가?

(A) 그들의 아들이 훌륭한 사람이 되도록 어떻게 도울지
(B) 그들의 아들이 얼마나 책임감이 없는지
(C) 언제 그들이 사무실에서 그녀의 편지를 가져올지
(D) 언제 아버지가 아들과 대화를 해볼지

2 대화에 대해 사실인 것은?

(A) 남자는 그의 아들과 얘기를 할 것이다.
(B) 여자는 그녀의 아들과 얘기를 할 것이다.
(C) 여자는 울 것이다.
(D) 여자는 아들에 대해 걱정하지 않는다.

Listening Task *04*

We think we know the people who are close to us. But sometimes they do things that we aren't expecting. It bothers me when that happens. We think someone is brave and kind-hearted, but that person sometimes acts in a cunning way. It can be a shock because we think we know the person. That's when I get upset because it seems as if the person is being dishonest.

▶ **bother** 괴롭히다, 성가시게 하다 **kind-hearted** 친절한, 마음이 따뜻한 **cunning** 교활한, 간사한 **shock** 충격, 쇼크 **get upset** 화가 나다 **dishonest** 부정직한, 불성실한

우리는 우리와 가까이 있는 사람을 잘 알고 있다고 생각한다. 하지만 그들은 때때로 우리가 예상하지 못하는 일들을 한다. 그런 일이 일어나면 나는 언짢아진다. 우리는 누군가가 용감하고 마음이 따뜻하다고 생각하지만 그들은 때때로 교활한 행동을 하기도 한다. 이는 우리가 그 사람을 알고 있다고 생각하기 때문에 충격이 될 수 있다. 그가 정직하지 않은 것 같기 때문에 나는 화가 난다.

1 화자를 놀라게 하는 것은 무엇인가?

(A) 사람들이 교활하게 행동할 때
(B) 친구들의 부정직
(C) 알고 있는 사람들이 친절할 때
(D) 알고 있는 사람들의 행동하는 방식이 바뀌었을 때

Listening Test

1

My friend Bill dislikes being criticized. He sees it as an insult. He believes in himself very strongly. He doesn't think anyone else's opinion matters. He is too self-confident and never admits when he is wrong. He never accepts help from anyone at work. He even shouts at his boss. Bill is a very difficult person.

▶ **criticize** 비평하다 **insult** 모욕 **matter** 문제가 되다, 중요하다

self-confident 자신 파잉의 **admit** 인정하다 **boss** 상사, 사장

내 친구 빌은 비판 받는 것을 싫어한다. 그는 그것을 모욕이라고 생각한다. 그는 자신을 너무 맹신하고 있다. 그는 다른 사람들의 의견을 고려하지 않는다. 그는 자신감이 너무 강해서 그가 틀렸을 때 절대 인정하지 않는다. 그는 일에 있어서 다른 사람의 도움도 받아들이지 않는다. 그는 심지어 그의 상사에게도 소리를 지른다. 빌은 아주 까다로운 사람이다.

빌을 가장 잘 묘사하고 있는 단어는?

(A) 용기 있는
(B) 부끄러워하는
(C) 거만한
(D) 자신감 있는

2

I may be too picky, but this guy is just full of himself. We have similar interests and backgrounds, but I found him to be conceited. I'm really disappointed. My ex-boyfriend was a man like that. I know how difficult it is for people to change their personalities. I may have to find a new boyfriend.

▶ **picky** 성미가 까다로운 **full of oneself** 자기 생각만 하는 **background** (사람의) 배경 **conceited** 우쭐대는, 자부심 강한 **personality** 성격, 개성

내가 너무 까다로운 것일지 모르지만, 이 남자는 자기 밖에 모른다. 우리는 비슷한 관심사와 배경을 가지고 있지만, 난 그가 우쭐거리는 사람이라는 것을 알게 됐다. 정말 실망스러웠다. 나의 전 남자 친구도 그랬다. 난 사람들이 자신의 성격을 바꾸는 것이 얼마나 어려운 일인지 알고 있다. 아무래도 새 남자 친구를 찾아야 할 것 같다.

화자는 누구에 대해서 얘기하고 있나?

(A) 그녀의 남자 형제
(B) 그녀의 전 남편
(C) 그녀의 현재 남자 친구
(D) 그녀의 새 남자 친구

3

I've tried to be patient, but I have to say this. One night a few weeks ago, after Tom had gone out, I was startled by the doorbell. It was Mr. Salvador, the landlord. He looked angry. "Your roommate promised to have the rent money three days ago," he said. It turned out that Tom had not paid him for two months.

▶ **patient** 인내심 있는 **startle** 깜짝 놀라게 하다 **doorbell** 초인종 소리 **landlord** 집주인 **rent money** 집세

난 참으려고 했지만, 말해야겠다. 몇 주 전 밤에 톰이 나간 후, 난 초인종 소리에 깜짝 놀랐다. 집주인인 살바도르 씨였다. 그는 화가 난 것처럼 보였다. "당신 룸메이트가 3일 전에 집세를 준다고 했소." 그가 말했다. 톰은 2달 동안 집세를 내지 않았던 것이다.

톰을 가장 잘 묘사하고 있는 단어는?

(A) 예의 없는
(B) 정직한
(C) 관대한
(D) 믿을 수 없는

4

Dan is my son's teacher. The kids really love him. Not only is he fun and entertaining, but he also really makes time to help the kids with their schoolwork. Sometimes he'll play with them on the basketball court for hours. Or he'll tell them a story and explain it to them until they understand it. I think they're really lucky to have a teacher like him.

▶ **make time** 시간을 내다

댄은 내 아들의 선생님이다. 아이들은 정말로 그를 좋아한다. 그는 재미있고 유쾌할 뿐만 아니라 아이들이 학교 일을 하는 것을 도와주기 위해 시간을 낸다. 때때로 그는 아이들과 몇 시간 동안 농구 코트에서 논다. 또는 그는 아이들에게 이야기를 해 주고 그들이 이해할 때까지 설명해 준다. 난 그와 같은 선생님을 만난 아이들이 정말로 행운이라고 생각한다.

댄을 묘사하는 단어가 <u>아닌</u> 것은?

(A) 인내심 있는
(B) 운이 좋은
(C) 도움을 주는
(D) 헌신적인

5

James is probably one of the top tennis coaches. Only a few players get to be coached by a guy like him. He understands the game very well. When he's on the court, he concentrates hard on the game. But as soon as he's off the court, he's a friend. He knows how to treat his players on and off the court.

▶ **coach** 지도하다, 코치하다   **concentrate** 집중하다   **treat** 다루다

제임스는 최고의 테니스 코치들 중 한 명이다. 오직 소수의 선수들만이 그와 같은 코치에게 배운다. 그는 경기를 아주 잘 이해한다. 그가 경기장에 있을 때, 그는 경기에 열심히 집중한다. 그러나 경기장에서 나오자마자 그는 친구가 된다. 그는 경기장 안팎에서 그의 선수들을 다루는 법을 알고 있다.

화자는 코치에 대해서 어떻게 느끼고 있나?

(A) 질투
(B) 애정
(C) 존경
(D) 실망

6

W When Steve comes home late at night, he's always very considerate of his sleeping neighbors and doesn't make any noise.

M That's very thoughtful of him.

W When people first meet him, they think he's a difficult person. Most are surprised to hear that he's so gentle.

M I'm very surprised. I always imagined he wouldn't care about other people at all.

▶ **considerate** 이해심 있는, 사려 깊은   **make noise** 소음을 내다   **thoughtful** 사려 깊은

여 스티브는 밤 늦게 집에 올 때, 항상 잠자고 있는 이웃들을 생각해서 어떠한 소리도 내지 않아.
남 참 사려 깊네.
여 사람들은 처음 그를 볼 때, 그가 까다로운 사람이라고 생각해. 대부분은 그가 매우 예의 바르다는 얘기를 듣고 깜짝 놀라곤 하지.
남 나도 깜짝 놀랐어. 난 항상 그가 다른 사람을 전혀 신경 쓰지 않을 거라고 생각했거든.

남자는 왜 놀랐나?

(A) 스티브가 소음을 냈기 때문에
(B) 스티브가 집에 늦게 오기 때문에
(C) 스티브가 보기와는 다르기 때문에
(D) 스티브가 다른 사람들에 대해서 신경 쓰지 않기 때문에

7

W That was such an amazing movie. I loved the ending.

M Are you crying because of that movie?

W Of course. It really moved me.

M Not me. I thought it was rather boring.

W I'm surprised. I thought you were more romantic than that.

▶ **move** 감동시키다   **rather** 어느 정도, 좀

여 저 영화 정말로 멋졌어. 엔딩이 정말로 마음에 들었어.
남 저 영화 때문에 지금 울고 있는 거야?
여 물론이지. 정말 감동적이었다고.
남 난 아니야. 난 좀 지루하다고 생각했는데.
여 놀랍다. 난 네가 그것보다는 좀더 로맨틱하다고 생각했어.

대화에 대해 사실인 것은 무엇인가?

(A) 여자는 진지하다.
(B) 여자는 감성적이다.
(C) 남자는 사려 깊다.
(D) 남자는 낭만적이다.

8

Ben is such a clever guy. He knows a lot about politics and history. He's also very sophisticated. He goes to the opera at least once a month and knows all of Shakespeare's plays. But he's so easy to get along with. He never makes me feel that I am less clever than he is nor shows off his intelligence in front of people.

▶ **politics** 정치, 정치학   **sophisticated** 세련된   **once a month** 한 달에 한 번   **play** 연극   **get along with** 잘 지내다, 잘 어울리다   **show off** 과시하다, 자랑하다

벤은 정말 똑똑한 남자다. 그는 정치와 역사에 대해서 많은 것을 알고 있다. 그는 또한 세련됐다. 그는 최소한 한 달에 한번은 오페라를 보러 가고 셰익스피어의 극들을 모두 알고 있다. 그러나 그는 사람들과 잘 어울린다. 그는 결코 내가 그보다 덜 똑똑하다고 느끼도록 하지 않고, 사람들 앞에서 자기의 똑똑함을 과시하지도 않는다.

화자의 말에 따르면, 벤은 어떤 사람인가?

(A) 야심이 있는 사람
(B) 겸손한 사람
(C) 조용한 사람
(D) 교양 없는 사람

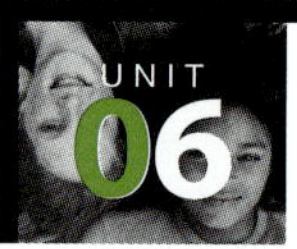

UNIT 06 Parties

정답 answer

Key Expressions

1　1 invitation　2 anniversary　3 guests
　　4 sense of humor　5 celebrates

2　1 ⓒ　2 ⓔ　3 ⓓ　4 ⓑ　5 ⓐ

3　1 ⓒ　2 ⓐ　3 ⓓ　4 ⓑ　5 ⓕ　6 ⓔ　7 ⓖ

Listening Practice

1 (B)　　　　**2** (A)

Check Up

Listening Task 01　1 (C)　2 (C)
Listening Task 02　1 1) ⓑ　2) ⓐ　3) ⓒ
Listening Task 03　1 (C)　2 (D)
Listening Task 04　1 (C)

Listening Test

1 (D)　**2** (B)　**3** (B)　**4** (D)　**5** (B)　**6** (D)
7 (B)　**8** (D)

스크립트 & 해석 script & translation

Key Expressions

1　표에서 가장 적절한 단어를 골라 빈칸을 채우시오.

　1 이 파티는 초대장을 가진 사람만 올 수 있다.

　2 당신의 부모님의 결혼 기념일은 언제입니까?

　3 손님들과 그들의 배우자들을 존경심을 갖고 대하세요.

　4 그의 유머 감각은 파티에 온 모두를 즐겁게 했다.

　5 추석은 풍년을 축하하는 한국의 전통적인 명절이다.

2　각각의 파티를 그것의 특징과 연결하시오.

　1 포틀럭 파티
　　ⓒ 참석자들은 음식을 가져와야 한다.

2 깜짝 파티
ⓔ 파티에 있는 누군가는 놀랄 것이다.

3 디너 파티
ⓓ 대개 짝수의 사람들이 초대된다.

4 브라이덜 샤워(신부를 위한 파티)
ⓑ 신부는 많은 선물을 받는다.

5 베이비 샤워(임산부를 위한 파티)
ⓐ 임신한 여자들은 많은 선물을 받는다.

3 다음 문장들을 가장 잘 어울리는 대답과 연결하시오.

1 암 연구를 위한 자선 디너야.
ⓒ 좋은 일인데. 2장 살게.

2 초대장 받았어?
ⓐ 응, 난 이미 내 RSVP 보냈어.

3 톰이 파티에 대해 알고 있어?
ⓓ 물론, 모르지. 깜짝 파티야.

4 장식이 너무 예쁘다.
ⓑ 고마워. 내가 직접 만들었어.

5 무슨 옷을 입어야 하지?
ⓕ 캐주얼 옷이면 돼.

6 춤 추시겠어요?
ⓔ 물론, 기꺼이요.

7 음식 맛있지 않아?
ⓖ 정말 맛있어! 굴 먹어봤어?

Listening Practice

1

Let me tell you about last night at Jim's house. He prepared a buffet, big fireworks, and even a live music band. On the rooftop, there was a fountain. Isn't that amazing? You should have joined us. Some people might say it's too luxurious, but I feel my life seems so boring now!

▶ **buffet** 뷔페 **fireworks** 불꽃놀이 **rooftop** 지붕, 옥상
fountain 분수대 **luxurious** 사치스러운

어젯밤 짐의 집에서 있었던 일을 얘기할게요. 그는 뷔페와, 불꽃놀이, 그리고 라이브 음악 밴드까지 준비했습니다. 지붕 꼭대기에는 분수도 있어요. 굉장하지 않습니까? 당신도 왔으면 좋았을 텐데요. 몇몇 사람들은 너무 사치스럽다고 말하겠지만 전 지금 제 삶이 너무 지루하게 느껴져요!

이 이야기의 요지는?

(A) 화자는 그의 새 집을 소개하고 있다.
(B) 화자는 파티에 대해 얘기하고 있다.
(C) 화자는 정말로 지루하게 느끼고 있다.

(D) 화자는 지붕을 묘사하고 있다.

2

M Hey, Jane. Do you know any good place for my birthday party?

W You mean like a restaurant?

M Not really. Somewhere different and a little fancy.

W I think any neighborhood café would be okay.

M A café may be a good idea. Actually, there's the Italian café on Main Street. What do you think about it?

W That's a good idea. They have two floors for private parties. And they're okay about people getting noisy.

▶ **fancy** 화려한, 장식적인 **private** 사적인, 개인적인

남 이봐, 제인. 내 생일 파티를 할 만한 좋은 곳을 알고 있어?
여 레스토랑 같은 것을 말하는 거야?
남 아니. 약간 다르고 화려한 곳.
여 근처에 있는 카페가 좋을 것 같은데.
남 카페 좋은 생각이다. 메인 스트리트에 실제로 이탈리아식 카페가 있거든. 어떻게 생각해?
여 좋은 생각이야. 사적인 파티를 위한 두 개 층이 있지. 또 사람들이 떠들어도 괜찮잖아.

대화에 대해 사실인 것은 무엇인가?

(A) 그들은 파티를 하기 위해 카페와 레스토랑 사이에서 선택하고 있다.
(B) 그들은 카페에서 떠들고 싶어 한다.
(C) 그들은 주위를 돌아다니고 싶어 한다.
(D) 그들은 레스토랑이 파티를 하기에 너무 화려하지 않을까 생각하고 있다.

Check Up

Listening Task *01*

From 7 p.m., a lot of cars and people made the long journey to Tom's house. At the busiest time of the evening, I would guess that there were over 50 people in his house. The party went very smoothly until the heating system stopped working at some point during the evening.

▶ **smoothly** 순조롭게, 매끄럽게 **heating system** 난방 시스템
point 지점, 장소

오후 7시부터 많은 차들과 사람들이 톰의 집으로 긴 행렬을 이뤘다. 저녁의 가장 바쁜 시간에, 그의 집에는 50명 이상의 사람들이 온 것 같다. 파티는 저녁의 어느 순간 난방 시스템이 작동을 멈출 때까지는 순조롭게 진행되었다.

1 파티에 대해 추측할 수 있는 것은?

    (A) 파티에 사람들이 거의 없었다.
    (B) 파티는 아주 지루했다.
    (C) 파티는 중반까지는 완벽했다.
    (D) 파티 중간쯤, 많은 사람들이 떠났다.

2 일어나지 않은 일은 무엇인가?

    (A) 난방 시스템이 작동을 멈췄다.
    (B) 많은 사람들이 파티에 갔다.
    (C) 50명 정도의 사람들이 여행을 떠났다.
    (D) 저녁에는 아주 바빴다.

Listening Task 02

ⓐ

Boy, I haven't been to a lunch party like that. There must have been 100 people jammed into Jim's yard all enjoying pizza and a barbecue.

▶ **jam into** 쑤셔 넣다, 채워 넣다

이런, 난 그런 런치 파티에 가 본 적이 없어. 짐의 마당에서 북적거리며 피자와 바비큐를 먹고 있는 사람들이 100명은 됐을 거야.

ⓑ

This party takes you to a fantastic club. The interior is elegant, yet relaxed, and decorated in bright colors with lots of mirrors so that people can watch themselves and others dancing.

▶ **interior** 내부 장식, 인테리어 **relaxed** 편안한
   decorated in ~으로 장식된

이 파티는 너를 환상적인 클럽으로 데리고 간다. 인테리어는 우아하지만 편안하고, 밝은 색깔로 장식되어 있으며, 많은 거울이 있어서 사람들이 춤추는 자신들과 다른 사람들을 볼 수 있다.

ⓒ

We had a party last Friday at the beach. Romantic moonlight, fresh wind, and beers. It was awesome.

▶ **moonlight** 달빛

우리는 지난 금요일에 해변에서 파티를 했다. 낭만적인 달빛, 신선한 바람, 그리고 맥주. 정말 굉장했다.

1 각 그림과 어울리는 이야기의 번호를 쓰시오.

  1)   2)   3)

Listening Task 03

A few days before my daughter turned three, we decided to have a party for her. We decided that it would be a big children's party with balloons and a clown. We bought a cake, some ice cream, and soda. We invited all the kids in the neighborhood. The weather was not perfect, but it didn't matter. A clown came to the party and made all the kids laugh. But my daughter was scared of the clown. She wouldn't stop crying until we sent him away.

▶ **turn** (나이를) 넘다, 초과하다 **clown** 광대
   be scared of ~에 겁을 먹은

내 딸이 세 살이 되기 며칠 전에, 우리는 딸을 위해 파티를 열기로 했다. 우리는 풍선과 광대가 있는 성대한 아이들 파티를 열어 주기로 했다. 우리는 케이크와 아이스크림 그리고 소다수를 샀다. 이웃에 있는 모든 아이들을 초대했다. 날씨가 좋지는 않았지만 문제가 되지 않았다. 광대가 파티에 왔고 모든 아이들을 웃게 만들었다. 하지만 내 딸은 그 광대를 무서워했다. 내 딸은 우리가 그를 보낼 때까지 울음을 그치려 하지 않았다.

1 아이들이 파티에서 먹지 않은 것은?

    (A) 케이크
    (B) 아이스크림
    (C) 사탕
    (D) 소다수

2 무엇이 파티를 망쳤나?

    (A) 아이들이 좋은 시간을 갖지 못했다.
    (B) 날씨가 안 좋았다.
    (C) 파티에 케이크가 없었다.
    (D) 그녀의 딸이 광대를 무서워했다.

Listening Task 04

Businesspeople attend dinner parties all the time. But they're not always for fun. They are useful ways to meet important people or others in the business world. It's called networking. It's really important for businesspeople to make connections. But it's more fun to get to know someone at a dinner party than at a meeting.

▶ **attend** 참여하다, 참석하다 **networking** 개인적 정보망
   connections 연고, 연줄 **get to know** 알게 되다

사업하는 사람들은 항상 디너 파티에 참석한다. 하지만 그것들이 항상 즐기기 위한 것은 아니다. 그러한 파티들은 비즈니스 세계에서 중요한 사람들이나 다른 사람들을 만날 수 있는 유용한 방법이다. 인맥 관리라고 불리는 것이다. 사업하는 사람들이 관계를 맺는 것은

아주 중요하다. 하지만 회의에서 보다 디너 파티에서 누군가를 알게 되는 것이 더 즐거운 일이다.

1 사업가들이 관계를 맺기에 즐거운 장소는 어느 곳인가?

(A) 비즈니스 회의
(B) 네트워크
(C) 디너 파티
(D) 커피숍

Listening Test

1

M Did you get invited to Jane's birthday party next week?

W Yes, I did. Looks like it will be a cool party.

M Great. Let's go together. I'll pick you up at 7.

W I won't make it to the party. I'm working until 10 p.m. that evening.

M Oh, that's terrible. Can you take the evening off?

W No, my boss is very strict.

M Everyone will be at the party. Why don't you come later?

▶ **invite** 초대하다 **pick up** (차로) 마중 나가다
make it 제시간에 도착하다 **strict** 엄한

남 다음 주에 있는 제인의 생일 파티에 초대 받았어?
여 응, 받았어. 멋진 파티가 될 것 같은데.
남 잘됐네. 같이 가자. 내가 7시에 데리러 갈게.
여 난 파티에 못 갈 것 같아. 그날 저녁에 밤 10시까지 일해야 해.
남 이런, 그거 안됐네. 저녁에 빠질 수 없어?
여 안 돼. 사장님이 엄하셔.
남 모두 파티에 올 거야. 늦게라도 오는 게 어때?

왜 여자는 파티에 갈 수 없는가?

(A) 그녀는 다음날 일할 것이다.
(B) 초대장이 없다.
(C) 그녀의 사장님이 무척 관대하시다.
(D) 밤 10시까지 일할 것이다.

2

M Hi, Kim. I'm going to a formal event in San Francisco next week. Can you tell me what I should wear?

W I think it's the same everywhere.

M I know a tuxedo will be proper. But I'm wondering if I could I get away with that black suit.

W Yes, I think so. But don't forget the black tie.

M Thanks for your advice.

▶ **formal** 공식적인, 격식 차린 **proper** 적당한, 예의바른

남 안녕, 킴. 내가 다음 주에 샌프란시스코에서 있는 공식 행사에 가려고 하는데. 무슨 옷을 입어야 할까?
여 어디서나 똑같지 않을까.
남 턱시도가 적절할 거라는 건 알아. 근데 검정 정장은 안 입어도 되나 해서.
여 응, 괜찮을 것 같은데. 하지만 검정색 타이는 매줘야겠지.
남 조언 고마워.

남자는 행사에서 무슨 옷을 입을 것인가?

(A) 
(B) 
(C) 
(D) 

3

Hello, Irene. How are you? Thank you so much for inviting us to John's birthday party last week. We had a fantastic time. You went to so much trouble. The birthday cake was really delicious. You know how much I love sweet things. I hope that you can come to dinner with us soon. Thanks again.

▶ **trouble** 노력, 수고

안녕, 이렌느. 어떻게 지내? 지난주에 존의 생일 파티에 초대해 줘서 정말 고마웠어. 정말 좋은 시간 보냈어. 네가 고생 많이 했네. 생일 케이크는 정말 맛있었어. 내가 단 것을 얼마나 좋아하는지 너 알지. 빠른 시일 내로 우리와 함께 저녁 먹으러 오면 좋겠다. 다시 한번 고마워.

이 이야기의 목적은 무엇인가?

(A) 파티에 초대하기 위해
(B) 파티 초대에 대한 감사함을 표현하기 위해
(C) 그녀가 좋아하는 것들에 대해 말하기 위해
(D) 불평하기 위해

4

My girlfriend and I went to a party last night, but we didn't enjoy it. First, the music was too loud, so we couldn't talk to anyone without yelling. Also, there wasn't enough food to eat. The food ran out quickly, so we didn't even get to eat. And we didn't see any of our friends either. We stayed for a short time and then went home immediately.

▶ **yell** 고함치다, 외치다 **run out** 고갈되다, 다 없어지다 **immediately** 즉시

여자 친구와 나는 어젯밤 파티에 갔는데, 정말 재미 없었다. 우선 음악이 너무 시끄러워서 우리는 소리치지 않고는 얘기를 나눌 수가 없었다. 또 먹을 음식이 충분치 않았다. 음식이 금새 바닥났기 때문에 우리는 먹으러 갈 수조차 없었다. 우리 친구들도 만나지 못했다. 우리는 잠깐만 있다가 바로 집으로 돌아갔다.

화자는 언제 음식을 먹었나?

(A) 그는 파티 초반에 음식을 먹었다.

(B) 그는 파티 내내 음식을 먹었다.

(C) 그는 파티가 끝날 때쯤 음식을 먹었다.

(D) 그는 아무것도 먹지 않았다.

5

M Hey, Peggy. Great party, isn't it?

W Yeah, pretty good.

M By the way, did you read about global warming? Scientists now have clear evidence.

W Yeah, I have heard that. The sea level is rising! Isn't it terrible?

M Just be careful when living in a house on the coast.

▶ **global warming** 지구온난화 **evidence** 증거 **sea level** 해수면 **coast** 연안, 해안

남 안녕, 페기. 멋진 파티야, 그렇지?

여 응, 정말 좋아.

남 그런데, 지구 온난화에 대해서 읽었어? 과학자들은 지금 명백한 증거를 갖고 있어.

여 응, 나도 들었어. 해수면이 상승하고 있다니! 끔찍하지 않니?

남 해안에 있는 집에 살면 조심해야겠더라.

왜 남자는 "해안에서 살 때 조심해라"라고 말하나?

(A) 그는 그녀가 물을 좋아하지 않는다는 것을 알고 있다.

(B) 그는 바다가 지구 온난화로 상승할 것이라고 생각한다.

(C) 그는 산에서 사는 것을 더 좋아한다.

(D) 과학자들이 해안에서 사는 것이 위험하다는 것을 증명했다.

6

W1 We have two weeks to find partners for the prom, Michelle.

W2 What are you going to do? I'm going to ask your brother.

W1 My brother? But he can't dance.

W2 It doesn't matter. I don't know who else to ask.

W1 What about the guy who sits next to you on the school bus every day?

W2 I'll ask him if he'll go with you.

W1 Great idea. Then we'll both have partners.

W2 Then we'll have to find pretty dresses to wear to the prom!

▶ **prom** (학년 말에 공식적으로 여는) 무도회, 댄스파티

여1 미쉘, 우리가 졸업 파티에 같이 갈 파트너를 찾는 데 2주가 남았어.

여2 어떻게 할 거야? 난 너희 오빠한테 물어보려고 하는데.

여1 우리 오빠? 하지만 춤 잘 못 추는데.

여2 상관없어. 물어볼 다른 사람이 없는걸.

여1 매일 스쿨버스에서 네 옆에 앉는 애는 어때?

여2 그가 너와 함께 갈 수 있는지 내가 물어볼게.

여1 좋은 생각이야. 그럼 우리 둘 다 파트너가 있겠네.

여2 이제는 우리 졸업 파티에서 입을 예쁜 옷을 찾아야 해!

두 여자가 졸업 파티 전에 필요로 하는 두 가지는 무엇인가?

(A) 새로운 헤어스타일과 파트너

(B) 자동차와 파트너

(C) 직업과 파트너

(D) 드레스와 파트너

7

An office party may seem like a great chance to get friendly with your employer, but your behavior can affect your career directly. According to Etiquette International, a company specializing in business etiquette, no matter how festive the party is, it's still about business.

▶ **get friendly with** ~와 친해지다 **employer** 고용주, 사용자 **behavior** 행동 **affect** 영향을 주다 **career** 경력, 이력, 직업 **according to** ~에 따르면 **specialize** 특수화하다, 전문화하다 **etiquette** 예의, 에티켓 **no matter how...** 얼마나 ~일지라도 하더라도

회사 파티는 당신의 고용주와 친해질 수 있는 좋은 기회인 것처럼 보이지만, 당신의 경력에 직접적으로 영향을 미칠 수 있다. 비즈니스 에티켓 전문 회사인 에티켓 인터내셔널에 따르면, 아무리 파티가 즐겁다 할지라도, 그 파티는 여전히 비즈니스에 관한 것이다.

이야기의 끝에 올 수 있는 문장으로 적절한 것은?

(A) 그러므로 당신은 회사 파티를 즐겨야 한다.

(B) 그러므로 회사 파티를 비즈니스의 연장선으로 생각하라.

(C) 그러므로 당신은 가족을 회사 파티에 데려가야 한다.

(D) 그러므로 당신은 회사 파티에서 친구들을 사귈 수 있다.

8

Dear friends, please join us for a potluck party

tomorrow evening. The theme is "Foods from around the world." Please bring your favorite dish from another country, not your traditional food. Snacks and drinks will be provided. But please bring a salad. After dinner, we'll serve your favorite desserts from around the world.

▶ **potluck party** 포틀럭 파티(각자 음식을 조금씩 마련해 오는 파티)
theme 주제 **provide** 제공하다 **serve** (음식을) 내다, 상을 차리다

친구들아, 내일 저녁에 있을 포틀럭 파티에 와줘. 주제는 '전세계의 음식'이야. 너희들의 전통 음식이 아닌 다른 나라의 네가 좋아하는 음식을 가져오면 좋겠어. 스낵과 음료는 제공될 거야. 하지만 샐러드는 가지고 와줘. 저녁 식사 후에는 너희들이 좋아하는 전세계의 후식이 제공될 거야.

파티에서 먹게 될 음식이 <u>아닌</u> 것은?

(A) 스낵
(B) 샐러드
(C) 다른 나라의 샐러드
(D) 손님들 나라의 전통 음식

Restaurants

정답 answer

Key Expressions

1 1 another cup 2 salad 3 allergic
   4 main dish 5 dessert

2 roast turkey, broiled salmon, roast pork

3 1 ⓓ 2 ⓔ 3 ⓐ 4 ⓑ 5 ⓕ 6 ⓒ 7 ⓖ

Listening Practice

1 (C)   **2** (B)

Check Up

Listening Task *01* 1 (C)   2 1) F 2) T 3) F
Listening Task *02* 1 (C)
Listening Task *03* 1 (B)   2 (C)
Listening Task *04* 1 (C)

Listening Test

1 (D)   **2** (B)   **3** (C)   **4** (A)   **5** (C)   **6** (C)
7 (C)   **8** (D)

스크립트 & 해석 script & translation

Key Expressions

1 표에서 가장 적절한 단어를 골라 빈칸을 채우시오.

   1 커피 한 잔 더 할 수 있을까요?

   2 샐러드가 정말로 신선하고 아삭아삭하다.

   3 나는 해산물 알레르기가 있다.

   4 로스트 비프가 주요리이다.

   5 디저트로 아이스크림 드시겠습니까?

2 채식주의자들이 먹지 않는 음식을 고르시오.

칠면조 구이	구운 감자	딸기잼	오이
연어 구이	시저 샐러드	돼지고기 구이	양송이 스프

<u>**3**</u> 다음 문장들을 가장 잘 어울리는 대답과 연결하시오.

1 디저트는 안 먹을래요. 너무 배불러요.
   ⓓ 저도요. 정말 성대한 만찬이었어요.

2 각자 계산할까요?
   ⓔ 아뇨. 제가 가자고 했으니까 제가 낼게요.

3 포장해 갈까, 여기서 먹을까?
   ⓐ 여기서 먹자. 바쁘지 않아.

4 어디에 앉으시겠어요?
   ⓑ 창가 쪽이요.

5 음료수 리필해 주시겠어요?
   ⓕ 예, 따라 드리겠습니다.

6 디저트 좀 먹고 싶은데.
   ⓒ 케이크나 파이는 어때?

7 주문하시겠습니까?
   ⓖ 예, 샐러드와 스프 주세요.

Listening Practice

<u>**1**</u>

I'm Jane, a chef. I've traveled all over the world to learn different cooking techniques and dishes. Europe is my favorite place, and my favorite ethnic foods to prepare are French and German. Both foods are rich and filled with so many variations.

▶ **chef** 요리사 **dish** 요리, 음식 **ethnic** 민족 특유의
rich 풍부한, 윤택한 **variation** 변화, 변동

전 제인입니다. 주방장이에요. 전 다양한 요리 기법과 음식들을 배우기 위해 전세계를 여행했어요. 유럽은 제가 가장 좋아하는 곳이고, 제가 가장 준비하기 좋아하는 민족 요리는 프랑스와 독일 음식이에요. 두 음식 모두 풍부하고 매우 다양한 변화가 가능하죠.

화자에 대해 사실이 <u>아닌</u> 것은 무엇인가?

(A) 그녀는 전세계를 여행했다.
(B) 그녀는 유럽을 가장 좋아한다.
(C) 그녀는 남은 여생을 유럽에서 보내고 싶어 한다.
(D) 그녀는 프랑스와 독일 요리를 가장 좋아한다.

<u>**2**</u>

M What is your favorite food?
W I love Italian food. I'm a big fan of pasta.
M What is your favorite dish then?
W I love spaghetti with seafood, especially shrimp.
M I see. My favorite is spaghetti with roasted vegetables.
W That's delicious, too!

▶ **shrimp** 새우 **roasted** 구운

남 어떤 음식 제일 좋아해?
여 이탈리아 음식을 좋아해. 파스타는 정말 좋아하지.
남 그럼 좋아하는 요리가 뭔데?
여 해산물, 특히 새우가 들어간 스파게티를 좋아해.
남 그렇구나. 난 구운 야채가 있는 스파게티를 좋아하는데.
여 그것도 맛있어!

대화에 대해 사실인 것은 무엇인가?

(A) 화자는 둘 다 프랑스 음식을 좋아한다.
(B) 남자와 여자는 그들이 좋아하는 이탈리아 요리를 비교하고 있다.
(C) 여자는 치킨을 곁들인 스파게티를 좋아한다.
(D) 남자는 해산물이 있는 스파게티를 좋아한다.

Check Up

Listening Task *01*

M Are you ready to order, ma'am?
W Yes. I would like the New York steak special with a salad.
M Excellent. How do you like your meat?
W Medium.
M Would you like the baked potato and vegetables?
W Yes, and go easy on the sour cream.
M Certainly. Anything else?
W No, that's all.

▶ **baked** 구운

남 주문하시겠습니까?
여 네. 뉴욕 스테이크 스페셜이랑 샐러드로 할게요.
남 좋아요, 고기는 어느 정도로 할까요?
여 미디엄이요.
남 구운 감자와 야채는요?
여 예, 주세요. 그리고 사워 크림을 좀 줄여 주세요.
남 알겠습니다. 다른 것은요?
여 아뇨, 그게 다에요.

1 **여자가 가장 신경 쓰는 것은 무엇인가?**

(A) 스테이크
(B) 샐러드
(C) 사워 크림
(D) 디저트

2 **맞으면 T, 틀리면 F에 체크하시오.**

1) 여자 손님은 중간 크기의 뉴욕 스테이크를 주문했다.
2) 그녀는 감자에 사워 크림을 약간만 원한다.
3) 그녀는 음료수도 주문했다.

Listening Task 02

If you're looking for good Mexican food, stay away from this restaurant. We came here for a Christmas party once. We were a big group of ten people. The server couldn't remember who had ordered what. He simply threw the plates of food on the table. The food is nothing special and is not a reason to go back there. There are better Mexican restaurants in the city.

▶ stay away from ~에서 떨어져 있다
server 근무자, 종업원   threw throw(던지다)의 과거

만약 좋은 멕시코 음식을 찾는다면, 이 식당은 가지 마세요. 우린 크리스마스 파티 때문에 한 번 여기 왔었어요. 10명의 대규모 인원이었죠. 종업원은 누가 뭘 주문했는지 기억하지 못했어요. 그는 테이블에 음식 접시를 던져놓을 뿐이었죠. 음식은 특별할 것도 없고 다시 갈 이유가 없어요. 이 도시에는 더 좋은 멕시코 식당들이 있어요.

화자가 이 식당을 좋아하지 않는 이유가 <u>아닌</u> 것은 무엇인가?

(A) 형편 없는 서비스
(B) 별 맛 없는 음식
(C) 비싼 가격
(D) 종업원들

Listening Task 03

M Well, we got the check. Since the dinner was my idea, I'll pay.
W No, that's not right. I should pay for my half.
M But I insist. Consider it a gift between two friends who haven't seen each other in ages.
W I still think it's not right though.
M Then the next time we go out, you can pay.
W That works for me.

▶ consider ~라고 생각하다

남 음, 내가 저녁 먹자고 했으니까, 내가 낼게.
여 아냐, 내 건 내가 낼게.
남 내가 낸다니까. 오랫동안 못 본 두 친구 사이의 선물이라고 생각해.
여 그래도 그러면 안 될 것 같은데.
남 그럼 다음에 만나면, 네가 사면 되잖아.
여 그래, 알았어.

1 대화 중 여자의 감정은 어떻게 변했나?

(A) 슬픈 → 기쁜
(B) 불편한 → 만족한
(C) 만족한 → 실망한
(D) 실망한 → 흥분한

2 대화에 대해 사실인 것은 무엇인가?

(A) 여자는 계산하기를 원하지 않는다.
(B) 남자는 여자가 계산하기를 원한다.
(C) 둘 다 지불하고 싶어 하지만, 남자가 지불한다.
(D) 저녁은 공짜였다.

Listening Task 04

M Have you been to that new Chinese restaurant?
W I guess so. Isn't it a kind of buffet?
M Yeah, it costs a fortune if you eat there though.
W It's open twenty-four hours, isn't it?
M I don't think so, but it's open really early.
W It doesn't really make sense, though. I mean, who wants to go for Chinese at nine a.m.?

▶ fortune 큰 돈, 재산   make sense 이치에 닿다, 뜻이 통하다

남 새로 생긴 저 중국 음식점에 가봤어?
여 그런 것 같은데. 뷔페 같은 거 아니야?
남 응, 근데 거기서 먹으면 돈이 많이 들어.
여 24시간 영업하지?
남 아닌 것 같은데. 하지만 굉장히 일찍 문을 열어.
여 그게 정말 이해가 안 가. 내 말은, 누가 아침 9시에 중국 음식을 먹으러 가겠냐고?

1 대화에 대해 사실인 것은 무엇인가?

(A) 여자는 아침에 중국 음식을 먹는 것이 좋은 생각이라고 생각한다.
(B) 이 음식점은 24시간 영업한다.
(C) 음식 가격이 비싸다.
(D) 그들은 이 음식점에 가 본 적이 없다.

Listening Test

1

I have owned my restaurant for the past five years. In that time, it has become more and more successful. I've learned what my customers like. I use only the freshest food and vegetables. I make sure that the food is tasty. The tables and dishes are always clean. Lastly, we always serve the customers in a polite manner to make them happy.

▶ tasty 맛 좋은   manner 태도, 몸가짐

저는 지난 5년간 레스토랑을 운영했습니다. 그 동안 레스토랑은 시간이 갈수록 더 성공적이었습니다. 전 고객이 무엇을 좋아하는지를 배웠습니다. 전 아주 신선한 음식과 야채들만 사용합니다. 음식이 맛있는지 확인합니다. 테이블과 접시는 항상 청결하게 유지합니다. 마지막으로, 우리는 고객님들이 행복하도록 항상 바르게 고객님을 응대합니다.

(A) 레스토랑이 음식을 어떻게 준비하나?
(B) 좋은 레스토랑이란 무엇인가?

(C) 성공적인 레스토랑을 어떻게 찾나?
(D) 레스토랑의 성공 요인은 무엇인가?

2

(A)

Bill and his friends are at Pizza Hut. They have decided to order two kinds of pizza. They get the cheese pizza and kimchi pizza. They are about to eat the pizzas.

▶ be about to 막 ~ 하려고 하다

빌과 그의 친구들은 피자헛에 있다. 그들은 두 종류의 피자를 시키기로 결정했다. 치즈 피자와 김치 피자가 나왔다. 그들은 피자를 먹으려고 한다.

(B)

Bill and his friends are sitting around at Pizza Hut. They are hungry, so they ordered two large pizzas. But they have been waiting for the pizza for over 40 minutes. They are upset now.

빌과 그의 친구들은 피자헛에 둘러 앉아 있다. 그들은 배가 고파서 두 개의 큰 사이즈 피자를 주문했다. 하지만 그들은 40분이 넘도록 음식을 기다리는 중이다. 그들은 화가 났다.

(C)

Bill and his girlfriend are at Pizza Hut. They ordered a pizza and some spaghetti, but the waiter brought them two pizzas. Bill is complaining to the manager about the waiter's mistake.

▶ complain 불만을 말하다, 불평하다

빌은 그의 여자 친구와 함께 피자헛에 있다. 그들은 피자 한 개와 스파게티를 주문했는데, 웨이터는 피자 두 개를 가져왔다. 빌은 웨이터의 실수에 대해 매니저에게 항의하고 있다.

그림의 상황을 가장 잘 묘사하고 있는 것은 무엇인가?

3

ⓐ

Peter and Samantha are at a fancy restaurant. They are sitting at a table with red roses and candles. Romantic music is playing softly. They are holding hands across the table while drinking their glasses of wine.

▶ softly 부드럽게   hold hands 손을 잡다
  across the table 테이블을 가로질러

피터와 사만다는 근사한 레스토랑에 있다. 그들은 빨간 장미와 양초가 있는 테이블에 앉아 있다. 낭만적인 음악이 감미롭게 흐르고 있다. 그들은 와인을 마시면서 테이블을 사이에 두고 손을 잡고 있다.

ⓑ

Samantha is waiting for Peter to show up at the restaurant. When he finally does, she scolds him for being late.

▶ show up 나타나다   scold 꾸짖다, 잔소리하다

사만다는 레스토랑에서 피터가 나타나기를 기다리고 있다. 그가 나타났을 때, 그녀는 그가 늦은 것에 대해 뭐라고 했다.

ⓒ

The waiter is taking Peter and Samantha's order. He brings them a bottle of fine wine and some glasses. He pours them some.

▶ take one's order ~의 주문을 받다   pour (액체를) 따르다, 붓다

웨이터는 피터와 사만다의 주문을 받고 있다. 그는 그들에게 좋은 와인과 잔을 가져다 주고 있다. 그는 와인을 따르고 있다.

상황의 순서가 올바른 것은?

(A) ⓐ – ⓑ – ⓒ
(B) ⓑ – ⓐ – ⓒ
(C) ⓑ – ⓒ – ⓐ
(D) ⓒ – ⓑ – ⓐ

4

W You know, they have excellent shrimp here.
M But I'm allergic to seafood.
W Really? That's a shame. Then, how about this chicken steak?
M That does sound delicious. And I know you have great taste in food.
W Okay, then I'll have the shrimp special while you have the steak.
M Yes, and salad and soup for appetizers.

▶ allergic 알레르기 체질의   That's a shame. 정말 안됐다.
appetizer 전채, 애피타이저

여   있지, 여기 새우가 정말 맛있어.
남   근데 나 해산물 알레르기 있는데.
여   정말? 정말 안됐다. 그럼 이 치킨 스테이크는 어때?
남   맛있겠다. 난 네가 음식에 일가견이 있다는 거 알고 있어.
여   됐다, 그럼 너는 스테이크를 먹고 난 새우 스페셜을 먹을게.
남   응, 그리고 애피타이저로 샐러드와 스프를 먹자.

대화에 대해 사실인 것은 무엇인가?

(A) 여자는 새우 요리를 먹을 것이다.
(B) 남자는 파이를 원한다.
(C) 남자는 새우를 먹을 것이다.
(D) 남자는 여자가 음식에 조예가 없다고 생각한다.

5

M   Here's your chicken pot pie.
W   But this is not what I ordered.
M   Oh! I apologize. I made a mistake on your order. We'll correct it at once.
------------pause------------
W   Here is your sweet and sour pork. I hope you enjoy it.
W   Thank you. I'm starving. It looks delicious.
M   I apologize for the mix up, ma'am.
W   ___________________

▶ make a mistake 실수하다   correct 정정하다, 바로잡다
mix up 혼란, 혼동

남   여기 주문하신 치킨 폿 파이 나왔습니다.
여   이건 제가 주문한 게 아닌데요.
남   오! 죄송합니다. 제가 실수했네요. 즉시 다시 가져 오겠습니다.

남   여기 스윗 앤 사워 포크 나왔습니다. 맛있게 드세요.
여   감사합니다. 배고파 죽을 것 같아요. 맛있어 보이네요.
남   혼동에 대해 사과 드립니다.
여   ___________________

여자가 다음에 할 말은 무엇인가?

(A) 당신과 상관없는 일이에요.
(B) 천만에요.
(C) 문제 없어요. 기다린 보람이 있네요.
(D) 저도 그 말을 들어서 기쁩니다.

6

I'm Max, and I work at my parent's restaurant. My job is to take orders from the customers and clean up tables. I've worked here for over a year now.

At first, I hated the job, but now I like it since it changed my life by teaching me to be responsible.

▶ clean up 깨끗이 청소하다   over a year 일 년 넘게

저는 맥스이고 부모님이 운영하시는 레스토랑에서 일합니다. 제 일은 고객의 주문을 받고 테이블을 치우는 것입니다. 전 여기서 1년 넘게 일했습니다. 처음에 저는 이 일을 싫어했지만, 지금은 제게 책임감을 가르쳐 줘서 제 인생을 바꿔 주었기 때문에 좋아한답니다.

이 이야기의 요지는 무엇인가?

(A) 그는 레스토랑에서 일하는 것을 싫어한다.
(B) 그는 자신의 일에 능숙하다.
(C) 그는 이 일로부터 책임감을 배웠다.
(D) 그는 3년 더 일하기를 원한다.

7

I'm Jane, and I am a vegetarian. I do not like to eat meat. I don't think that it tastes good at all. I love tofu, bean sprouts, broccoli, and other vegetables. I don't even like to eat fish. Sometimes it's hard for me to eat when I go out to restaurants. Lots of places don't offer dishes that have no meat. To be a vegetarian is a challenge, but I like it.

▶ vegetarian 채식주의자   tofu 두부   bean sprouts 콩나물
offer 제공하다   challenge 도전

전 제인이고, 채식주의자입니다. 전 고기 먹는 것을 좋아하지 않습니다. 전 두부, 콩나물, 브로콜리, 그리고 다른 야채를 좋아합니다. 전 심지어 생선도 안 먹습니다. 레스토랑에서 식사를 하는 것은 때론 제게 어려운 일이죠. 많은 식당들이 고기가 들어가지 않은 음식을 팔지 않죠. 채식주의자가 되는 것은 도전이지만, 전 좋아합니다.

여자가 이야기에서 생선을 언급한 이유는 무엇인가?

(A) 왜 그녀가 채식주의자가 되었는지 설명하기 위해
(B) 채식주의자가 되는 것이 얼마나 어려운 일인지 설명하기 위해
(C) 그녀가 채식주의자라는 것을 강조하기 위해
(D) 고기를 먹지 않는 다이어트가 도전이라는 것을 강조하기 위해

8

M   Cindy, I know of a good restaurant for you.
W   Really? Where is it?
M   About two miles away from our office.
W   How are the prices there?
M   Reasonable. Not that expensive.
W   How about the food and the service?

| M | The food is great, and they have excellent service. I highly recommend it. |
| W | All right. Thanks! |

▶ reasonable (값이) 비싸지 않은, 적당한   recommend 추천하다

남 신디, 널 위한 좋은 레스토랑을 알고 있어.
여 정말? 어디야?
남 사무실에서 한 2마일 정도 떨어져 있어.
여 가격은 어때?
남 적당해. 그렇게 비싸지 않아.
여 음식하고 서비스는?
남 음식은 맛있고, 서비스는 정말 좋아. 정말 추천해 주고 싶어.
여 알았어. 고마워!

여자가 레스토랑에 대해서 물어보지 <u>않은</u> 것은 무엇인가?

(A) 위치
(B) 서비스
(C) 음식의 질
(D) 청결함

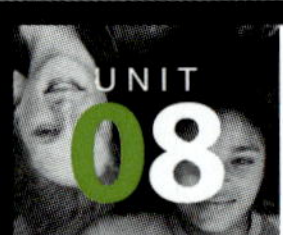

Entertainment

Key Expressions

1 1 up-to-date   2 sold out   3 plot
    4 front row   5 concert
2 1 ⓐ   2 ⓑ   3 ⓓ   4 ⓒ
3 1 ⓖ   2 ⓐ   3 ⓔ   4 ⓑ   5 ⓓ   6 ⓕ   7 ⓒ

Listening Practice

1 (C)   **2** (C)

Check Up

Listening Task *01*   1 (A)   2 (D)
Listening Task *02*   1 1) ⓒ   2) ⓑ   3) ⓐ
Listening Task *03*   1 (D)   2 (C)
Listening Task *04*   1 (C)

Listening Test

1 (C)   **2** (B)   **3** (C)   **4** (D)   **5** (B)   **6** (B)
7 (B)   **8** (B)

Key Expressions

1 표에서 가장 적절한 단어를 골라 빈칸을 채우시오.
    1 난 항상 최신 영화 정보를 위해 온라인을 검색한다.
    2 그 쇼는 너무 인기 있어서 이미 표가 매진됐다.
    3 너는 이 영화 줄거리 이해하겠어?
    4 앞줄에 앉고 싶지 않아. 너무 가까워.
    5 클래식 음악을 좋아한다면, 이 콘서트를 놓쳐서는
      안 돼요.

2 각각의 영화 장르를 가장 잘 설명하고 있는 것과 연
    결하시오.
    1 로맨스
      ⓐ 러브 스토리를 얘기해 주는 영화

2 공포
ⓑ 관중들을 무섭게 하는 영화
3 액션
ⓓ 위험과 흥분으로 가득찬 빠른 움직임이 있는 영화
4 코미디
ⓒ 사람들을 웃게 만드는 영화

3 다음 문장들을 가장 잘 어울리는 대답과 연결하시오.

1 벌써 네 티켓 샀어.
ⓖ 고마워. 언제 갈 거야?
2 우리는 모두 10분간 박수를 쳤어.
ⓐ 와우. 정말 좋았나 보네.
3 요즘 드라마들은 너무 지루해.
ⓔ 응, 우는 장면이 많아.
4 오스카 시상식이 오늘밤이야.
ⓑ 정말? 2년간 시상식하는 거 못 봤는데.
5 금요일 저녁에 뭐해?
ⓓ 보통 친구들하고 외출해.
6 영화랑 연극 중에서 어떤 게 더 좋아?
ⓕ 잘 모르겠어. 둘 다 좋아하는데.
7 내일 소풍에 대해서 생각하는 거 있어?
ⓒ 강변 공원에 가는 게 어때?

Listening Practice

1

There is going to be a concert this Saturday night. I can't wait for it. My favorite group is going to be playing. I saved up all my money for a few months so that I could buy a ticket. My father is going to take my best friend and me to the hall. I have all of the group's CDs, but this is the first concert for me to go to. This is going to be great.

▶ **save up** 저축하다　**take** ~을 데리고 가다

이번 주 토요일 밤에 콘서트가 열릴 예정이다. 나는 그것이 너무나 기다려진다. 내가 가장 좋아하는 그룹이 연주할 예정이다. 나는 몇 달 동안 돈을 모두 모아서 티켓을 샀다. 아빠가 내 제일 친한 친구와 나를 콘서트 홀에 데리고 가 주실 예정이다. 나는 그 그룹의 모든 CD를 가지고 있지만 콘서트에 가는 것은 이번이 처음이다. 정말 멋질 것이다.

소년이 지금 느끼는 기분을 가장 잘 표현하고 있는 것은 무엇인가?

(A) 화가 난
(B) 실망한
(C) 흥분한
(D) 피곤한

2

W　So, how did you enjoy the movie, Dad?
M　I thought it was really exciting. And the soundtrack was pretty good, too.
W　Yeah, I agree. And I really loved the chase scenes. They seemed to be totally realistic.
M　I thought that the special effects were well done, too.
W　Exactly. What did you think of the acting?
M　_______________________________

▶ **exciting** 흥분시키는, 신나는　**soundtrack** 사운드트랙, 영화음악　**chase** 추격; 쫓다　**scene** (영화, 연극의 특정) 장면, 씬　**realistic** 현실적인, 실제 같은　**special effects** 특수 효과　**acting** 연기, 연출

여　영화 어땠어요, 아빠?
남　정말 재밌구나. 영화 음악도 꽤 좋았고 말이야.
여　맞아요. 저도 그렇게 생각해요. 추격신이 정말 마음에 들었어요. 진짜 실제 같아 보였다니까요.
남　특수 효과도 좋았어.
여　정말 그래요. 연기는 어땠다고 생각하세요?
남　_______________________________

아버지가 마지막에 할 말로 가장 적절한 것은?

(A) 영화가 마음에 들었어.
(B) 마지막 부분이 좋았어.
(C) 평균 이상이더구나.
(D) 아니, 괜찮았어.

Check Up

Listening Task *01*

I really like listening to music when I have a hard day at school. It makes me feel relaxed and happy. I like pop music the best because it is fun. I sing and dance with the music. But I don't like rap. Sometimes I listen to rock or even classical music. I like to listen to classical music when I study. I have a big test next week, and classical music helps me stay focused on my work.

▶ **relaxed** 긴장을 푼, 느슨한　**focus** ~에 집중하다

나는 학교에서 힘들 때 음악 듣는 것을 정말 좋아한다. 음악은 날 편안하고 행복하게 한다. 난 신이 나기 때문에 팝 음악을 가장 좋아한다. 음악을 들으면서 노래도 부르고 춤도 춘다. 랩은 좋아하지 않는다. 공부할 때는 록이나 클래식 음악 듣는 것도 좋아한다. 다음 주에 큰 시험이 있는데 클래식 음악은 내가 공부하는 데 집중할 수 있도록 도와준다.

1 화자가 좋아하지 않는 것은?

(A) 랩 (B) 팝 (C) 록 (D) 클래식

2 이야기 속에서 언급되지 않은 것은?

(A) 그가 음악을 좋아하는 이유
(B) 그가 가장 좋아하는 음악
(C) 그가 클래식 음악을 듣는 이유
(D) 그가 랩 음악을 싫어하는 이유

Listening Task 02

ⓐ

Oh, no! Look at the long line to buy tickets. I wish we had come earlier. It's so cold out here, and the line is not moving. What if the tickets are all sold out when we get to the front?

▶ What if...? ~하면 어쩌지? sold out 매진된

오, 이런! 표 사려고 기다리는 줄 좀 봐. 좀 더 일찍 왔어야 했는데. 여긴 너무 춥고 줄은 안 줄어드는데. 매표소에 갔을 때 표가 다 매진되면 어쩌지?

ⓑ

Welcome back to the game show *Unbelievable Nonsense*! Jennifer Smith is the finalist today. But she will still have to answer five questions correctly to win our big prize, $30,000 in cash.

▶ finalist 결승 진출자 correctly 정확하게 in cash 현금으로

'언빌리버블 넌센스' 퀴즈 쇼에 오신 걸 환영합니다. 제니퍼 스미스가 오늘의 최종 참가자입니다. 하지만 큰 상인 현금 3만 달러를 얻기 위해서는 5개의 질문에 정확하게 대답해야만 합니다.

ⓒ

That magician we went to see last night was really good. He did some interesting magic tricks with cards, but the most exciting part was when he made a whole car disappear. I don't know how he did it.

▶ magician 마술사

우리가 어젯밤에 보러 갔던 마술사는 정말 훌륭했다. 그는 카드를 가지고 재미있는 마술 묘기를 보여 주었지만, 가장 흥미로웠던 것은 그가 자동차를 통째로 사라지게 할 때였다. 어떻게 그가 그걸 했는지 모르겠다.

1 각 그림과 어울리는 이야기의 번호를 쓰시오.

1)  2)  3) 

Listening Task 03

W I stayed up all night reading my new book. It was so good I didn't want to stop reading.

M You must be tired.

W Not really. It was so interesting that it kept me awake.

M Well, it's a good thing you don't have to go to school today.

W Yes, after breakfast I am going to start reading a new book!

M Wow, that's amazing! I never knew that you enjoyed reading so much.

W Ever since I read *Harry Potter*, I have just loved reading books.

▶ stay up all night 밤을 새다 ever since ~ 이후로 줄곧

여 책 읽느라 어젯밤 꼬박 샜어. 너무 재미 있어서 멈출 수가 없었어.
남 피곤하겠네.
여 그렇지 않아. 너무 재미있어서 깨어 있었던 거야.
남 오늘 학교 가지 않아도 되니까 다행이구나.
여 응, 아침 먹은 후에 새 책을 읽으려고!
남 굉장하구나! 네가 책 읽는 걸 그렇게 좋아하는지 몰랐어.
여 '해리 포터'를 읽은 후로 난 독서를 좋아하게 됐어.

1 여자는 왜 밤을 샜는가?

(A) 피곤하지 않았다.
(B) 다음 날이 휴일이었다.
(C) 그 날 학교에 가야만 했다.
(D) 책을 읽었다.

2 여자를 설명하는 가장 알맞은 말은?

(A) 카우치 포테이토
(B) 만물박사
(C) 책벌레
(D) 운동선수

Listening Task 04

M Let's go outside and play in the snow. This television show is boring.

W Sounds like fun. Let me get my coat and gloves.

M We can make a snow sculpture.

W What will we make?

M A snowman?

W We did that last year. What about making a snow angel?

M If there's enough snow, why not? Let's go outside and see.

W   Don't forget to bring the camera as well.

▶ sculpture 조각; 조각하다

남   밖에 나가서 눈 속에서 가지고 놀자. 텔레비전이 지루해.
여   재미있겠는데. 코트랑 장갑 가져올게.
남   눈 조각 만들자.
여   뭐 만들 건데?
남   눈사람?
여   작년에 만들었잖아. 눈천사는 어때?
남   눈만 많다면, 왜 안되겠어? 밖에 나가서 보자.
여   카메라 가져 오는 거 잊지마.

1   화자들은 눈 쌓인 곳에 나가기 전에 무엇을 하고 있었나?

   (A) 그들은 잠을 자고 있었다.
   (B) 그들은 저녁을 먹고 있었다.
   (C) 그들은 텔레비전을 보고 있었다.
   (D) 그들은 사진을 찍고 있었다.

Listening Test

1

M   This theme park is amazing!

W   It sure is. I don't think we have enough time to go on all the rides.

M   Probably not. So what ride should we go on first?

W   How about the roller coaster? I love them.

M   Uh, no thanks. I'm afraid of heights. How about doing something else?

W   Well, the bumper cars are nearby. Or we could go on the flume.

M   Hmm… How about the bumper cars?

W   Great. Let's get in line.

▶ theme park 테마 파크, 놀이공원   ride (유원지 등의) 탈것   height 높이, 높음   flume (유원지의) 워터슈트

남   이 놀이공원 굉장하다!
여   정말 그래. 놀이기구를 전부 다 타볼 시간이 있을지 모르겠네.
남   아마 시간 모자랄 걸. 제일 먼저 뭘 탈까?
여   롤러코스터 어때? 나 그거 정말 좋아해.
남   음, 아냐. 나 고소공포증 있어. 다른 게 어떨까?
여   흠, 범퍼카가 가까이에 있네. 아니면 워터슈트를 타러 갈 수도 있고.
남   흠…. 범퍼카 타러 갈까?
여   좋아. 가서 줄 서자.

이 대화가 끝난 후에 화자들은 무엇을 할 것인가?

(A) 워터슈트를 탄다.
(B) 다음 롤러코스터를 기다린다.
(C) 범퍼카를 타기 위해 줄을 선다.
(D) 모든 놀이기구를 타러 간다.

2

M   I'd like to reserve two tickets for the comedy show tonight, please.

W   There are two shows, one at 6 p.m. and one at 8:30 p.m.

M   I'd like tickets for the six o'clock show.

W   There are only a couple of seats left. I'm afraid they are right in the back.

M   That's no good. What about the show at 8:30?

W   We have some seats left in the middle and near the back.

M   This must be a popular show.

W   Yes, audiences love the comedian.

▶ reserve 예약하다, 지정해 두다   audience 관중, 관객

남   오늘밤에 하는 코미디 쇼 티켓 2장 예약하려고요.
여   6시랑 8시 30분 쇼가 있는데요.
남   6시 쇼 티켓이 좋겠군요.
여   몇 석밖에 안 남아 있습니다. 뒤쪽 오른쪽이에요.
남   별로네요. 8시 30분 쇼는요?
여   중앙과 뒤쪽에 몇 좌석 남아 있네요.
남   쇼가 인기있나봐요.
여   네, 관객들이 그 코미디언을 좋아해요.

왜 남자는 8시 30분 쇼를 보려고 하는가?

(A) 6시에 하는 코미디 쇼는 별로다.
(B) 6시 쇼에서 뒤쪽 자리에 앉고 싶어 하지 않는다.
(C) 그는 6시에 하는 쇼에 제시간에 오지 못할 것이다.
(D) 8시 30분에 하는 쇼가 더 낫다.

3

M   Hey, Jane. Chris told me he watched *Star Wars* with you last weekend.

W   Yeah, we did.

M   How was it? I plan to watch it with my family this Saturday.

W   Please, don't ask about it. Chris and I just wasted our time.

M   I don't believe it. Everyone says it's a great movie.

W   I fell asleep during the movie. It was so bad. There was no action in the movie.

▶ fall asleep 잠이 들다   during ~사이에, ~하는 중에

남   안녕, 제인. 크리스가 지난주말에 너랑 '스타 워즈' 봤다고 하던데.
여   응, 봤어.
남   어땠어? 이번 토요일에 가족과 함께 보려고 하는데.
여   얘기하지도 마. 크리스와 나는 시간만 낭비했어.

남　믿을 수가 없어. 다른 사람들은 다 그 영화가 좋다고 하던데.

여　난 영화 상영 중에 잠들었어. 정말 별로였어. 영화에 액션이 없어.

여자는 영화에 대해서 어떻게 느꼈는가?

(A) 즐거웠다
(B) 신났다
(C) 지루했다
(D) 무서웠다

4

▶ theater 극장

난 샐리와 함께 연극을 보러 갔어. 너무나도 좋은 시간을 보내서 너도 그것을 보면 좋아할 거야. '나잇 앤 데이'라는 연극인데 새로 나온 영국 연극이야. 엔딩이 너무 슬퍼. 배우들이 너무 연기를 잘해서 난 거의 울 뻔했어. 많이 비싸지도 않아. 연극이 시작하기 30분 전에 극장에서 표를 사기만 하면 돼.

여자는 무엇에 대해 얘기하고 있는가?

(A) 어쩌다가 연극 관람료를 내는 것을 잊었는지
(B) 연극을 보러 갈 계획
(C) 그녀가 보고 있는 연극
(D) 볼 만한 좋은 연극

5

M　The weather's going to be great this weekend. Let's do something fun.

W　Yes, let's go away to a place near the beach for the weekend.

M　Oh, there's a company picnic on Saturday. That might be great.

W　Oh, that sounds boring. Let's go to the music concert in the park in the evening.

M　Okay, then I can catch the baseball game in the afternoon. What will we do on Sunday?

W　We'll have lunch in the park and then see a movie.

M　That sounds good.

▶ catch (TV 프로그램 등을) 보다

남　이번 주말은 날씨가 좋대. 재미있는 거 하자.
여　그래, 주말에 해변 근처로 놀러가자.
남　토요일에는 회사 소풍이 있는데. 재미있을 거야.

여　그거 지루할 것 같은데. 저녁에 공원에서 하는 음악 콘서트에 가자.
남　알았어. 그럼 난 오후에 야구 경기 볼 수 있겠다. 일요일에는 뭐하지?
여　공원에서 점심 먹고 영화보러 가자.
남　그거 좋은 생각인데.

이들은 토요일에 무엇을 함께 할 것인가?

(A) 그들은 해변에 갈 것이다.
(B) 그들은 공원에서 하는 음악 콘서트에 갈 것이다.
(C) 그들은 야구 경기를 볼 것이다.
(D) 그들은 공원에서 점심을 먹을 것이다.

6

M　Are you watching that TV program again?

W　Yes. I like it. Don't you?

M　It's been on about twenty times already.

W　Twenty times? That's not true. Anyway, it's still funny.

M　Why don't you change the channel? I'm sure there's something better on.

W　Why don't you sit down and watch the program with me? You might enjoy it.

M　I have better things to do with my time. I'd rather wash the car.

남　그 TV 프로그램 또 보고 있는 거야?
여　응, 난 이거 정말 좋아해. 넌?
남　20번은 봤겠다.
여　20번? 그건 아니다. 어쨌든, 아직도 재미있어.
남　채널을 돌리는 게 어때? 더 재미있는 거 할 거야.
여　그냥 앉아서 나와 같이 이 프로그램 보는 게 어때? 아마 너도 재미있어 할 거야.
남　그 시간에 난 더 나은 일을 할래. 난 세차나 해야겠다.

남자는 프로그램에 대해서 어떻게 느끼고 있나?

(A) 다시 보고 싶어 한다.
(B) 그것을 보는 것에 싫증났다.
(C) 재미있다고 생각한다.
(D) 흥미롭다고 생각한다.

7

W　Hey, Chris, can you go out to the snack bar and get me a drink before the movie starts? I'm really thirsty.

M　Yeah, I can do that for you. What do you want? Coke or juice?

W　Coke. Can you me get some popcorn, too?

M　Great, and I'll get some popcorn for myself as

well. Oh, do you want an ice cream?

W You can get one for yourself, and I'll help you eat it.

여 크리스, 스낵 바에 가서 영화 시작하기 전에 음료수 좀 사다 줄래? 목이 너무 말라.

남 그래, 사다 줄게. 뭐 마실래? 콜라 아니면 주스?

여 콜라. 팝콘도 사다 줄래?

남 알았어. 내가 먹을 팝콘도 좀 사야겠다. 아, 아이스크림 먹을래?

여 네 것만 사와. 난 네 거 조금만 먹을래.

여자가 원하지 <u>않는</u> 것은 무엇인가?

(A) 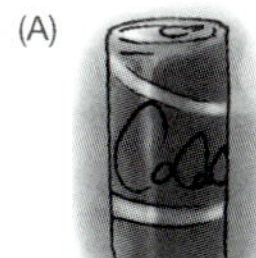

(B) 

(C) 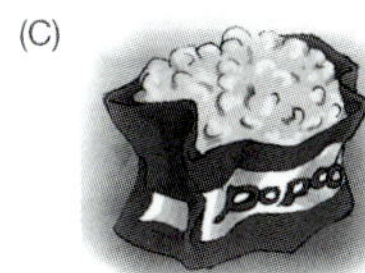

(D) 

8

M Hi, may I help you?

W I would like to rent some DVDs. How much does it cost to rent them?

M The price depends upon the DVD itself. New releases are three dollars, and others are two dollars.

W I want to rent these three DVDs. Are they new releases?

M Let me take a look at them. Only one of them is new. The others are not.

▶ **depend upon** ~에 달려 있다   **release** 공개, 개봉(물), 발표(물)

남 안녕하세요, 무엇을 도와 드릴까요?

여 DVD를 빌리려고 하는데요. 빌리는 데 얼마에요?

남 가격은 DVD에 달렸어요. 신작은 3달러이고 다른 것들은 2달러에요.

여 이렇게 세 개를 빌리고 싶은데요. 신작들인가요?

남 제가 좀 볼게요. 하나만 신작이네요. 나머지는 아니에요.

여자는 얼마를 지불해야 하나?

(A) 3달러

(B) 7달러

(C) 8달러

(D) 10달러

Transportation

Key Expressions

1   1 intersection   2 speeding   3 traffic jam
      4 seatbelt   5 accident

2   go straight, go two blocks, turn right, on your right

3   1 ⓑ   2 ⓔ   3 ⓓ   4 ⓖ   5 ⓒ   6 ⓕ   7 ⓐ

Listening Practice

1 (B)   **2** (A)

Check Up

Listening Task *01*   1 (A)   2 (C)

Listening Task *02*   1 (C)

Listening Task *03*   1 (C)   2 (C)

Listening Task *04*   1 (B)

Listening Test

1 (A)   **2** (C)   **3** (D)   **4** (A)   **5** (B)   **6** (C)

7 (B)   **8** (C)

Key Expressions

1   표에서 가장 적절한 단어를 골라 빈칸을 채우시오.

   1 남자는 재빨리 교차로를 건너고 있다.

   2 집에 오는 길에 과속 딱지를 뗐다.

   3 러시아워의 교통체증에 걸렸다.

   4 안전 벨트를 매주세요.

   5 나는 어제 교통사고를 당했지만 다친 곳은 전혀 없다.

2   지도 위의 학교에 가기 위한 길을 설명하는 데 필요한 표현들을 고르시오.

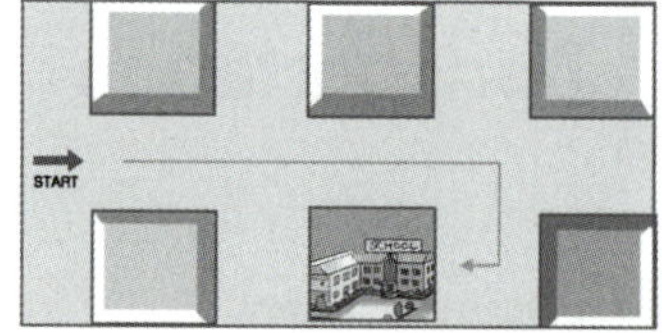

3 다음 문장들을 가장 잘 어울리는 대답과 연결하시오.

1 표는 얼마야?
ⓑ 900원 정도 해.

2 몇 정거장 더 가야 해?
ⓔ 7번째 정거장에서 내려.

3 여기서 도서관으로 가려면 어떻게 해야 하나요?
ⓓ 93번 버스를 타야 해요.

4 미안해, 늦었어.
ⓖ 괜찮아. 오늘 교통이 혼잡하잖아.

5 주차 공간이 있나요?
ⓒ 이쪽에는 없어요.

6 버스 정류장이 어디 있나요?
ⓕ 저쪽 모퉁이에요.

7 이태원에서 공원까지는 얼마나 걸리나요?
ⓐ 버스로 30분쯤 걸려요.

Listening Practice

1

Hi, I'm James Park. I'm in my senior year of high school. I've been going to school by bus for three years. My house is an hour away from school. When I was younger, I used to talk with my friends all the time. But these days, I have to study. It's also the best time to listen to audio books. I listen to books about history or politics, and I'm even learning a new language.

▶ **senior** 상급자인; 상급자 **used to** (과거에) ~하곤 했다

안녕, 난 제임스 박이야. 고등학교 3학년에 재학중이야. 나는 3년 동안 버스로 학교에 갔어. 우리집은 학교에서 1시간 정도 떨어져 있어. 좀 더 어렸을 때는, 친구들과 항상 이야기를 나누곤 했지. 하지만 요즘에는 공부해야 해. 오디오 북을 듣기에 가장 좋은 때이기도 해. 난 역사와 정치에 관한 책을 듣고, 심지어 새 언어도 배워.

이야기의 주제는 무엇인가?

(A) 학교까지 버스 타는 법
(B) 학교 가는 시간을 보내는 법
(C) 그가 오디오 북 듣기를 좋아하는 이유
(D) 새 언어를 배우는 법

2

M How should we go to the restaurant?
W I don't know. Where is it again?
M It's downtown.
W Well, then, we can get there by bus or subway.
M Let's take the subway. No traffic.
W True, but I like the bus better since you can see where you are.
M Well, it's up to you.

▶ **downtown** 도심지, 시내 **traffic** 교통, 교통량
up to ~가 해야 할, ~가 하기 나름인

남 레스토랑까지 어떻게 가야 하지?
여 모르겠는데. 거기가 어디라고?
남 시내야.
여 음, 그럼, 버스나 지하철을 타면 되겠네.
남 지하철 타자. 교통체증이 없잖아.
여 맞아, 하지만 난 버스가 더 좋을 것 같은데. 그래야 네가 어디 있는지 알 수 있잖아.
남 뭐, 네 뜻대로 하자.

대화에 대해 사실인 것은 무엇인가?

(A) 그들은 목적지에 어떻게 가는지에 대해 얘기하고 있다.
(B) 남자는 전철이 버스보다 안 좋다고 얘기하고 있다.
(C) 레스토랑은 걸어갈 만한 거리에 있다.
(D) 여자는 전철을 좋아한다.

Check Up

Listening Task *01*

W Have you seen my new car?
M No, I haven't.
W It's that small one over there.
M It's neon green!
W Yes, now I can easily spot it!
M True. Mine is a black one, so it blends in with the other cars.

▶ **spot** 발견하다, 분간하다 **blend in** ~와 섞이다, 조화되다

여 내 새 차 봤니?
남 아니, 못 봤는데.
여 저쪽에 있는 소형차야.
남 형광 초록색이구나!
여 응, 이제 내 차를 쉽게 찾을 수 있어!
남 그래. 내 차는 검은 색이라서 다른 차들과 섞이거든.

1 여자는 자신의 차에 대해 어떻게 느끼고 있나?

(A) 만족한   (B) 무관심한

(C) 슬픈 　　　　　(D) 역겨운

2　남자는 차의 ~때문에 놀랐다.

(A) 크기 　　　　　(B) 흔한 색깔
(C) 독특한 색깔 　　(D) 모양

Listening Task *02*

M　How could you run into my car like that? Didn't you see me turning into the road?
W　I'm sorry. I was on my mobile phone.
M　So you weren't watching the road?
W　I was watching the car in front of you.
M　My car looks terrible.
W　I'll pay for the damage. I'm so sorry.

▶ **run into** 달려들다, (차가) 충돌하다　**damage** 손상, 손해, 피해

남　어떻게 내 차로 그렇게 돌진할 수가 있어요? 내가 도로로 진입하는 거 못 봤나요?
여　죄송합니다. 통화 중이었어요.
남　그래서 도로도 안 보고 있었다는 거에요?
여　당신 앞에 있는 차는 봤어요.
남　내 차가 끔찍해 보여요.
여　제가 보상해 드리겠습니다. 죄송합니다.

1　남자가 느끼는 바를 가장 잘 나타낸 것은?

(A) 실망한 　　　　(B) 좌절한
(C) 화가 난 　　　　(D) 절망적인

Listening Task *03*

M　We have a little problem.
W　What happened?
M　The car has a flat tire.
W　Oh no! Can you fix it?
M　Yes, I have a spare tire.
W　Then I'll help you so we can get to the movie on time.
M　Thank you!

▶ **flat tire** 바람 빠진 타이어　**spare** 예비의, 여분의
　on time 제 시간에, 시간 맞춰

남　약간의 문제가 생겼어.
여　무슨 일인데?
남　자동차 타이어가 펑크났어.
여　오 이런! 수리할 수 있겠어?
남　응, 스페어 타이어가 있거든.
여　그럼 내가 도울게. 그래야 영화 보러 제시간에 갈 수 있을 거야.
남　고마워.

1　대화에 대해 사실인 것은 무엇인가?

(A) 타이어가 펑크나서 견인 트럭을 불러야 한다.
(B) 남자는 혼자서 타이어를 교체할 것이다.
(C) 여자와 남자는 함께 펑크난 타이어를 교체할 것이다.
(D) 스페어 타이어가 펑크났다.

2　왜 여자는 남자를 도우려 하는가?

(A) 그러고 싶었기 때문에
(B) 잘하기 때문에
(C) 일이 좀 더 빨리 끝날 테니까
(D) 돈을 받기 때문에

Listening Task *04*

I always drive home from work, but I really hate the traffic. In the evening, it often takes me over one hour to get home. There are just too many drivers on the roads these days. It really makes me frustrated to sit in traffic for a long time and not go anywhere. I think I'm going to start taking the subway to work. That way, my travel time will be much shorter.

▶ **frustrated** 실망한, 좌절한

나는 늘 자가용으로 퇴근하는데, 교통체증이 정말로 싫다. 저녁 때는 집에 오는 데 한 시간이 넘게 걸리기도 한다. 요즘엔 도로에 차가 너무나 많다. 아무 데도 갈 수 없는 채 차 안에서 오래도록 앉아 있어야 하는 것은 정말 기운이 빠진다. 지하철을 이용해서 회사에 갈까 생각중이다. 그러면 출퇴근 시간이 훨씬 단축될 것이다.

1　남자는 무엇을 할 예정인가?

(A) 퇴근길에 운전할 것이다.
(B) 지하철을 타기 시작할 것이다.
(C) 교통체증 속에서 오래 기다릴 것이다.
(D) 저녁 때까지 회사에 있을 것이다.

Listening Test

1

I'm George, and I'm twenty years old. I'll be getting my driver's license soon. I drive well, but I still have trouble with a few things. I'm glad that my parking is nearly perfect. It's worth twenty-five percent of the test. I'm sure I can pass that part easily. But I still need to work on it. I also need to work on backing up.

▶ **driver's license** 운전면허증　**parking** 주차, 주차 장소
　worth ~의 가치가 있는　**back up** (차를) 후진시키다, 후원하다

난 조지이고 스무살이다. 곧 있으면 운전 면허증을 딸 것이다. 난 운전을 잘하지만, 몇가지 어려움이 있다. 주차는 거의 완벽하다. 주차

는 시험의 25퍼센트를 차지한다. 난 주차는 쉽게 통과할 것이라고 확신한다. 하지만 계속 연습해야 한다. 또한 후진하는 것도 연습할 필요가 있다.

이야기의 요지는 무엇인가?

(A) 조지는 운전 면허증을 따기 위해 준비하고 있다.
(B) 그는 주차를 잘 못한다.
(C) 시험의 주차 부분은 25퍼센트가 안 된다.
(D) 그는 스무살 청년이다.

2

M   What is the fare for two people to Seoul Land?
W   Do you have a student card?
M   No, I'm not a student. But my brother is only ten years old.
W   Children only pay half the price.
M   That's good. How much is the adult fare?
W   It's ten thousand won.

▶ fare 운임, 요금, 통행료   adult fare 성인 요금

남   서울랜드에 가는 데 두 사람에 얼마에요?
여   학생증이 있나요?
남   아뇨, 전 학생이 아니에요. 제 남동생은 단지 10살이에요.
여   아이들은 요금의 반만 내면 됩니다.
남   그거 잘됐군요. 성인 요금은 얼마인가요?
여   만원이에요.

서울랜드에 가는 티켓의 총 비용은 얼마인가?

(A) 만원   (B) 2만원
(C) 만 오천원   (D) 5만원

3

I just flew on an airplane for the first time ever. It was such an exciting event. First, I got to sit next to the window, so I could see everything really clearly. When we took off, we were going down the runway so quickly. Suddenly, we flew up in the air. The flight was so nice and smooth. We watched a movie. And then I got to have dinner — it was really delicious. Finally, after a few hours, we landed. I couldn't believe how quickly we traveled across the country. I can't wait to fly again soon.

▶ take off 이륙하다   runway 활주로, 활주대   fly up 날아오르다
  land 착륙하다, 상륙하다

나는 방금 생애 처음으로 비행기를 타봤다. 그건 정말 신나는 일이었다. 우선 나는 창가에 앉아서 모든 것을 생생하게 볼 수 있었다. 이륙할 때 우리는 정말로 빠르게 활주로를 내달렸다. 그리고서는 갑

자기 공중에 날아올랐다. 비행은 굉장히 멋지고 부드러웠다. 우리는 영화를 보았다. 그리고나서 기내식을 먹었는데 그건 정말 맛있었다. 마침내 몇 시간 후 우리는 착륙했다. 나는 우리가 얼마나 빨리 나라를 횡단했는지 믿을 수가 없다. 빨리 또 비행기를 타고 싶다.

여자가 기내에서 하지 <u>않은</u> 것은 무엇인가?

(A)    (B) 

(C)    (D) 

4

M   Hello, I'd like a ticket for Chicago, please.
W   Sure. There is a train leaving in one hour.
M   Great. I'll take that. How much does the ticket cost?
W   It will cost fifty dollars. Will you be paying with cash or a credit card?
M   Cash. Oh, one more question. What gate is it leaving from?
W   Go to gate seven. It's right behind us.

▶ for (목적지) ~로 가는, ~로 가기 위한

남   안녕하세요, 시카고 행 표를 사고 싶습니다.
여   네, 한 시간 뒤에 떠나는 기차가 있어요.
남   좋군요. 그걸 타겠습니다. 티켓이 얼마죠?
여   50달러입니다. 현금으로 계산하시겠어요, 신용카드로 하시겠어요?
남   현금으로 하죠. 아, 질문 하나만 더 할게요. 기차가 몇 번 게이트에서 출발하죠?
여   7번 게이트로 가세요. 바로 뒤에 있습니다.

이 대화가 일어나고 있는 곳은 어디인가?

(A) 기차역   (B) 버스 정류장
(C) 주유소   (D) 영화관

5

W   Alex, you should really purchase a transit card.
M   Why? These tickets are more convenient.
W   But the cards are cheaper than the tickets.
M   Really?

W Yes, and you can also use the cards on public buses!

M You're right. It's also easier to scan the card when you go through the gate.

W Let's go to the counter and get one for you then!

▶ **purchase** 사다, 구입하다 **transit** 통과, 통행 **convenient** 편리한, 사용하기 좋은 **go through** 통과하다, 지나가다

여 알렉스, 너 교통카드 사야 해.
남 왜? 이 표가 더 편리한데.
여 그렇지만 카드가 표보다 더 싸.
남 정말?
여 응, 그리고 그 카드로 버스에서도 사용할 수 있어!
남 네 말이 맞다. 게이트를 통과할 때도 카드를 스캔하는 게 더 쉽겠구나.
여 매표소에 가서 하나 사자!

왜 여자는 카드가 더 좋다고 생각하나?

(A) 가지고 다니기에 더 가볍기 때문에
(B) 더 싸고 버스에서도 사용할 수 있기 때문에
(C) 카드 회사를 소유하고 있기 때문에
(D) 표를 싫어하기 때문에

6

M So we're going to the Coex Mall?

W Yes.

M What subway stop is that at?

W It's on line number two, the green line, at Samsung Station.

M How far is that from here at Sadang Station?

W It's seven stops away, so it will take us about fifteen minutes to get there.

M Then let's go!

남 우리 코엑스 몰에 가는 거야?
여 응.
남 거기는 무슨 역에 있어?
여 초록색 2호선 라인의 삼성역에 있어.
남 사당역에서 얼마나 멀지?
여 일곱 정거장 더 가야 해. 거기 가는 데 한 15분이 걸릴 거야.
남 그럼 가 보자!

대화에 대해 사실이 <u>아닌</u> 것은?

(A) 남자는 코엑스 몰이 어디 있는지 모른다.
(B) 삼성역은 2호선인 초록색 노선에 있다.
(C) 여자는 50분 이상 걸릴 것이라고 말한다.
(D) 그들은 사당역에 있다.

7

The subway is a very convenient form of transportation. It's a lot quicker than buses or sometimes even taxis. It's cheaper than driving your car everywhere and then looking for a parking space. Most major cities have a subway system. It's probably the best way to get around in a big city, which is usually crowded with cars and people.

▶ **transportation** 운송, 교통 기관 **parking space** 주차 공간 **get around** 돌아다니다 **crowded** 붐비는, 혼잡한

전철은 아주 편리한 운송 수단이다. 버스, 때로는 택시보다도 훨씬 빠르다. 차를 타고 다니면서 주차 공간을 찾는 것보다 훨씬 비용이 덜 든다. 대부분의 대도시들은 전철 시스템을 가지고 있다. 전철은 사람과 차로 붐비는 대도시를 돌아다니는 가장 좋은 방법일 것이다.

이 이야기는 무엇에 대해 답하고 있는가?

(A) 가장 저렴한 교통 수단은 무엇인가?
(B) 대도시에서 가장 좋은 교통 수단은 무엇인가?
(C) 버스나 비행기보다 여행하기 더 좋은 방법은 무엇인가?
(D) 가장 안전한 교통 수단은 무엇인가?

8

W Are you going on a long plane trip?

M Yes, I'm going to Boston, Massachusetts, my hometown.

W That will be a long flight.

M I know, and I have three layovers.

W Where are they?

M They're at Narita, Los Angeles, and Chicago.

W Well, I hope you have a safe trip.

M Thank you.

▶ **go on a trip** 여행을 가다 **layover** 도중하차

여 장기 비행기 여행을 할 예정인가요?
남 네, 전 제 고향인 메사추세츠주의 보스턴에 가려고 해요.
여 긴 여행이 되겠네요.
남 그렇죠. 세 곳을 경유해요.
여 어디죠?
남 나리타, 로스엔젤레스, 시카고요.
여 안전한 여행되길 바래요.
남 고마워요.

남자는 보스턴에 도착하기 전에 몇 대의 비행기를 탈 것인가?

(A) 두 대 (B) 세 대
(C) 네 대 (D) 다섯 대

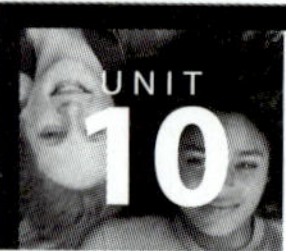

UNIT 10 Hobbies

정답 answer

Key Expressions

1 1 outdoor 2 garden 3 comic books
   4 surfing the Internet 5 hobby

3 1 ⓑ 2 ⓒ 3 ⓔ 4 ⓐ 5 ⓓ 6 ⓕ 7 ⓖ

Listening Practice

1 (C)   **2** (B)

Check Up

Listening Task 01 1 (A)   2 1) F 2) T 3) T
Listening Task 02 1 (C)
Listening Task 03 1 (A)   2 (A)
Listening Task 04 1 (B)

Listening Test

1 (C)   **2** (A)   **3** (B)   **4** (B)   **5** (C)   **6** (C)
7 (D)   **8** (D)

스크립트 & 해석 script & translation

Key Expressions

1 표에서 가장 적절한 단어를 골라 빈칸을 채우시오.

1 나는 하이킹, 캠핑, 낚시와 같이 야외에서 하는 활동을 좋아한다.

2 우리는 정원에서 야채를 기른다.

3 나는 소설과 만화책, 시를 읽는 것을 좋아한다.

4 요즘 많은 젊은 사람들은 책을 읽는 것보다 인터넷 서핑하는 것을 더 좋아하는 것 같다.

5 최근에 나는 새로운 취미를 찾았다.

---

2 당신이 여가 시간에 하고 있는 활동들을 고르시오.

정원 손질	요리	밴드에서 연주
하이킹	인터넷 서핑	영화 보기
쇼핑	컴퓨터 게임하기	음악 듣기
독서	운동하기	채팅하기

3 다음 문장들을 가장 잘 어울리는 대답과 연결하시오.

1 요리하는 거 좋아해?
   ⓑ 한 번도 해 본 적 없는데.

2 어떤 종류의 잡지 좋아해?
   ⓒ *News Weekly* 좋아해.

3 축구하는 거 좋아해?
   ⓔ 아니, 난 스포츠 안 좋아해.

4 너희 아버지 취미 있으셔?
   ⓐ 응, 골프 치셔.

5 여가 시간에 뭐해?
   ⓓ 보통 책 보는데.

6 내 친구는 나랑 같은 취미를 가지고 있어.
   ⓕ 그거 좋구나.

7 야외활동과 실내활동, 뭘 더 좋아하니?
   ⓖ 당연히 후자지.

Listening Practice

1

Most people have some sort of hobby. Hobbies help people to relax and give them opportunities to meet new people. They can also give people things to talk about. In addition, learning something new is good for keeping the mind active. There are many excellent reasons to develop a hobby that interests you.

▶ opportunity 기회, 호기 in addition 게다가, 더구나
active 활기찬, 활발한 develop 발달시키다, 개발하다

대부분의 사람들은 취미를 가지고 있다. 취미는 사람들의 정신적 긴장을 풀어주고 새로운 사람들을 만날 수 있는 기회를 제공해 준다. 또한 얘깃거리를 제공해 준다. 게다가 새로운 것을 배우는 것은 정신을 활기차게 유지하는 데 좋다. 당신이 관심을 갖고 있는 취미를 발전시킬 많은 좋은 이유들이 있다.

이야기의 주제는 무엇인가?

(A) 긴장을 푸는 법
(B) 새로운 취미를 배우는 방법들
(C) 취미를 갖는 것의 이점들
(D) 왜 새로운 사람들을 만나야 하는가

2

W   I have a lot of free time these days.

M   So, what are you going to do?

W   I am thinking of learning to ride a motorbike.

M   Oh yeah? Isn't it too dangerous for women?

W   I don't think so as long as I keep alert.

▶ **as long as** ~하기만 하면, ~하는 한   **alert** 방심하지 않는, 경계하는

여   요즘 시간이 많이 나.
남   그럼, 뭐 할 거야?
여   모터바이크를 탈까 생각 중이야.
남   뭐라고? 여자가 타기에는 너무 위험하지 않아?
여   조심하면 그렇게 위험하지 않아.

남자는 여자의 새로운 취미에 대해 어떻게 생각하는가?

(A) 그도 같은 취미를 원한다.
(B) 그는 그것이 그녀가 하기에 알맞지 않다고 생각한다.
(C) 그는 자기 자신에게 그것이 너무 위험한 취미라고 생각한다.
(D) 그는 모터바이크 타는 것을 두려워한다.

Check Up

Listening Task 01

Finally, I have discovered a couple of things I really like doing. The first one is listening to music. The other thing is photography. However, I think the latter may be a future hobby. I can't afford a good digital camera right now. I also have to take courses to learn more about it.

▶ **photography** 사진술, 사진 촬영   **the latter** 후자의, 후자 *cf.* the former 전자   **afford** (경제적, 시간적) 여유가 있다. ~할 수 있다

마침내 난 내가 정말로 좋아하는 것들을 찾아냈다. 첫 번째는 음악을 듣는 것이다. 다른 것은 사진을 찍는 것이다. 하지만 사진 찍는 것이 앞으로의 취미가 될 것이다. 난 지금 당장 좋은 디지털 카메라를 살 여유가 없다. 또한 사진 찍는 것을 좀 더 배우기 위해 수업을 들어야 한다.

1 **화자는 무엇에 관해 이야기하고 있는가?**

(A) 그녀가 무엇을 즐겨하는지
(B) 왜 그녀가 좋아하는 것을 할 수 없는지
(C) 왜 그녀가 음악을 듣는 것을 좋아하는지
(D) 어떻게 훌륭한 사진 작가가 될 것인지

2 **맞으면 T, 틀리면 F에 체크하시오.**

1) 그녀는 음악을 좋아하지 않는다.
2) 그녀는 사진술에 대해 배우기를 원한다.
3) 그녀는 지금 좋은 디지털 카메라를 살 여유가 없다.

Listening Task 02

M   Do you want to go hiking with me this weekend?

W   Hiking? I'm not sure.

M   It'll be fun. You'll see.

W   I'm not in great shape right now. I won't be able to keep up with you.

M   Nonsense. It's easy, and it's good exercise. Besides, we can enjoy the scenery.

W   Okay, I'll give it a try. But we'll have to take it slowly.

▶ **go hiking** 하이킹 가다   **in shape** 건강이 좋은
keep up with 뒤떨어지지 않다, 지지 않다
scenery 풍경, 배경   **give a try** 시도해 보다, 한번 해보다

남   이번 주말에 나랑 하이킹 갈래?
여   하이킹? 잘 모르겠는데.
남   재미 있을 거야. 너도 알게 될 거야.
여   난 지금 몸 상태가 안 좋아. 널 따라갈 수 없을 거야.
남   말도 안 돼. 하이킹은 쉽고 좋은 운동이야. 게다가 우리는 경치도 즐길 수 있잖아.
여   알았어, 한번 해보자. 하지만 천천히 가야 해.

1 **왜 여자는 하이킹 가는 것을 원하지 <u>않았는가</u>?**

(A) 일이 바쁘다.
(B) 하이킹보다 등산하는 것을 더 좋아한다.
(C) 몸 상태가 좋지 않다.
(D) 남자를 잘 알지 못한다.

Listening Task 03

W   I like doing ordinary things like cooking, reading, and camping.

M   What about your brother?

W   He likes skydiving. He has jumped several times, and he can't wait to go again.

M   Wow, that's pretty scary.

W   He asked me if I wanted to go next time, and I said, "Surely you aren't serious?"

▶ **ordinary** 평범한, 보통의, 평상의   **serious** 진지한, 진담의

여   난 요리, 독서, 캠핑처럼 평범한 일을 하는 것을 좋아해.
남   네 오빠는 어때?
여   그는 스카이다이빙 하는 것을 좋아해. 그는 몇 번이나 다이빙을 했고, 다시 또 하고 싶어서 안달이 났어.
남   와우, 꽤 무서울 텐데.
여   다음 번에 갈 때 같이 가고 싶은지 나한테 묻길래, "진심은 아니지"? 라고 얘기했어.

1 대화에 따르면 '꽤 무서운' 것은 무엇인가?

  (A) 스카이다이빙
  (B) 여자의 오빠
  (C) 평범한 일들
  (D) 또 다시 점프하는것

2 여자의 마지막 말에서 추론할 수 있는 것은 무엇인가?

  (A) 그녀는 오빠와 함께 스카이다이빙 하러 가지 않을
      것이다.
  (B) 그녀는 운동을 즐겨하지 않는다.
  (C) 그녀는 확실히 오빠와 함께 스카이다이빙을 하러
      갈 것이다.
  (D) 그녀의 오빠는 스카이다이빙을 하는 것에 대해 진
      지하지 않다.

Listening Task 04

When I was a young boy, I used to have many pets. I had two dogs, a cat, a parrot, and a rat. My hobby was taking care of them. I was always busy. I had to feed them, keep them clean, and play with them. Now my job keeps me busy. I have no time for pets. I'd love to get a cat. But I live alone, and sometimes I travel. I miss having animals around.

▶ **parrot** 앵무새 **rat** 쥐 **feed** (동물 등에) 먹이를 주다, 먹이다

내가 어렸을 때, 난 많은 애완동물들을 갖고 있었다. 두 마리의 개와 한 마리의 고양이, 앵무새, 그리고 쥐를 가지고 있었다. 내 취미는 그들을 돌보는 것이었다. 난 항상 바빴다. 난 그들에게 먹이를 주고, 깨끗이 씻기고 그들과 놀아 주었다. 지금은 일이 너무 바쁘다. 애완동물들을 돌볼 시간이 없다. 난 고양이를 갖고 싶다. 그러나 나는 혼자 살고 때때로 여행을 한다. 난 애완동물을 갖고 있던 때가 그립다.

1 지금 화자가 고양이를 갖지 못하는 것은 왜인가?

  (A) 다른 취미들이 있다.
  (B) 그는 일로 바쁘다.
  (C) 이미 애완동물이 많이 있다.
  (D) 그는 매주 여행한다.

Listening Test

1

(A)

If you have a lot of patience, then consider miniatures. It is an interesting hobby. Making miniature trains, cars, or toy soldiers will include painting, construction work, crafts, and more.

▶ **patience** 인내, 인내심 **miniature** 축소 모형; 소형의
construction 건설, 축조, 구조 **craft** 공예, 기능, 기교

당신이 인내심이 많다면, 취미로 미니어처를 취미를 생각해 보길 바란다. 그것은 재미있는 취미이다. 미니어처 기차, 자동차, 또는 장난감 군인들을 만드는 것에는 색칠, 조립 작업, 공예 등이 포함될 것이다.

(B)

Anyone can enjoy drawing or painting as a hobby even if that person doesn't have any special talents. There are no rules for art. You can draw or paint whatever you like. It is an activity that allows you to relax.

▶ **even if** 비록 ~하더라도 **whatever** ~하는 것은 무엇이든지

어느 누구든 특별한 재능이 없더라도 그림 그리기를 취미로 즐길 수 있다. 미술에는 어떤 규칙도 없다. 당신은 원하는 것은 무엇이든지 그릴 수 있다. 그것은 정신적으로 긴장을 풀어주는 활동이다.

(C)

Make sure your hobby will not take away from the time you need to spend with your family. Ask them to come and watch you play sports. They can even play with you. It will be more relaxing.

▶ **make sure** ~을 확인하다, 다짐받다

취미가 가족과 함께 보낼 시간을 뺏지 않도록 해라. 그들에게 당신이 운동하는 것을 보라고 얘기하라. 그들이 당신과 함께 운동할 수도 있다. 훨씬 더 편안할 것이다.

다른 사람들과 취미를 즐기는 법에 관한 이야기는 무엇인가?

(A)
(B)
(C)

2

W Why does Laurie collect coins? It seems pretty boring to me.

M She has always been fascinated with old money.

W I'm more fascinated with new money. I can spend it.

M Some of that old money could bring you a lot of new money.

W If you're lucky, then it could. But I'd rather just spend my money instead of saving it.

▶ **be fascinated with** ~에게 반한, ~에 매혹된
instead of ~ 대신에

여 로리는 왜 동전을 수집한대? 나한테는 상당히 지루해 보이는데.
남 항상 옛날 동전에 매력을 느꼈대.
여 난 새 동전이 더 좋던데. 쓸 수 있잖아.

남 옛 동전 중 어떤 것은 많은 새 돈을 가져다 줄 수도 있어.

여 운이 좋다면 말이지. 하지만 나라면 그걸 모으느니 써버리겠어.

상황을 가장 잘 묘사하고 있는 것은?

(A) 그들은 로리의 취미에 대해 얘기하고 있다.

(B) 그들은 돈에 대해 얘기하고 있다.

(C) 여자는 돈을 빌려 달라고 부탁하고 있다.

(D) 남자는 옛날 돈을 찾고 있다.

3

Are you tired of spending money on your hobby? You could try turning your hobby into a business! Maybe you have a hobby that other people find interesting. If you are really good at it, people might want to learn more about this hobby from you. You might be able to earn some money teaching your hobby to others while still doing something you enjoy.

▶ turn A into B A를 B로 만들다, 바꾸다

취미에 돈을 쓰는 것에 지쳤습니까? 당신은 당신의 취미를 사업으로 바꿀 수도 있습니다! 당신은 어쩌면 다른 사람들이 관심 있어하는 것을 취미로 갖고 있을지도 모릅니다. 만약에 당신이 그것에 능숙하다면, 그들은 당신으로부터 그 취미에 대해 더 배우고 싶어 할지도 모릅니다. 당신은 여전히 당신이 좋아하는 것을 하면서 당신의 취미를 다른 사람들에게 가르치고 약간의 돈을 벌 수 있을 것입니다.

이 이야기에 따르면, 당신은 당신의 취미로부터 어떻게 돈을 벌 수 있나?

(A) 우표를 모아서 그것들을 판다.

(B) 다른 사람들에게 그것을 하는 방법을 가르쳐 준다.

(C) 그것에 돈을 조금만 쓴다.

(D) 훨씬 더 많은 취미를 갖는다.

4

M I became interested in gardening after my mother told me about my grandmother.

W Oh really? Was your grandmother a gardener?

M Yes, that's why we always had flowers in the house.

W I see. So can I expect to receive flowers from you soon?

M I only started my garden two months ago. Maybe I'll have flowers next year.

W I suppose it's a lot of work.

M Yes, this is the kind of hobby that keeps you very busy.

▶ gardening 원예, 정원 가꾸기 suppose 추측하다, 가정하다

남 어머니가 내게 할머니에 대해서 말씀해 주신 이후 난 정원 가꾸는 것에 관심을 갖게 됐어.

여 정말? 할머니가 정원사셨어?

남 응, 그래서 우리 집에 항상 꽃들이 있었던 거야.

여 그렇구나. 그럼 내가 곧 너한테 꽃을 받을 수 있는 거야?

남 겨우 2달 전에 시작했을 뿐이야. 내년에 꽃들이 필 거야.

여 손이 많이 가겠구나.

남 응, 정원 가꾸기는 사람을 매우 분주하게 하는 취미야.

왜 남자는 올해 여자에게 꽃을 주지 <u>못하나</u>?

(A) 그는 정원 가꾸는 것을 잘 하지 못한다.

(B) 정원을 가꾸기 시작한 지 얼마 되지 않았다.

(C) 정원이 너무 작다.

(D) 그는 그저 꽃을 주기를 원하지 않는다.

5

Building your own simple furniture items can be an easy weekend activity. It's best to begin with small projects, such as a bookcase or a table. "Doing it yourself," or DIY, is not as hard as it may seem. There is information on the Internet or in books on the subject of DIY. It will tell you what materials to buy and then guide you as to how to use the materials. After a few tries, DIY furniture making will become a good hobby.

▶ activity 활동, 운동, 활약 such as 예컨대, 이를테면
 subject 주제, 과제, 문제 material 재료, 자재, 원료
 as to ~에 대하여, ~에 관하여

간단한 가구를 직접 만드는 것은 쉬운 주말 활동이 될 수 있다. 책장이나 테이블 같이 작은 과제로 시작하는 것이 좋다. "너 스스로 해라" 또는 DIY는 보이는 것처럼 어렵지는 않다. DIY 주제에 관한 책이나 인터넷에 정보가 있다. 그것은 무슨 재료를 사야 하고 재료를 어떻게 사용할지 알려줄 것이다. 몇 번 해보면, DIY 가구 만드는 것은 취미가 될 것이다.

DIY 가구를 만드는 것에 능숙하도록 해주는 것은 무엇인가?

(A) 전문가들에게 배우는 것

(B) 올바른 재료

(C) 인터넷과 책에 있는 정보

(D) 당신의 이웃

6

M Rose, what are you doing this weekend?

W How about a movie?

M We saw *Star Wars* last week. How about riding our bikes?

W Biking? That's boring.

M   Then, what do you want to do?

W   I'd like to go shopping.

M   I don't think that will be fun for me. How about a museum?

W   Okay.

▶ How about...? ~하는 것이 어때?

남   로즈, 이번 주말에 뭐할 거야?
여   영화보는 건 어때?
남   지난 주에 '스타 워즈' 봤잖아. 자전거 타는 건 어때?
여   자전거? 좀 지루한데.
남   그럼 넌 뭐하고 싶은데?
여   쇼핑하고 싶어.
남   나한테는 재미 없을 것 같아. 박물관 가는 건 어때?
여   좋아.

그들은 이번 주말에 무엇을 할 것인가?

(A) 쇼핑을 갈 것이다.
(B) 자전거 타러 갈 것이다.
(C) 박물관에 갈 것이다.
(D) '스타 워즈'를 볼 것이다.

7

M   Hi, may I help you?

W   Yes, please. I'm looking for a baseball glove.

M   I see. How about this one?

W   That looks good. How much is it?

M   It's 125 dollars.

W   Great. Come to think of it, I need a bat, too.

M   This one is 60 dollars.

W   Perfect. I'll take both.

▶ come to think of it 생각해보니, 생각해보자니

남   어서 오세요, 무엇을 도와 드릴까요?
여   네, 야구 글러브를 찾고 있어요.
남   알겠습니다. 이건 어떤가요?
여   좋아 보이는데요. 얼마에요?
남   125달러입니다.
여   좋아요. 생각해 보니 배트도 필요해요.
남   이건 60달러입니다.
여   좋아요. 두 개 다 살게요.

여자는 얼마를 지불할 것인가?

(A) 60달러
(B) 125달러
(C) 131달러
(D) 185달러

8

What's the difference between a hobby, a habit, and an interest? What are some common hobbies from around the world? Do males and females have different hobbies? All these questions and more will be answered in our class "Hobbies and Leisure." If you take this class, you'll get hands-on experience in many different activities. You'll learn lots of different things. So be sure to sign up now.

▶ common 공통의, 일반의, 보통의   male 남성; 남성의
   female 여성; 여성의   leisure 자유 시간, 여가
   hands-on 실제의, 실무적인   sign up (클럽 등에) 참여하다, 가입하다

취미, 습관, 관심의 차이는 무엇입니까? 전세계적 공통적인 취미로는 무엇이 있을까요? 남자와 여자는 서로 다른 취미를 가지고 있을까요? 이 질문들을 비롯한 다른 질문에 대해서 우리의 "취미와 레저" 수업 시간에 답변을 들을 수 있습니다. 이 수업을 듣는다면 여러분은 많은 다양한 활동들에 대한 실질적인 경험을 얻을 수 있습니다. 많은 다양한 것들을 배우실 겁니다. 지금 등록하세요.

이 워크샵에서 얘기하지 않을 주제는 무엇인가?

(A) 남자와 여자들의 취미의 차이점
(B) '관심'은 무엇인가
(C) 전세계의 공통적인 취미
(D) 좋은 언어 습관을 발전시키는 법

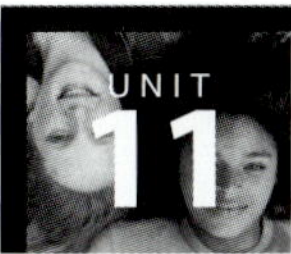

U N I T 11 Interesting Places

정답 answer

Key Expressions

1 1 amusement park   2 zoo   3 lake
   4 hot springs   5 snake park

3 1 ⓑ 2 ⓐ 3 ⓔ 4 ⓓ 5 ⓒ 6 ⓕ 7 ⓖ

Listening Practice

1 (C)   **2** (C)

Check Up

Listening Task *01* 1 (C)   2 1) T   2) T   3) F   4) F
Listening Task *02* 1 1) ⓑ   2) ⓒ   3) ⓐ
Listening Task *03* 1 (D)   2 (C)
Listening Task *04* 1 (D)

Listening Test

1 (B)   **2** (C)   **3** (B)   **4** (C)   **5** (C)   **6** (C)
7 (D)   **8** (A)

스크립트 & 해석 script & translation

Key Expressions

1 표에서 가장 적절한 단어를 골라 빈칸을 채우시오.
   1 내 아들은 놀이공원에서 놀이기구를 타는 것을 좋
     아한다.
   2 난 공원에서 코끼리와 원숭이 사진을 많이 찍었다.
   3 오늘 오후에는 보트 타고 호수를 건너자.
   4 난 휴식을 취하기 위해 가끔 온천에 간다.
   5 내 딸은 뱀 공원에서 겁에 질렸다.

2 새로운 도시에 방문할 때 무엇을 하는가? 아래에서
   고르시오.

박물관을 방문한다	교회나 사원을 방문한다
버스 투어를 한다	지역 음식을 먹어 본다
동물원에 간다	기념품을 산다
쇼핑을 한다	지역 문화 행사에 참여한다

3 다음 문장들을 가장 잘 어울리는 대답과 연결하시오.
   1 수영장 중 한 곳에서 휴식을 취하자.
     ⓑ 기다리는 사람들이 너무 많아.
   2 난 어제 남자 친구랑 박물관에 갔었어.
     ⓐ 재미있었겠는데.
   3 놀이공원 무료 입장표가 두 장 있어.
     ⓔ 나랑 같이 안 갈래? 놀이기구 타는 것 좋아해.
   4 오늘밤 극장에 가는 게 어때?
     ⓓ 좋아. 내가 표 예매할게.
   5 내가 가장 좋아하는 활동은 공원에서 자전거를 타
     는 거야.
     ⓒ 하지만 거기 여름에는 자전거 타는 사람들이 너
       무 많아.
   6 입장료가 얼마죠?
     ⓕ 애들은 10달러인 것 같아요.
   7 등산갈까?
     ⓖ 응. 정상에서의 경치가 보고 싶어.

Listening Practice

1

This is a fun place for children and adults.
Customers can go on lots of different rides at this
place. The most exciting ride for most people is
the roller coaster. This goes up and down very fast
and sometimes even makes loops. There are also
other rides like bumper cars, the haunted house,
and merry-go-rounds.

▶ loop 고리, 고리 모양으로 생긴 것   haunted 귀신 붙은, 귀신이 나오는
merry-go-rounds 회전목마

이곳은 아이들과 어른들에게 재미있는 장소이다. 손님들은 이곳에
서 많은 다양한 놀이기구를 탈 수 있다. 대부분의 사람들에게 가장
신나는 놀이기구는 롤러코스터이다. 이것은 위아래로 빠르게 움직
이며 때때로 회전을 한다. 범퍼카, 귀신의 집, 회전목마와 같은 다른
놀이기구들도 있다.

이 이야기의 주제는 무엇인가?

(A) 어떤 사람의 놀이공원 나들이
(B) 최초의 놀이공원 이야기
(C) 놀이공원의 묘사
(D) 놀이공원은 왜 그렇게 재미있는가

W How often do you go to the ski resort?

M In winter, I go almost every weekend.

W You must be really good at skiing.

M Not really. But it's very pretty in winter. My family enjoys walking in the snow.

W Maybe I will take my family to visit the ski resort this weekend.

M You should go because they would really love it.

▶ resort 행락지

여 스키장에는 얼마나 자주 가세요?

남 겨울에는 거의 매 주말마다 가요.

여 스키 잘 타시겠네요.

남 그렇지는 않아요. 하지만 겨울에는 너무 아름다워요. 제 가족은 눈 속에서 산책하는 것을 좋아한답니다.

여 이번 주말에는 저도 가족과 함께 스키장에 가려고요.

남 아마 가족들이 정말 좋아할 테니 꼭 가세요.

대화에 대해 사실인 것은?

(A) 여자는 스키장에 가는 것을 좋아한다.

(B) 남자는 스키를 잘 탄다.

(C) 남자는 그의 가족을 스키장에 데려가는 것을 좋아한다.

(D) 남자는 사실은 스키 타는 것을 좋아하지 않는다.

Check Up

Listening Task *01*

The first department store was established in Paris. It offered a wide selection of goods in one building. At first, other merchants laughed at the idea of selling so many different goods. But, as the customers were happy with lower prices and a wider selection, other merchants increasingly chose to shop there instead of at traditional shops.

▶ establish 설립하다, 수립하다   selection 선발된 것, 정선물
merchant 상인   laugh at 비웃다   increasingly 점점, 더욱 더

첫 번째 백화점은 파리에 세워졌다. 그 백화점은 한 건물에서 다양한 상품들을 제공했다. 처음에 다른 상인들은 그렇게나 많은 다양한 물건들을 파는 생각을 비웃었다. 하지만 고객들이 낮은 가격과 넓은 선택의 폭에 만족하자, 다른 상인들도 점차 전통적인 가게 대신에 그곳에서 쇼핑하기를 선택했다.

1 화자는 어느 질문에 대해 답하고 있는가?

(A) 왜 당신은 백화점에서 물건을 사는가?

(B) 좋아하는 쇼핑 장소는 어디인가?

(C) 백화점의 역사에 대해 말해 줄 수 있는가?

(D) 백화점을 마지막으로 방문한 때가 언제인가?

2 맞으면 T, 틀리면 F에 체크하시오.

1) 백화점은 판매를 위한 다양한 상품들을 가지고 있다.

2) 다른 상인들은 결국 새로운 백화점을 좋아했다.

3) 고객들은 새로 생긴 백화점을 좋아하지 않았다.

4) 백화점은 다른 가게보다 더 비쌌다.

Listening Task *02*

ⓐ

This place offers a broad selection of indoor activities. You can run, play tennis, or play basketball.

▶ offer 제공하다, 제출하다   indoor 실내의

이곳은 실내 활동의 더 넓은 선택권을 제공해 줍니다. 당신은 달릴 수도 있고, 테니스를 칠 수도 있고, 농구를 할 수도 있습니다.

ⓑ

Here you will find the most inspiring landscape of ancient temples and tombs on Earth. If you walk into one of them, you will visit the greatest civilization of the ancient world.

▶ inspiring 영감을 주는, 고무하는   landscape 풍경, 경치
civilization 문명, 문명세계

여기서 당신은 고대 사원들과 지구상에 있는 무덤들의 가장 가슴 설레이는 광경을 보게 될 것입니다. 만약 그곳들 중 한 곳에 들어간다면 당신은 고대의 가장 위대한 문명을 방문하게 될 것입니다.

ⓒ

I love this place. It's my favorite because there's so much to do there. You can go shopping, eat, and even watch movies.

전 이곳을 좋아합니다. 이곳에서는 할 일이 많기 때문에 제가 좋아하는 곳입니다. 당신은 쇼핑할 수도 있고, 음식을 먹을 수도 있고 영화를 볼 수도 있습니다.

1 각 그림과 어울리는 이야기의 번호를 쓰시오.

1)    2)    3)  

Listening Task *03*

I went to Paris on a short holiday last year. I was very impressed by the Eiffel Tower. It's more amazing than any picture I've ever seen of it. The weather was terrible that day, so I did not go up the tower. That was a little disappointing. But I took many pictures of myself standing right next to the tower. I look so small because the tower is huge.

▶ be impressed by ~에 감동하다, 깊은 인상을 받다
disappointing 실망시키는, 기대에 어긋나는

난 지난해 짧은 휴가로 파리에 갔다. 나는 에펠 타워를 보고 큰 감명을 받았다. 내가 여태껏 본 어떤 사진보다도 훌륭했다. 그날은 날씨가 좋지 않아서, 탑에는 올라가지 못했다. 약간 실망스러웠다. 하지만 타워 옆에서 사진을 많이 찍었다. 타워가 컸기 때문에 나는 굉장히 작아 보인다.

1 남자는 왜 타워에 올라갈 수 없었나?

(A) 올라가고 싶지 않았기 때문에
(B) 고소 공포증이 있어서
(C) 카메라에 필름이 없어서
(D) 날씨가 좋지 않아서

2 남자가 에펠 타워를 보고 느낀 점에 대해 가장 잘 나타낸 것은 무엇인가?

(A) 매우 실망했다.
(B) 너무 작아서 놀랐다.
(C) 그것을 보고 감명을 받았다.
(D) 너무 커서 충격을 받았다.

Listening Task *04*

M Hey, Jane. Is this your first visit to the ice festival?

W Yes. These sculptures are huge. I can't believe they're made of ice.

M That's why this is a famous festival. Every year, people come to see the animal sculptures and the ice palaces.

W Yes, it's really crowded. Wow, look at the enormous sculpture of that Siberian tiger!

M I've never seen anything like that before. Let's go check out some of the other exhibits.

▶ sculpture 조각, 조각술 be made of ~으로 만들어지다(재료의 형태를 보존하고 있을 경우) *cf.* be made from (재료의 형태를 알 수 없게 되었을 경우) ~으로 만들어지다

남 이봐, 제인. 얼음 축제에는 처음 온 거야?
여 응. 이 조각들 굉장히 크다. 얼음으로 만들어졌다니 믿을 수 없어.
남 그게 바로 이 축제가 유명한 이유야. 매년 사람들은 동물 조각들과 얼음 궁전을 보러 와.
여 응, 정말 사람들이 많다. 와우, 저기 커다란 시베리아 호랑이 조각상 좀 봐!
남 난 저런 거 본 적이 없어. 다른 전시물들도 보러 가자.

1 대화의 주제는 무엇인가?

(A) 얼음 조각을 만드는 법
(B) 세계의 유명한 이벤트
(C) 얼음 축제에 있는 군중들
(D) 얼음 축제 방문

Listening Test

1

W How long have you been in Korea?

M About a week.

W I have to take you to Seoul Tower while you're here.

M It's the place at the top of Namsan, isn't it?

W Yes, you can see amazing views of Seoul from the tower.

M Let's go in the afternoon. I'd like to take some photographs of the city.

여 한국에는 얼마나 있었나요?
남 일주일 정도요.
여 여기 있는 동안에 당신을 서울 타워에 데리고 가야 할 텐데 말이에요.
남 남산 꼭대기에 있는 거, 맞죠?
여 네, 타워에서 서울의 멋진 경치를 볼 수 있어요.
남 오후에 가죠. 도시의 사진을 찍고 싶어요.

화자들은 언제 서울 타워에 갈 것인가?

(A) 다음날
(B) 오후에
(C) 다음 주에
(D) 남자가 한국을 떠나기 전날에

2

For surfers, the only interesting places are those with great surfs. And, as we all know, the best surf is in Hawaii. All waves lead to Hawaii, and Hawaii's north shore especially is a surfer's paradise. Even many pizza delivery cars have surfboard pictures on their doors and roofs.

▶ surf (해안으로) 밀려드는 파도 lead to ~로 통하다, ~로 이르다

서핑하는 사람들에게 유일한 흥미로운 곳은 파도가 좋은 곳입니다. 그리고 모두 알다시피, 가장 좋은 파도는 하와이에 있습니다. 모든 파도들이 하와이로 통하고 특히 하와이의 북쪽 해안은 서퍼들의 천국입니다. 많은 피자 배달 차들조차 문과 지붕에 서프보드의 그림이 그려져 있습니다.

왜 화자는 피자 배달 차를 언급했는가?

(A) 피자가 하와이에서 유명하다는 것을 보여 주기 위해

(B) 하와이에서 파도 타는 법을 설명하기 위해

(C) 하와이의 파도타기 문화가 얼마나 강한지 보여 주기 위해

(D) 왜 서핑이 하와이에서 인기가 있는지 설명하기 위해

3

Welcome to the Seoul Metro Museum. Our museum lets you experience how ancient Koreans lived. We are open from 10 a.m. to 6 p.m., Monday to Friday. Admission is 20 dollars for adults and 10 dollars for kids younger than 10 years old. You can get a 10% discount for groups of more than 5 people and 30% for groups of more than 10 people.

▶ admission 입장료, 입장

서울 메트로 박물관에 오신 것을 환영합니다. 저희 박물관은 고대 한국인들이 어떻게 살았는지를 체험할 수 있게 해드립니다. 월요일 부터 금요일까지 오전 10시에서 오후 6시까지 개관합니다. 입장료 는 어른은 20달러, 10살이 안 된 아이들은 10달러입니다. 5명 이상 인 경우는 10퍼센트의 할인을 받을 수 있고 10명 이상인 경우에는 30퍼센트의 할인을 받을 수 있습니다.

제인은 이번 금요일에 부모님과 세 명의 남동생들과 함께 서 울 메트로 박물관을 방문하려고 한다. 남동생 중 두 명은 10 살 이하이다. 그들은 총 얼마를 지불해야 하나?

(A) 80달러

(B) 90달러

(C) 100달러

(D) 108달러

4

Students at the University of Michigan speak proudly of the famous football stadium on their campus. It is one of the largest college football stadiums, with seats for more than 110,000 fans. Most fans have season tickets. This makes it really difficult to get tickets to see the games, most of which have been sold out for more than 30 years.

▶ season ticket (시즌 내) 정기 입장권

미시간 대학 학생들은 그들의 대학 내에 있는 유명한 미식 축구 경 기장을 자랑스럽게 얘기한다. 그것은 11만명 이상의 관중을 위한 좌석이 있는 가장 큰 대학 미식 축구 경기장 중 하나이다. 대부분의 팬들은 시즌 입장권을 가지고 있다. 이것은 경기를 보기 위한 표를 사는 것을 어렵게 한다. 이 중 대부분은 이미 30년 전에 팔렸다.

경기 입장권을 사는 것이 왜 어려운가?

(A) 경기장이 충분히 크지 않다.

(B) 너무 비싸다.

(C) 시즌 티켓 소유자들이 많이 있다.

(D) 주변에 너무 많은 사람들이 있다.

5

M   Jane, I heard you are visiting Cape Town during vacation.

W   Yes, it will be my first time in South Africa.

M   There's a famous mountain in Cape Town, isn't there?

W   Yes, it's called Table Mountain because its top is as flat as a table.

M   I hope you take pictures. I've never seen anything like that before.

W   I know. It's the only mountain in the world with a flat top.

M   I'm sure you'll see beautiful beaches there, too.

▶ flat 평평한, 평탄한

남   제인, 이번 연휴 동안에 케이프 타운에 간다면서.

여   응, 첫 번째 남아프리카 여행이 될 거야.

남   케이프 타운에 유명한 산이 있지, 그렇지?

여   응, 꼭대기가 테이블처럼 평평하다고 해서 테이블 산이라고 불 려.

남   사진 찍어 와. 전에 그런 걸 본 적이 없거든.

여   알겠어. 평평한 꼭대기를 가진 전세계에서 유일한 산이래.

남   거기서 아름다운 해변도 볼 수 있을 거야.

남자는 여자가 무슨 사진을 찍어 오기를 바라는가?

(A) 케이프 타운의 해변

(B) 와인을 만드는 계곡

(C) 유명한 테이블 산

(D) 케이프 타운의 호텔

6

The Museum of Magic is a good place to see special magic shows. The best magicians will show their audiences some of their most famous tricks. Not only is it great fun, but it is also educational and motivational for young people. Many young people leave here wanting to study magic. The magicians are very daring. Their shows are not for those who get nervous very easily or who have weak hearts! The shows are often sold out. You should reserve your seat early so that you are not disappointed.

▶ trick 재주, 요술, 묘기   educational 교육적인, 교육상의
motivational 동기 유발하는   daring 대담한, 용감한
get nervous 긴장하다   heart 심장, 마음, 감정

마술 박물관은 특별한 마술쇼를 보기에 좋은 곳이다. 최고의 마술사들이 그들이 가장 잘하는 유명한 마술을 청중들에게 보여 줄 것이다. 그것은 재미있을 뿐만 아니라, 젊은 사람들에게 교육적이고 동기 유발도 된다. 많은 젊은 사람들이 마술을 공부하기 위해 여기에 남는다. 마술사들은 대담하다. 그들의 쇼는 쉽게 긴장하거나 심장이 약한 사람들에게는 적절하지 못하다! 쇼는 종종 매진된다. 실망하지 않기 위해서는 미리 좌석을 예약해야 한다.

화자는 왜 이 쇼가 쉽게 긴장하는 사람들에게 적합하지 않다고 얘기하는가?

(A) 사람들이 이 쇼를 좋아하지 않을까 걱정한다.
(B) 사람들이 이 쇼를 보고 지겨워한다고 생각한다.
(C) 이 쇼가 극적일 것이라고 생각한다.
(D) 쇼가 너무 시끄럽다고 생각한다.

7

The Inca Trail trek is known as probably the most spectacular short hiking trail in the world. Many people around the world visit here annually. You can walk along a path on rocks built more than 500 years ago. You can also see the remarkable city of Cusco, which was the capital of the Inca Empire, and the unique traditional market at Chinchero.

▶ trek 길고 힘든 여행   spectacular 구경거리의, 장관의
annually 매년   walk along 계속 걷다
remarkable 놀랄 만한, 주목할 만한

잉카 트레일 트랙은 아마도 세계에서 가장 멋진 단거리 하이킹 트레일로 알려져 있을 것이다. 매년 전 세계의 많은 사람들이 이곳을 방문한다. 당신은 500년 이상 이전에 지어진 돌길을 따라 걸을 수 있다. 당신은 또한 잉카제국의 수도였던 훌륭한 도시 쿠스코와 친체로의 독특한 전통 시장을 볼 수 있다.

잉카 트레일 트랙에 대해 사실이 <u>아닌</u> 것은 무엇인가?

(A) 그 코스는 돌 위에 지어졌다.
(B) 트렉 도중에 오래된 시장을 경험할 수 있다.
(C) 많은 사람들이 매년 그곳을 방문한다.
(D) 잉카 제국의 역사를 체험할 수 있다.

8

The Great Wall of China was built over 2,000 years ago. It is almost 7,000 kilometers long. Can you imagine walking along the entire wall? It would take you a long time. Thousands of people visit the wall every year. It is difficult to walk there, and a few people have even been injured. But everyone agrees that it is one of the most incredible manmade wonders of the modern world.

▶ The Great Wall 만리장성   injure 상처를 입히다, 부상을 입히다
incredible 놀라운, (믿기 어려울 만큼) 굉장한
manmade 인공의, 인조의   wonder 불가사의, 경탄할 만한 것

중국의 만리장성은 2000년 전에 지어졌다. 길이가 거의 7000킬로미터에 달한다. 전체 벽을 따라 걷는 것을 상상할 수 있는가? 오랜 시간이 걸릴 것이다. 수천 명의 사람들이 매년 만리장성을 방문한다. 그곳을 걷는 것은 힘든 일이며 몇몇 사람들은 부상을 당하기도 했다. 그러나 모든 사람들은 만리장성이 현대 세계의 인류가 만든 가장 놀랄 만한 경이들 중 하나라는 것에 동의한다.

중국의 만리장성에 대해 사실이 <u>아닌</u> 것은 무엇인가?

(A) 2000년 전에 기계를 이용해 지어졌다.
(B) 벽을 따라 걷도록 허용되었다.
(C) 세계의 불가사의한 것들 중 하나이다.
(D) 길이가 거의 7000킬로미터에 달한다.

UNIT 12 Shopping

Key Expressions

1 1 looking for   2 exchange   3 impulse
4 bargain   5 deals

2 1 clothing   2 furniture   3 groceries
4 toys

3 1 ⓒ   2 ⓔ   3 ⓖ   4 ⓑ   5 ⓓ   6 ⓕ   7 ⓐ

Listening Practice

1 (B)   **2** (C)

Check Up

Listening Task *01* 1 (C)   2 1) T   2) F   3) F
Listening Task *02* 1 (B)
Listening Task *03* 1 (D)   2 (A)
Listening Task *04* 1 (D)

Listening Test

1 (C)   **2** (D)   **3** (C)   **4** (C)   **5** (C)   **6** (B)
7 (D)   **8** (D)

스크립트 & 해석 script & translation

Key Expressions

1 표에서 가장 적절한 단어를 골라 빈칸을 채우시오.
1 나는 아버지의 날 선물을 찾고 있다.
2 이 스웨터 다른 것으로 교환하실 수 있습니다.
3 신용카드는 충동 구매를 이끌 수 있다.
4 너무 싸서, 이것이야말로 진짜 특가이다.
5 이곳에서 보통 가장 좋은 거래를 할 수 있다.

2 각 단어 그룹에 맞는 올바른 카테고리 단어들을 박스 안에서 고르시오.

식료품	가구	주류	장난감	의류

1 셔츠, 바지, 스웨터, 재킷
2 의자, 소파, 테이블, 책상
3 우유, 달걀, 빵, 채소
4 인형, 블록, 기차 세트, 모형 비행기

3 다음 문장들을 가장 잘 어울리는 대답과 연결하시오.
1 무엇을 도와 드릴까요?
ⓒ 그냥 구경하고 있어요.
2 신용카드도 받나요?
ⓔ 네, 하지만 비자 카드와 마스터 카드만 받습니다.
3 이거 얼마죠?
ⓖ 가게에 있는 모든 물건에 대해 30퍼센트 할인해서 25달러입니다.
4 이거 환불을 받을 수 있을까요?
ⓑ 네, 영수증만 있으면요.
5 보증이 되나요?
ⓓ 네, 6개월간 됩니다.
6 더 저렴한 것이 있습니까?
ⓕ 이것이 훨씬 더 저렴합니다.
7 난 충동 구매를 하는 경향이 있어.
ⓐ 쇼핑리스트 만드는 것을 잊지 마.

Listening Practice

1

I love shopping at K–Mart. I can easily find some nice shoes from a reputable manufacturer for a good price there. K–Mart sells overstocked and out-of-season shoes, so its prices are generally terrific. Come to K–Mart, and get discounts on shoes.

▶ reputable 평판이 좋은, 이름 높은   manufacturer 제조업자, 제조 회사   overstock 너무 많이 사들이다, 지나치게 공급하다
out-of-season 제철이 아닌   terrific 훌륭한, 멋진, 아주 좋은

난 케이마트에서 쇼핑하는 것을 좋아합니다. 그곳에서 나는 브랜드 제품의 좋은 신발을 좋은 가격에 쉽게 찾을 수 있어요. 케이마트는 재고품과 시즌이 지난 신발을 팔아서 가격이 대개 저렴하죠. 케이마트에 오셔서 신발 할인을 받으세요.

이 이야기의 목적은 무엇인가?

(A) 상가의 형편 없는 서비스를 불평하기 위해서
(B) 케이마트를 광고하기 위해서
(C) 케이마트를 어떻게 찾는지 설명하기 위해서
(D) 좋은 신발 브랜드를 소개하기 위해서

2

W	Hey, Mike. I can't resist buying beautiful jewelry.
M	So do you buy a lot of jewelry?
W	Yes. If I see something nice, I always imagine myself wearing it. Then I am not satisfied until I buy it.
M	That sounds like an expensive habit.
W	I know. It is a kind of obsession, but I can't seem to help myself.

▶ resist ~에 저항하다, 반항하다 obsession 강박 관념, 집념

여 이봐, 마이크, 난 예쁜 보석만 보면 사고 싶어져.
남 그래서 보석을 많이 사니?
여 응. 좋은 보석만 보면 내가 차고 있는 모습을 상상해. 그럼 그것을 살 때까지는 만족할 수 없어.
남 너무 돈이 많이 드는 습관인 것 같구나.
여 나도 알아. 일종의 강박관념인데, 나도 나를 어찌할 수가 없어.

대화의 주제는 무엇인가?

(A) 쇼핑 문제를 극복하는 법
(B) 보석을 사는 법
(C) 여자의 쇼핑 문제
(D) 그들이 쇼핑하는 장소

Check Up

Listening Task 01

Hong Kong is a perfect place for shopping. It is not just because Hong Kong has many modern shopping malls that sell expensive designer clothes. Hong Kong also offers cheap and exotic goods from old markets. This variety adds excitement to any shopping day by providing opportunities for all shoppers.

▶ exotic 이국적인, 색다른 goods 상품, 물품
variety 다양성, 변화 add 보태다, 더하다

홍콩은 쇼핑하기에 완벽한 곳이다. 홍콩에 값비싼 디자이너 옷을 파는 현대적인 쇼핑몰들이 많기 때문만은 아니다. 홍콩은 또한 재래 시장에서 값싸고 이국적인 제품들을 판매한다. 이러한 다양함이 모든 쇼핑하는 사람들에게 기회를 제공함으로써, 어떤 쇼핑 날에든 재미를 부여해 준다.

1   이 이야기는 무슨 질문에 대한 답인가?

(A) 홍콩에서 쇼핑하기에 가장 좋은 때는 언제인가?
(B) 홍콩에서 쇼핑하는 가장 좋은 방법은 무엇인가?
(C) 해외에서 쇼핑하기에 가장 좋은 곳은 어디인가?

(D) 홍콩에서 어떤 종류의 물건들을 살 수 있는가?

2   맞으면 T, 틀리면 F에 체크하시오.

1) 홍콩의 재래 시장은 재미를 제공해 준다.
2) 홍콩에서 재래 시장을 찾는 것은 쉬운 일이 아니다.
3) 홍콩에는 브랜드 상점들이 많이 없다.

Listening Task 02

W	I remember when my friends would say, "Let's go shopping," and I'd be all excited.
M	So?
W	But now I just get bored with all the shops, to be honest.
M	I know what you mean.
W	I tried to shop for a new pair of shoes the other day, but I got bored. So I just went home after only visiting two shops.

▶ to be honest 솔직히 말하면

여 난 친구들이 "쇼핑하러 가자"라고 말했을 때, 내가 항상 흥분했던 것을 기억해.
남 그런데?
여 근데, 지금은 솔직히 말해서 모든 쇼핑에 지루함을 느껴.
남 무슨 말하는지 알 것 같아.
여 요 전날 새 신발을 사려고 쇼핑을 했는데 지루해졌어. 그래서 가게 두 군데만 갔다가 돌아왔어.

1   여자가 남자에게 말하려고 하는 것은 무엇인가?

(A) 그녀는 쇼핑하는 것을 좋아하지 않는다.
(B) 그녀는 변했다.
(C) 그녀는 새 신발을 필요로 하지 않는다.
(D) 그녀는 너무 정직하다.

Listening Task 03

M	I still think the CD player I bought from K-Mart was too expensive.
W	I agree that some of their stuff is high priced, but at least you know the quality is guaranteed. And nowhere else has such a wide selection.
M	I think Hi-Mart has got a pretty good selection.
W	No way. Last time I went there, they had about ten MP3 players and still no iPods.

▶ guarantee 보증하다, 보증

남 난 아직도 케이마트에서 샀던 CD플레이어가 너무 비싸다고 생각해.
여 거기 제품들 중에 몇 개는 가격이 좀 비싸긴 하지만, 어쨌든 품질은 보장되잖아. 그리고 그렇게 선택의 폭이 넓은 곳도 없어.

남　하이마트에도 꽤 다양한 물건이 있는 것 같은데.
여　말도 안돼. 지난 번에 거기 갔었는데, 10개 정도의 MP3플레이어만 있고 아이팟은 있지도 않았어.

1　여자가 "말도 안 돼"라고 말한 이유는 무엇인가?

(A) 남자가 케이마트에서 CD플레이어를 샀기 때문에
(B) 케이마트에 다양한 물건이 없기 때문에
(C) 하이마트가 합리적인 가격을 제공하기 때문에
(D) 하이마트에 다양한 물건이 없기 때문에

2　대화에 대해 사실인 것은 무엇인가?

(A) 여자는 돈을 더 지불하고 품질이 좋은 제품을 사는 것이 낫다고 생각한다.
(B) 여자는 남자와 똑같은 의견을 가지고 있다.
(C) 남자는 하이마트에 간 것을 후회하고 있다.
(D) 남자는 MP3플레이어를 할인해줘야 한다고 생각한다.

Listening Task 04

The most convenient way to shop these days is on the Internet. But be careful since it's very easy to spend too much money shopping that way. Internet shopping is really quick. In no time, you can spend twice as much money as you had expected. I do most of my shopping on the Internet. But these days, I think carefully before deciding to buy something.

▶ in no time 곧, 바로

요즘에 쇼핑하기 가장 편리한 방법은 인터넷에서 사는 것이다. 하지만 인터넷에서 쇼핑을 하는 것은 너무 많은 돈을 쓸 수 있기 때문에 조심해야 한다. 단숨에 당신이 생각했던 것보다 2배나 많은 돈을 쓸 수 있다. 난 대부분의 쇼핑을 인터넷에서 한다. 하지만 요즘에는 어떤 것을 사려고 결정하기 전에 신중히 생각한다.

1　화자가 말하려 하는 것을 가장 잘 나타낸 것은?

(A) 그녀는 인터넷 쇼핑이 위험하다고 생각한다.
(B) 그녀는 인터넷 쇼핑에 대하여 사람들에게 경고하려고 한다.
(C) 그녀는 인터넷 쇼핑을 하다가 안 좋은 경험을 한 적이 있다.
(D) 그녀는 인터넷 쇼핑을 즐기지만 사람들이 좀 더 신중해야 한다고 생각하고 있다.

Listening Test

1

W　Hi, can I help you?
M　Yes, please. I am looking for a gift for my girlfriend.
W　How about this skirt?
M　How much is it?
W　At the regular price, it is 80 dollars, but we are having a special today. If you spend more than 100 dollars, you get a 10 percent discount.
M　How much is this hat?
W　It is 40 dollars.
M　Then, I'll take both.

▶ regular 통상의, 보통의

여　안녕하세요, 도와 드릴까요?
남　네, 부탁합니다. 제 여자 친구에게 줄 선물을 찾고 있는데요.
여　이 스커트는 어때요?
남　얼마죠?
여　원래 가격은 80달러인데, 오늘 특별 행사를 해요. 100달러 이상을 사시면, 10퍼센트 할인을 받으실 수 있어요.
남　이 모자는 얼마에요?
여　40달러입니다.
남　그럼 두 개 다 살게요.

남자는 얼마를 지불할 것인가?

(A) 80달러
(B) 120달러
(C) 108달러
(D) 90달러

2

W　The final thing we want to tell you about is the discount stores. You can go whenever you're out of something. There are several around campus.
M　That's right. And they have everything you need.
W　They don't usually have milk, though, so you need to walk down to the convenience store close by the dormitory.
M　Yeah, she said everything I wanted to say to you.

▶ out of ~가 떨어진, 물건이 바닥난　convenience store 편의점
dormitory 기숙사

여　우리가 마지막으로 당신에게 말하고 싶은 것은 할인점들에 대해서요. 뭔가가 다 떨어졌을 때 언제든 갈 수 있죠. 캠퍼스 주변에 몇 군데가 있어요.
남　맞아요. 그리고 필요한 모든 것을 구비하고 있죠.
여　하지만 보통 우유는 없으니까 기숙사 근처에 있는 편의점까지 걸어가야 할 거예요.
남　맞아요. 내가 하고 싶은 얘기를 그녀가 다 했군요.

이 상황을 가장 잘 설명하고 있는 것은?

(A) 그들은 오늘 어디에서 쇼핑할지 결정하고 있다.

(B) 남자는 여자가 어디에서 쇼핑해야 하는지 말하고 있다.

(C) 여자는 남자가 캠퍼스 근처에서 쇼핑하는 것을 돕고 있다.

(D) 그들은 새로운 학생에게 쇼핑하는 법을 말해 주고 있다.

3

W   Here we are. I'm going to stop by Hyundai Department Store first. I might just get lucky today. Who knows, some of their dresses might be on sale.

M   Hyundai?

W   It's a fairly well-known department store. Sort of like Lotte. They've got some quality stuff. Do you want to check it out?

M   Why not?

W   _______________________

▶ **fairly** 꽤, 상당히   **quality** 상질의, 훌륭한; 특성, 품질

여   다 왔다. 난 먼저 현대 백화점에서 쇼핑하려고 해. 오늘 운이 좋을지도 몰라. 누가 알아. 몇몇 드레스를 세일할지도 모르잖아.

남   현대?

여   꽤 유명한 백화점이야. 롯데처럼. 좋은 품질의 물건들이 있어. 확인하러 가 볼래?

남   왜 안되겠어?

여   _______________________

여자가 다음에 할 말은 무엇인가?

(A) 그럼 롯데 가자.

(B) 다른 생각은?

(C) 실망하지 않을 거야.

(D) 문제 없어.

4

M   Excuse me. I purchased these earrings last week. I'd like to exchange them for another pair.

W   Do you have the receipt?

M   Unfortunately not. But I only purchased these last week. They're still in the wrapping.

W   Our store policy requires a receipt in order for you to exchange them.

M   But that's ridiculous. They are in perfect condition. May I speak to your manager?

▶ **exchange** 교환하다, 바꾸다   **receipt** 영수증, 영수
wrapping 포장, 쌈   **ridiculous** 터무니없는, 우스꽝스러운

남   실례합니다. 지난주에 이 귀걸이들을 구매했는데요. 다른 걸로 교환하고 싶어서요.

여   영수증은 가지고 계시나요?

남   아니요. 하지만 전 지난주에 이것들을 구입했어요. 여전히 포장된 상태고요.

여   저희 가게 정책상, 물건을 교환해 드리기 위해서는 영수증이 필요합니다.

남   그건 말도 안 돼요. 이것들은 상태가 아주 좋다구요. 매니저와 얘기할 수 있을까요?

남자는 어떻게 느끼고 있을까?

(A) 실망한

(B) 당황한

(C) 화가 난

(D) 놀란

5

Look, I just saw the same camera at the store down the road. It's on sale, and it's about half the price of this one. It's exactly the same. It would be silly to buy that camera here when you could save so much elsewhere. I hope they have not all sold out. I'll be so happy if I could save some money. I can buy myself a new handbag with the money.

▶ **elsewhere** 다른 곳에서

봐봐, 난 길 아래쪽에 있는 가게에서 똑같은 카메라를 봤어. 세일 중이라서 이것의 반 가격이야. 완전 똑같아. 돈을 그렇게나 절약할 수 있는데 여기서 카메라를 사는 건 바보짓일 거야. 아직 다 안 팔렸기를 바랄 뿐이야. 돈을 절약할 수 있으면 좋겠어. 난 그 돈으로 새 핸드백을 살 수 있을 거야.

여자는 다음에 무엇을 할 것인가?

(A) 지금 있는 가게에서 카메라를 살 것이다.

(B) 새 핸드백을 살 것이다.

(C) 길 아래쪽에 있는 가게로 갈 것이다.

(D) 저축을 시작할 것이다.

6

I need a new computer. I am not looking for a desktop PC because I don't do much on my current one except play games and watch movies. I don't really want to spend more than $800. I know that is cheap, but that is all I think I can afford. So call me back if you think you have something for me.

▶ **current** 지금의, 현재의
afford (경제적, 시간적으로) 여유가 있다, ~할 수 있다

전 새 컴퓨터가 필요합니다. 현재의 컴퓨터로 게임하고 영화 보는 것 외에는 잘 사용하지 않으니까 데스크탑 컴퓨터를 찾는 것은 아니에요. 전 800달러 이상은 쓰고 싶지 않아요. 그 가격이 싸다는 것을 알지만 그 정도가 제가 지불할 수 있는 전부예요. 제게 적당한 것이 있으면 연락 주세요.

화자는 어떤 종류의 컴퓨터를 원하는가?

(A) 1000달러 데스크탑 컴퓨터

(B) 750달러 랩탑 컴퓨터

(C) 750달러 데스크탑 컴퓨터

(D) 1000달러 랩탑 컴퓨터

7

Hey, Bill, you want my advice on what to get Emily for her birthday? Well, a handbag or a T-shirt might be nice. Designer perfume is another option. Wait a minute! I have a 15% discount coupon for Penny's Jewelry. I hardly ever shop there, so go ahead and use the coupon if you can. Here it is.

▶ **hardly ever** 거의 ~하지 않다, 좀처럼 ~하지 않다
go ahead (망설이지 않고) 진행시키다

빌, 에밀리 생일에 무엇을 사 줄지에 대한 내 조언이 필요해? 음, 핸드백이나 티셔츠가 좋을 것 같은데. 디자이너 향수도 괜찮을 것 같고. 잠시만! 나 페니 쥬얼리 15퍼센트 할인 쿠폰 있는데. 나 그 가게 잘 안 가거든. 그러니까 필요하면 이거 가지고 가서 사용해. 여기 있어.

빌은 에밀리의 생일에 무엇을 살까?

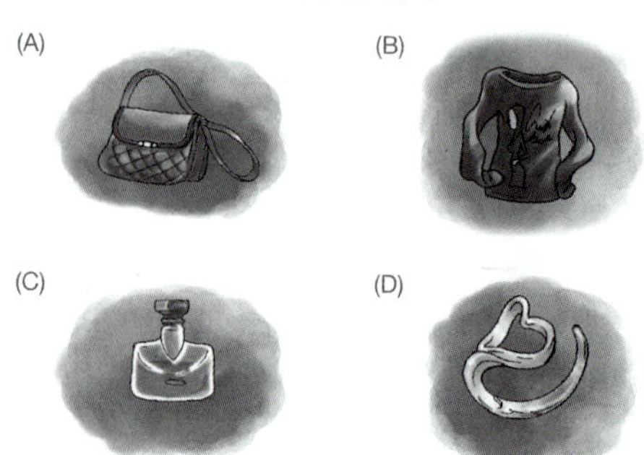

(A)　　(B)
(C)　　(D)

8

Sometimes you may pay more than the original price for a product. In order to avoid this problem, be sure to shop at places where the products' prices are clearly displayed. You should also compare prices to get a better idea of a product's price and features before purchasing it. You should also make sure you understand exactly

what you are buying.

▶ **display** 나타내다, 드러내다, 전시하다　**compare** 비교하다, 비유하다
feature 특징, 특색

때때로 당신은 제품의 원래 가격보다 더 많은 돈을 지불할지도 모른다. 이런 문제를 피하기 위해서는, 제품 가격이 명확히 표시된 곳에서 물건을 사야 한다. 또한 구매하기 전에 제품의 가격과 특징에 대해 알아보기 위해 가격을 비교해 봐야 한다. 그리고 사려고 하는 것을 정확히 알고 있어야 한다.

화자에 의해 추천되지 <u>않은</u> 것은 무엇인가?

(A) 가격이 명확히 표시된 곳에서 물건을 사는 것

(B) 가격을 비교하는 것

(C) 사려고 하는 것을 이해하는 것

(D) 가격이 할인되었을 때 물건을 사는 것

UNIT 13 Traveling

정답 answer

Key Expressions

1 1 paradise 2 vacation 3 cruise
   4 travel agent 5 destination

3 1 ⓔ 2 ⓐ 3 ⓓ 4 ⓑ 5 ⓖ 6 ⓕ 7 ⓒ

Listening Practice

1 (D)   **2** (A)

Check Up

Listening Task *01* 1 (C)   2 1) T 2) F 3) T 4) T
Listening Task *02* 1 (C)
Listening Task *03* 1 (B)   2 (C)
Listening Task *04* 1 (A)

Listening Test

1 (B)   **2** (B)   **3** (A)   **4** (C)   **5** (C)   **6** (C)
7 (C)   **8** (D)

스크립트 & 해석 script & translation

Key Expressions

1 표에서 가장 적절한 단어를 골라 빈칸을 채우시오.

1 푸른 물이 있는 아름답고 하얀 백사장. 천국에 오신 걸 환영합니다.

2 휴가 가기 전에, 나는 항상 철저하게 여행을 계획한다.

3 당신의 모험은 남극으로의 크루즈를 포함할지도 모릅니다.

4 좋은 여행사는 당신의 여행 계획을 짜 줄 수 있습니다.

5 먼저, 목적지로 가는 티켓을 사야 해요.

2 여행 동안에 필요한 물건들에 동그라미 치시오.

신혼 여행	바지	랜턴	출장	백팩
텐트	예약	지도	양말	여권

---

3 다음 문장들을 가장 잘 어울리는 대답과 연결하시오.

1 가장 좋아하는 휴가지가 어디인가요?
   ⓔ 제주도를 가장 좋아해요.

2 나는 일 때문에 많은 곳을 여행해야 합니다.
   ⓐ 얼마나 자주 가나요?

3 기차 여행은 끔찍했어요.
   ⓓ 왜요? 무슨 일이 있었는데요?

4 저는 이번 여름에 크루즈 여행을 갔었어요.
   ⓑ 어디 갔었나요?

5 해외로 여행한 적 있나요?
   ⓖ 예, 지난 여름 휴가 동안 유럽을 여행했어요.

6 언젠가 방문하고 싶은 나라는 어디에요?
   ⓕ 언젠가 스페인을 방문하고 싶어요.

7 한국에서 여행하기에 가장 좋은 계절은 언제죠?
   ⓒ 전 봄에 여행하는 것을 좋아해요.

Listening Practice

1

Summer vacation is coming. I'm so excited. My family and I are going to Thailand for three weeks. This is our first vacation as a family in thirteen years. My husband is a businessman. He travels frequently. When he takes a break, he wants to stay at home. But I stay home with the kids every day. It's so boring for me. I plan to go to the beach every day and have fun with my family.

▶ **frequently** 자주, 종종, 빈번하게 **take a break** 휴식을 취하다

여름 휴가가 다가오고 있다. 난 너무 들떠 있다. 우리 가족과 나는 3주간 태국에 갈 예정이다. 이것은 13년만에 처음으로 가는 가족 여행이다. 내 남편은 사업가이다. 그는 자주 여행을 한다. 그는 휴식을 취할 때, 집에 있고 싶어 한다. 하지만 난 매일 아이들과 집에 있는다. 내게는 너무 지루하다. 난 매일 해변에 가서 가족과 함께 즐겁게 보낼 계획을 하고 있다.

이야기에 대해 사실이 <u>아닌</u> 것은 무엇인가?

(A) 그녀는 남편과 아이들과 함께 휴가를 갈 것이다.

(B) 그녀는 매일 아이들과 함께 집에 있다.

(C) 그녀는 13년간 가족과 휴가를 가지 못했다.

(D) 그녀의 남편은 휴가 동안에 여행하는 것을 좋아한다.

2

W How is the weather in England in July?

M During the day, the temperature is around 31 degrees Celsius, and at night, it's about 18.

W   Okay. And what tours do you have?

M   We offer trips from London to Liverpool, Manchester, and Oxford.

W   What can we see in London?

M   The main attractions are Buckingham Palace and Big Ben.

▶ temperature 온도, 체온   Celsius 섭씨의
attraction 인기거리, 매력

여   7월의 영국 날씨는 어때요?

남   낮 동안에는 섭씨 31도 정도 되고, 밤에는 18도 정도 되요.

여   알겠습니다. 어떤 여행이 있나요?

남   런던에서부터 리버풀, 맨체스터, 옥스포드로 가는 여행이 있습니다.

여   런던에서는 무엇을 볼 수 있나요?

남   주요 관광지로는 버킹엄 궁전과 빅벤이 있어요..

대화가 일어난 곳은 어디인가?

(A) 여행사

(B) 공항

(C) 지하철 역

(D) 학교

Check Up

Listening Task 01

Backpacking overseas can be an inexpensive way to travel if you stay at cheap hotels and youth hostels. It can also provide great language and cultural training. Rather than learning about a culture and language in the classroom, you can meet people from around the world and improve your language skills that way.

▶ backpack 배낭을 메고 걷다; 배낭   overseas 해외로 가는, 해외의
rather than ~라기 보다도   improve 개선하다, 향상시키다

당신이 저렴한 호텔과 유스호스텔에 머문다면, 해외로 배낭 여행을 가는 것은 여행하는 데 있어 경비가 적게 드는 방법이 될 수 있다. 그것은 또 훌륭한 언어와 문화 훈련을 제공해 줄 수도 있다. 교실에서 문화와 언어에 대해서 배우기보다는, 전세계에서 온 사람들을 만날 수 있고, 그런 방법으로 언어 기술도 향상시킬 수 있다.

1   **이야기의 제목으로 가장 좋은 것은 무엇인가?**

  (A) 다른 문화를 배우는 방식

  (B) 휴식을 취하기에 좋은 곳들

  (C) 배낭 여행의 좋은 점들

  (D) 다른 문화에서 온 사람들을 만나는 방법

2   **맞으면 T, 틀리면 F에 체크하시오.**

  1) 배낭 여행은 비용이 별로 안 든다.

  2) 교실에서 배낭 여행에 대해 배울 수 있다.

  3) 배낭 여행 중에 새 언어를 배울 수 있다.

  4) 배낭 여행하는 사람들은 유스호스텔에 머무를 수 있다.

Listening Task 02

M   Here are the postcards and photographs that my dad sent 10 years ago.

W   Where was he? Do you remember?

M   I'm not sure. He traveled a lot back then. He was in France, and I think he was in Canada as well.

W   That's wonderful.

M   I also remember him talking about India. Oh, he mentioned Japan, too. But then he didn't go on a trip after that.

▶ mention 언급하다, 간단히 말하다

남   여기 아버지가 10년 전에 보낸 엽서와 사진들이 있네.

여   어디 계셨는데, 기억해?

남   확실히는 모르겠어. 그때 여행을 많이 하셨거든. 프랑스에 계셨고, 캐나다에도 계셨어.

여   멋지다.

남   난 아버지가 인도에 대해서 얘기했던 것도 기억해. 오, 일본도 얘기했었다. 그리고 그 후에는 여행을 가지 않으셨어.

1   **남자의 아버지가 방문하지 <u>않았던</u> 대륙은 어디인가?**

  (A) 아시아

  (B) 북아메리카

  (C) 오세아니아

  (D) 유럽

Listening Task 03

M   Ah, here we are. What do you think?

W   Wow! Just looking at it from the outside, this hotel is great. It has an outdoor swimming pool, a view of the beach, and free breakfast.

M   Unfortunately, that's not our hotel. Uh, it's the one next door.

W   What? That place? You've got to be joking. I mean that place looks so old.

M   Sorry.

W   I can't believe it!

▶ outdoor 야외의, 집 밖의   view 경치, 전망, 관점

남   자, 도착했다. 어때?

여 와! 밖에서 본 것만으론 이 호텔 좋은데. 야외 수영장도 있고, 해변도 보이고 아침 식사도 무료야.

남 아쉽게도, 거기가 우리 호텔이 아니야. 옆에 있는 거야.

여 뭐라고? 저거? 너 농담하는 거지. 저기는 너무 낡았어.

남 미안해.

여 믿을 수 없어!

1 왜 여자는 "믿을 수 없어"라고 얘기했나?

(A) 그녀는 마침내 도착해서 기뻤다.

(B) 그녀는 호텔이 생각했던 것보다 안 좋다고 생각한다.

(C) 그녀는 그들이 운이 좋다고 생각한다.

(D) 그녀는 그 호텔이 수영장이 있을 거라고 기대하지 않았었다.

2 대화에 대해 사실인 것은 무엇인가?

(A) 남자와 여자는 그들의 호텔에 만족하고 있다.

(B) 남자는 호텔에서 본 해변 풍경을 좋아한다.

(C) 여자는 그들의 호텔에 만족하지 못한다.

(D) 남자와 여자는 농담을 즐기고 있다.

Listening Task *04*

I'm a little worried about traveling in Egypt. Traveling in other Middle Eastern countries is very dangerous, but Egypt is supposed to be safer than other countries in the Middle East. Still, I'll have to prepare for culture shock by reading up on Egypt and gathering information on the Internet.

▶ **Middle Eastern** 중동의 **supposed** 상상된, 가정의
culture shock 문화적 충격 **read up** 연구하다, 복습하다

나는 이집트로 여행가는 것에 대해서 약간 걱정이 된다. 중동 국가로 여행하는 것은 아주 위험하지만, 이집트는 중동에 있는 다른 나라들보다 안전하다. 그래도 나는 이집트에 관한 책을 읽고, 인터넷에서 정보를 수집함으로써 문화 충격에 대비해야만 한다.

1 남자가 그의 여행에서 걱정하는 것은?

(A) 문화 충격

(B) 안전 문제

(C) 너무 많은 여행객들

(D) 의사 소통

Listening Test

1

Some parts of the world are medically safer than others. This is partly because of diseases but mainly due to the gap between countries' medical services. These two things could influence your choice of destinations. When planning a trip, you should ask an expert to find out of what you must be careful. This will make your trip safe and enjoyable.

▶ **medically** 의학상으로, 의학적으로 **partly** 어느 정도는, 부분적으로
due to ~ 때문인, ~에 기인하는 **gap** 큰 차이, 격차
influence 영향을 끼치다, 좌우하다 **destination** 목적지, 행선지
expert 전문가, 달인

세계의 몇몇 지역은 다른 곳보다 의학적으로 안전하다. 이는 부분적으로는 질병 때문이지만, 주로 의학 서비스의 차이 때문이다. 이 두 가지 것들이 당신의 목적지 선택에 영향을 줄 수 있다. 여행을 계획할 때, 무엇을 조심해야 하는지 알기 위해 전문가에게 자문을 구해야 한다. 이렇게 해야 당신의 여행이 안전하고 즐거울 수 있을 것이다.

화자는 무엇에 관해 얘기하고 있나?

(A) 의학적으로 안전한 곳을 선택하는 방법

(B) 의학적으로 안전한 여행을 하는 방법

(C) 외국에서 의료 시설들을 이용하는 방법

(D) 외국에서 질병을 치료하는 법

2

W I'd like to go to Peru this year. I heard you have traveled there.

M Yeah, I was there last year.

W Did you use a travel agency or plan everything on your own?

M I just did it all myself. All the package tours were so expensive, but, if you do it yourself, it's much cheaper.

W Okay, that sounds like good advice.

▶ **travel agency** 여행사 **on one's own** 혼자서, 스스로의 힘으로

여 올해 페루에 가고 싶어. 너 거기 갔었다면서.

남 응, 작년에 갔었어.

여 여행사를 이용했어, 아니면 혼자 계획했어?

남 전부 나 혼자서 했어. 모든 패키지 여행은 굉장히 비싸지만, 혼자서 하면 훨씬 싸잖아.

여 알았어. 좋은 조언이야.

여자는 다음에 무엇을 할 것인가?

(A) 여행사를 이용한다.

(B) 모든 것을 혼자 계획한다.

(C) 패키지 여행을 간다.

(D) 다른 곳을 간다.

3

It's best to travel when others are not traveling. Just ask your travel agent. An airline can tell you which times of year are slower and therefore offer lower prices and better seats. Hotels and resorts also know when they will have fewer guests. Sometimes, the difference is only a week. If you travel just a week earlier or later, you could enjoy a much cheaper holiday.

▶ travel agent 여행사 직원 airline 항공사, 정기 항공
slow 활기가 없는, 경기가 나쁜, 둔한

다른 사람들이 여행하지 않을 때 여행하는 것이 가장 좋다. 여행사에 물어 보라. 항공사는 언제가 한가한 때라 좀 더 저렴하고 좋은 좌석을 제공해 줄 수 있는지 알려 준다. 여행사는 호텔과 리조트도 언제 손님이 적은지를 알고 있다. 때때로 그 차이는 단지 일주일이 되기도 한다. 일주일 빨리 여행하거나 늦게 여행한다면 훨씬 더 저렴한 휴가를 즐길 수 있다.

이 이야기의 주제는 무엇인가?

(A) 여행하기 가장 좋은 때
(B) 편리하게 혼자 여행하는 법
(C) 여행사에 물어 볼 것
(D) 더 저렴한 가격으로 사는 법

4

W　Excuse me. Can you help me? Can you tell me where the tourist information center is?

M　It's not far. Walk straight on this road for about five minutes. Then turn right, and walk straight for another minute. The information center is next to the bookshop.

W　Thank you so much.

M　Don't worry. You can't miss it.

W　It sounds simple, but I don't know the city.

▶ tourist information center 여행자 안내소

여　실례합니다. 저 좀 도와 주시겠어요? 여행 안내소가 어디 있는지 알려주시겠습니까?

남　멀지 않아요. 약 5분간 이 길을 따라 죽 가세요. 그 다음에 오른쪽으로 꺾어서 또 1분간 걸어가요. 여행 안내소는 서점 옆에 있어요.

여　고맙습니다.

남　걱정하지 마세요. 찾으실 수 있을 거에요.

여　간단한 것 같은데 제가 이 도시를 잘 몰라서요.

상황을 가장 잘 나타낸 것은?

(A) 여자는 잘못 돌아서 길을 잃었다.
(B) 남자가 여자에게 잘못 길을 가르쳐 줘서 여자는 길을 잃었다.
(C) 남자가 여행 안내소로 가는 길을 알려 주고 있다.
(D) 여자는 문제가 생겨서 경찰서에 가야 한다.

5

I was on holiday in Mongolia last month. At first, I had a great time. I thought it would be the best experience of my life. But, on the third day, my tour guide demanded that I pay him more money. I had already paid for a guided tour and didn't have enough money. He left me in my hotel, and I was stuck there for a week because I didn't know how to get around. All I could do was walk around the city where the hotel was.

▶ Mongolia 몽골, 몽골국 demand 요구하다, 청구하다
stuck stick(~에 달라붙다, ~에 계속 머무르다)의 과거

지난달에 몽골에서 휴가를 보냈다. 처음에는 좋은 시간을 보냈다. 내 인생의 가장 좋은 경험이 될 것이라고 생각했었다. 하지만 셋째 날에, 내 여행 가이드는 내가 돈을 더 지불해야 한다고 했다. 나는 이미 가이드 여행에 대하여 지불을 했고 충분한 돈이 없었다. 그는 호텔에 나를 남겨 뒀고, 난 거기에 일주간 갇혀 있었다. 난 돌아다니는 법을 알지 못했다. 내가 할 수 있었던 것은 호텔이 있는 도시 주위를 걸어 다니는 것이었다.

남자는 휴가 후에 어떤 기분일까?

(A) 신이 난
(B) 걱정하는
(C) 실망한
(D) 지친

6

W　Excuse me. Do you need any help?

M　Oh, thanks. I'm trying to get to the airport.

W　You have to go to City Hall Station and transfer to the airport shuttle bus. It costs about five dollars.

M　Get off at City Hall Station?

W　Yeah. It's only three stops from here.

M　Great, thanks a lot.

▶ transfer 갈아타다, 이동하다 get off (차에서) 내리다, 하차하다

여　실례합니다. 도와 드릴까요?

남　오, 고맙습니다. 공항에 가려고 하는데요.

여　시청역으로 가서 공항 셔틀 버스로 갈아타셔야 합니다. 5달러 정도 비용이 듭니다.

남　시청역에서 내리라고요?

여　네. 여기서 세 정거장만 가면 되요.

남　좋습니다, 정말 고맙습니다.

이 대화가 일어나고 있는 곳은?

(A) 공항에서
(B) 시청역에서

(C) 버스 또는 전철에서
(D) 공항 셔틀 버스 정류장에서

7

M Where should we go for our family vacation this year? I hear that Portugal and Spain are very nice. But in March there could be heavy rains.

W Last year in March, my family spent a long weekend there. The weather was perfect. We spent the whole weekend on the beach.

M Well, I hope the weather will be the same as it was last year.

W You never know, but I recommend that you go there.

▶ heavy rain 폭우 recommend 추천하다, 권하다

남 올해는 가족 여행으로 어디로 가지? 포르투갈하고 스페인이 좋다고 하던데. 근데 3월에는 비가 많이 온다네.
여 작년 3월에 가족이랑 주말 여행 갔었는데. 날씨가 아주 좋았어. 주말 내내 해변에서 보냈는데.
남 작년처럼 올해도 날씨가 좋으면 좋겠다.
여 알 수 없지만, 난 거기 가는 거 추천해.

남자와 그의 가족은 이번 휴가에 무엇을 할 것인가?

(A) 포르투갈과 스페인보다 날씨가 더 좋은 곳을 찾을 것이다.
(B) 그의 부모님에게 방문할 장소를 선택해 달라고 부탁할 것이다.
(C) 그들은 휴가 동안에 포르투갈과 스페인으로 갈 것이다.
(D) 그들은 여행사를 방문할 것이다.

8

The travel agent told us that cruises serve different travelers, including singles, honeymooners, and families. Therefore, each cruise has different activities and services onboard the ship. Since we were going on our honeymoon, we did not want a family cruise. We chose a cruise for people like ourselves so that we could have time alone together.

▶ cruise 순항, 배로 하는 여행 serve (손님을) 접대하다, 시중들다
onboard the ship 선내에서

여행사는 크루즈가 싱글들, 신혼 여행객들, 그리고 가족들을 포함하여 다양한 여행자들에게 이용된다고 했다. 그러므로 각 크루즈는 배 위에서 다양한 활동들과 서비스를 제공한다. 우리는 신혼여행을 가는 길이기 때문에, 가족 크루즈는 원하지 않았다. 우리는 우리와 같은 사람들을 위한 크루즈를 선택해서 우리만의 시간을 가질 수 있었다.

화자가 크루즈를 선택하는 데 있어서 가장 중요하게 생각한 것은?

(A) 다양한 활동들을 하는 것
(B) 새로운 사람들을 만나는 것
(C) 비용
(D) 다른 사람들에게 방해 받지 않는 것

UNIT 14 Hotel

Key Expressions

1　1 situated　2 separate　3 charge
　　　4 cancel　5 accommodation

2　1 ⓓ　2 ⓑ　3 ⓒ　4 ⓐ

3　1 ⓓ　2 ⓒ　3 ⓔ　4 ⓐ　5 ⓕ　6 ⓑ

Listening Practice

1 (B)　　　　　**2** (B)

Check Up

Listening Task 01　1 (C)　2 1) T　2) T　3) F　4) F
Listening Task 02　1 1) ⓑ　2) ⓐ　3) ⓒ
Listening Task 03　1 (C)　2 (A)
Listening Task 04　1 (C)

Listening Test

1 (C)　**2** (D)　**3** (C)　**4** (A)　**5** (C)　**6** (C)
7 (B)　**8** (A)

Key Expressions

1　표에서 가장 적절한 단어를 골라 빈칸을 채우시오.

　　1 그것은 상가와 박물관 가까운 곳에 위치해 있다.

　　2 모든 방에는 독립된 응접실, 침실 공간이 있다.

　　3 주차에 추가 비용을 내야 하는지 말해 주세요.

　　4 죄송한데 계획이 바뀌어서 예약을 취소해야 할 것
　　　같아요.

　　5 아이들에게 적당한 숙박 시설인가요?

2　박스에서 올바른 질문을 골라 빈칸을 채우시오.

> ⓐ 어떻게 지불하시겠습니까?
> ⓑ 예약하셨나요?
> ⓒ 성함이 어떻게 되시나요?
> ⓓ 어서 오세요. 도와 드릴까요?

A: 1 <u>어서 오세요. 도와 드릴까요?</u>

B: 예, 체크인 하려고 하는데요.

A: 2 <u>예약하셨나요?</u>

B: 예, 했습니다.

A: 3 <u>성함이 어떻게 되시나요?</u>

B: 존슨입니다.

A: 싱글룸 2박이시죠?

B: 예, 맞아요.

A: 4 <u>어떻게 지불하시겠습니까?</u>

B: 현금이요.

A: 고맙습니다. 여기 열쇠가 있습니다. 5번 방입니다.

B: 감사합니다.

3　다음 문장들을 가장 잘 어울리는 대답과 연결하시오.

　　1 오늘밤 예약했는데요.
　　　ⓓ 예약 확인해 드리겠습니다.

　　2 아침 식사가 포함되나요?
　　　ⓒ 예, 포함됩니다.

　　3 프론트 데스크 직원이 너무 무례했어요.
　　　ⓔ 매니저에게 말씀하세요.

　　4 어떤 방을 원하시나요?
　　　ⓐ 트윈 베드가 있는 방이요.

　　5 제 방이 너무 작아요.
　　　ⓕ 다른 방으로 바꾸시겠습니까?

　　6 얼마나 머무르실 건가요?
　　　ⓑ 이틀 밤이요.

Listening Practice

1

You can make hotel reservations in several ways. The easiest ways are through the phone and over the Internet. These days, the Internet is becoming more and more important for hotel bookings. There are a number of advantages to using the Internet, such as reduced costs.

▶ booking (좌석의) 예약　reduced 할인된, 축소된

당신은 몇 가지 방법으로 호텔 예약을 할 수 있다. 가장 쉬운 방법은 전화로 하거나 인터넷으로 하는 것이다. 요즘에 인터넷은 호텔 예약

에 있어서 점점 더 중요해지고 있다. 할인된 가격처럼 인터넷을 사용하면 많은 장점들이 있다.

화자는 무엇에 대해 얘기하고 있는가?

(A) 호텔 예약하는 법
(B) 호텔 예약을 하는 새로운 방법
(C) 전화로 호텔을 예약하는 것의 장점들
(D) 좋은 호텔을 선택하는 법

2

W Excuse me. We asked for a double bed, but we only have a single bed in our room.
M Oh, I'm sorry. Let me see if we can change that.
W I made a special request when we booked.
M I see. Ah, here we are. Room 812. But we'll have to ask you to pay extra as that room has an ocean view.
W That's not good enough. It wasn't our mistake.

▶ pay extra 추가 요금을 내다   ocean view 바닷가 경치

여 실례합니다, 우리는 더블 침대를 요청했는데, 방에는 싱글 침대만 있네요.
남 오, 죄송합니다. 바꿀 수 있는지 알아보겠습니다.
여 저희가 예약할 때 특별히 요청했는데요.
남 아, 알겠습니다. 여기 있네요. 812번 방이죠. 하지만 그 방이 바다의 전경이 한 눈에 보이는 방이라서 추가 요금을 내셔야 합니다.
여 그건 옳지 않아요. 저희 실수가 아니잖아요.

여자는 무엇을 하고 있는가?

(A) 방을 예약하고 있다.
(B) 방에 대해 불평하고 있다.
(C) 바다의 전경이 보이는 곳을 요청하고 있다.
(D) 자신의 실수를 바로 잡고 있다.

Check Up

Listening Task *01*

I have a new job at a five-star hotel. It's exciting, but I work really hard. I am responsible for managing the hotel restaurant and bar. We serve breakfast at 6 in the morning, lunch at 12 p.m., and then dinner at 5 in the evening. The bar is open from 3 p.m. until midnight. I have to make sure that we have enough staff working, that the quality of the food is good, and that the guests are happy.

▶ responsible (~에 대해) 책임이 있는, 신뢰할 수 있는

나는 한 5성 호텔에서 새 직업을 구했다. 재미있지만 난 정말로 열심히 일하고 있다. 난 호텔 레스토랑과 바를 경영하는 책임을 맡았다. 우리는 오전 6시에 아침 식사를 제공하고, 12시에 점심을 제공하며, 저녁 식사는 5시에 제공한다. 바는 오후 3시에 열어서 자정까지 영업한다. 난 일하는 직원이 충분한지, 음식의 맛이 좋은지, 손님들이 만족하는지 확인해야 한다.

1 남자의 직업은 무엇인가?

(A) 5성 호텔의 매니저
(B) 호텔 레스토랑의 웨이터
(C) 호텔 레스토랑과 바의 매니저
(D) 호텔 레스토랑의 요리사

2 맞으면 T, 틀리면 F에 체크하시오.

1) 남자는 한 호텔에서 새 직장을 가졌다.
2) 레스토랑은 하루 세 번 식사를 제공한다.
3) 남자는 손님들이 만족하고 있는지 확인할 필요가 없다.
4) 남자의 일은 쉬워서 열심히 일하지 않는다.

Listening Task *02*

ⓐ

The Hotel Palomar opens today. Guests can expect a classic Texan look. The hotel has high ceilings, wooden floors, and a grand fireplace. It is cozy yet modern. Guests can enjoy the view of the mountains from the 26-foot windows.

▶ classic 고전적인, 고전의, 고상한   fireplace 벽난로
cozy 아늑한, 편안한   foot 길이의 단위 피트

호텔 파로마가 오늘 오픈했습니다. 숙박객들은 고전적인 텍사스의 모습을 볼 수 있습니다. 호텔에는 높은 천장과, 나무로 된 마루, 그리고 웅장한 벽난로가 있습니다. 아늑하지만 현대식입니다. 26피트의 창문으로 산의 전경을 즐길 수 있습니다.

ⓑ

Every time you see a guest, smile and greet the guest before the guest greets you. Never say "no" to a guest. Treat all colleagues with respect, just as you would want to be treated.

▶ greet ~에게 인사하다, 환영하다   treat 대우하다, 다루다
colleague (직업상의) 동료

손님을 볼 때마다, 손님이 인사하기 전에 웃으면서 인사하십시오. 손님에게 절대로 "안 된다"라고 말해서는 안 됩니다. 여러분이 대접받고 싶듯이, 모든 동료들을 존경을 가지고 대해야 합니다.

ⓒ

The Chandra Hotel was dark because it was dimly lit. The old wooden floors creaked, and my room was tiny. The staff was rude and indifferent to me. I cannot say that my stay was pleasant.

► **dimly** 어둑하게, 희미하게 **lit** 불이 켜진, 불 밝힌
creak 삐걱거리다 **indifferent** 무관심한, 냉담한

찬드라 호텔은 불이 희미하게 밝혀져 있어서 어두웠다. 오래된 나무 바닥은 금이 갔고 내 방은 작았다. 종업원들은 무례하고 내게 무관심했다. 그것이 좋았다고 말할 수 없다.

1 각 이야기의 목적을 연결하시오.

1) 충고하기 위해
2) 광고하기 위해
3) 불만을 말하기 위해

Listening Task 03

W Good morning, sir. Are you ready to leave?

M Yes, but I think my bill seems a little high.

W Let me check it. Oh, I see you've been charged for watching a cable channel that you didn't use.

M Have I?

W Yes, here it is. I'll correct it right now, Mr. Black. We don't want you leaving here unhappy!

M Thank you. And I don't want to pay for things I didn't use.

► **bill** 계산서, 청구서 **charge** 요금을 청구하다, 값을 매기다

여 좋은 아침입니다, 손님. 출발할 준비가 다 되셨나요?

남 네, 근데 제 청구서가 좀 더 나온 것 같은데요.

여 확인해 보겠습니다. 아, 고객님께서 사용하지 않으신 케이블 채널을 본 것에 대한 비용이 부과되었군요.

남 그랬나요?

여 여기요. 제가 지금 수정해 드릴게요, 블랙 씨. 저희는 손님께서 불쾌한 기분으로 떠나시길 원치 않습니다.

남 고맙습니다. 저도 제가 사용하지 않은 것에 대해서는 지불하고 싶지 않습니다.

1 상황을 가장 잘 설명하고 있는 것은?

(A) 남자는 호텔에 체크인하고 있다.
(B) 남자는 호텔에서 체크아웃하고 있다.
(C) 남자는 케이블 요금에 대해서 묻고 있다.
(D) 남자는 호텔 방을 예약하고 있다.

2 직원이 발견한 실수는 무엇이었나?

(A) 남자는 자신이 사용하지 않았던 것에 대해 요금을 부과 받았다.
(B) 점원은 청구서에 보험료를 추가하는 것을 잊었다.
(C) 남자는 케이블 방송을 본 것에 대해 지불하지 않았다.
(D) 직원이 추가 비용을 청구하는 것을 잊었다.

Listening Task 04

I'm a businessman, and I travel a lot. But, every time I travel to a city for the first time, I'm a little nervous about things like changing money for a taxi, finding my hotel, and not getting lost. Some of the bigger hotels will arrange for hotel staff to fetch you at the airport. That's so convenient, especially when my flight lands late at night.

► **arrange** 준비하다, 마련하다 **fetch** 데리고 오다, 가지고 오다

난 사업가이고 여행을 많이 다닌다. 하지만 처음 가는 도시를 여행할 때마다, 나는 택시를 타기 위해 환전을 하고, 호텔을 찾고, 길을 잃어버리지 않기 위해 약간 긴장이 된다. 큰 호텔들 중 몇몇은 호텔 직원들이 당신을 데리러 공항으로 올 것이다. 그것은 특히 비행기가 밤 늦게 도착했을 때에 아주 편리하다.

1 새로운 도시에서 남자를 긴장하게 만드는 것은 무엇인가?

(A) 안 좋은 호텔에 머무르는 것
(B) 택시 요금을 바가지 쓰는 것
(C) 호텔에 가는 길을 잃어버리는 것
(D) 공항에서 짐을 잃어버리는 것

Listening Test

1

M Are you sure they didn't make a mistake with our reservation? This room is great.

W There's no mistake. The hotel isn't busy, so they upgraded our room.

M Well, this is fantastic. We have a great view from the balcony.

W The bath is huge. We're so lucky.

M Are you sure they won't charge us extra?

W I don't think so. But why don't you ask the manager?

► **extra** 추가 요금; 추가의, 여분의

남 우리 예약에 뭔가 실수가 있는 거 아닐까? 방이 너무 좋잖아.

여 실수는 없어. 호텔이 붐비지 않아서 방을 업그레이드 시켜준 거야.

남 정말 멋지다. 발코니 전망도 좋아.

여 욕실도 크고. 우린 참 운이 좋구나.

남 우리에게 추가 비용을 청구하지 않을까?

여 그럴 거 같지는 않아. 하지만 매니저에게 물어보는 게 어때?

왜 남자는 호텔이 그들에게 추가 요금을 요청할 것이라고 생각하나?

(A) 호텔이 예약과 관련하여 실수를 했다.
(B) 호텔이 바쁘지 않다.
(C) 호텔이 그들의 방을 업그레이드 해줬다.
(D) 큰 욕조가 있다.

2

W Hi, may I help you?

M Yes, I would like to know if there is a discount rate for agents.

W Yes, there is. I think it's 10%, but I can check that for you.

M Okay, do you mind if I book it for now and call you back later to confirm? I just need to check one or two details.

W That's fine, sir.

▶ discount rate 할인율 confirm 확인하다, 확증하다
detail 세부, 항목

여 안녕하세요. 도와 드릴까요?
남 예, 직원에 대한 할인율이 있는지 알고 싶어서요.
여 예, 있습니다. 10퍼센트인 것 같은데 제가 확인해 보겠습니다.
남 제가 지금 예약하고 나중에 확인하러 다시 전화해도 될까요? 한 두 개 사항만 확인하면 되거든요.
여 예, 그렇게 하세요.

대화에 대해 사실인 것은 무엇인가?

(A) 직원에 대한 할인은 없다.
(B) 남자는 10퍼센트 할인이 너무 낮다고 생각한다.
(C) 남자는 예약을 확인하지 않을 것이다.
(D) 남자는 예약하기 전에 몇 가지 사항들을 확인할 것이다.

3

W Hey, Chris. I'm going to be visiting New York City soon. What hotels have you stayed at there?

M I always look for something inexpensive. I like the Four Seasons on 51st. It used to have a shared bathroom between two rooms.

W I've never been there. But I stayed at the Holiday Inn once before, and I really liked it. Maybe I'll just stay there again.

▶ shared bathroom 공용 욕실

여 안녕, 크리스. 나 뉴욕에 갈 예정이야. 너는 거기서 어느 호텔에 묵었어?
남 난 항상 비싸지 않은 곳을 찾아. 난 51번가에 있는 포 시즌즈를 좋아해. 두 개의 방에 공유할 수 있는 욕실이 있어.
여 난 거기 가 본 적 없는데. 하지만 난 전에 홀리데이 인에서 머물렀는데 정말 괜찮았어. 그냥 거기 다시 묵을까봐.

이들은 무엇에 대해서 얘기하고 있나?

(A) 뉴욕에 있는 유명한 호텔들
(B) 뉴욕에 있는 안 좋은 호텔들
(C) 그들이 머물렀던 호텔들
(D) 그들의 호텔에 가는 방법

4

We arrived at the hotel late last night. The hotel staff made a terrible mistake with my reservation and didn't have a room for me. Lenny and Sam had to share a room, and I took Lenny's room. To apologize for the mistake, the hotel manager treated us to drinks and dinner. This morning, they moved my luggage to the new room they had arranged for me.

▶ share 함께 나누다, 공유하다; 몫, 할당몫 treat 대접하다, 한 턱 내다
luggage 수하물(= baggage)

우리는 어젯밤 늦게 호텔에 도착했다. 호텔 직원이 내 예약과 관련하여 끔찍한 실수를 해서 방이 없었다. 레니와 샘은 방을 같이 써야 했고, 난 레니의 방을 썼다. 실수에 대해 사과하기 위해서, 호텔 매니저는 음료와 저녁 식사를 제공해 주었다. 오늘 아침, 그들은 내 위해 마련한 새 방으로 내 짐들을 옮겨 주었다.

화자의 감정 변화를 가장 잘 보여 주고 있는 것은 무엇인가?

(A) 화가 난 → 만족한
(B) 행복한 → 화가 난
(C) 화가 난 → 실망한
(D) 흥분한 → 행복한

5

W Front Desk. How can I help you?

M The air conditioner in my room isn't working. Cold air doesn't come out when I turn it on.

W How long did you wait after you turned it on?

M I'm not sure. Maybe a minute.

W You have to wait more than 5 minutes to get cold air after you turn it on.

M I'm sorry. Aha, there's cold air coming out now. Thank you.

W My pleasure.

▶ turn on 틀다, 켜다

여 프론트 데스크입니다. 무엇을 도와 드릴까요?
남 제 방에 있는 에어컨이 작동을 하지 않아요. 에어컨을 켰는데 찬 바람이 나오지 않네요.
여 켜고 나서 얼마나 기다리셨나요?
남 잘 모르겠는데요. 아마 1분쯤?

여　작동시키고 나서 찬 바람이 나오려면 5분 이상은 기다리셔야
　　해요.
남　죄송합니다. 아, 이제 찬 바람이 나오네요. 감사합니다.
여　천만에요.

에어컨의 문제는 무엇이었나?

(A) 적절하게 연결되어 있지 않았다.
(B) 켜는 법을 알지 못했다.
(C) 충분히 기다리지 않았다.
(D) 바람이 충분히 시원하지 않았다.

6

I've been the owner of my little youth hostel for about eight years now. It's small and simple. But it's already famous among backpackers around the world. They know that it's very cheap but also clean and comfortable. It's in the city's center, which is a great location for travelers. Some people prefer hotels, but I think they are too expensive and unnecessary.

▶ backpacker 배낭여행자　location 위치, 장소, 주소

난 약 8년 동안 이 작은 유스호스텔의 주인이었다. 이곳은 작고 심플하다. 하지만 전세계의 배낭 여행객들에게는 이미 유명하다. 그들은 이곳이 싸지만 깨끗하고 편하다는 것을 알고 있다. 도시 중심에 위치해 있어서 여행객들에게는 아주 좋은 위치이다. 몇몇 사람들은 호텔을 선호하지만, 난 그곳들이 너무 비싸고 불필요하다고 생각한다.

이 이야기의 주제는 무엇인가?

(A) 값비싼 호텔들
(B) 유스호스텔들
(C) 남자가 소유하고 있는 유명한 유스호스텔
(D) 남자가 갖고 싶어 하는 작은 호텔

7

M　Excuse me. I checked in late, and I'm really hungry.
W　Would you like dinner or just a snack?
M　I'd like a snack and something to drink. Is that possible?
W　Of course. This is the number for room service. They will help you.
M　Is room service still available?
W　Yes, it's a 24-hour service.
M　Oh, I'm so glad to hear that. Thanks.

▶ available 이용할 수 있는, 입수할 수 있는

남　실례합니다. 전 체크인을 늦게 했는데 배가 너무 고파서요.

여　저녁 식사를 하시겠어요, 아니면 그냥 간식을 원하세요?
남　간식과 마실 것을 원해요. 가능한가요?
여　물론이죠. 이게 룸서비스 전화번호에요. 도움이 될 거에요.
남　아직 룸서비스 이용이 가능한가요?
여　네, 24시간 서비스에요.
남　오, 그 말을 들으니 정말 반갑네요. 고마워요.

남자가 다음에 할 일은 무엇인가?

(A) 그는 룸서비스 저녁 식사와 와인을 주문할 것이다.
(B) 그는 룸 서비스로 간식을 주문할 것이다.
(C) 그는 레스토랑에 갈 것이다.
(D) 그는 호텔에서 체크아웃할 것이다.

8

I wasn't sure what to expect, but I do really like my room. The carpet is old and worn, but you can really sense the history of the place. I like the fact that I have a Roman-style balcony that I can go out on. The staff here even wears medieval-style uniforms. It makes me feel like I'm in a different time period. Of course, all of the services are modern. That's what I liked most. After all, I don't think I would really want to stay in a real Roman-style hotel.

▶ worn 써서 낡은, 닳아 해진　sense 느끼다; 감각
medieval-style 중세풍의, 중세 스타일의　period 시대, 시간, 시

내가 기대한 것이 어떤 것이었는지 확실하지 않았지만, 정말로 내 방이 맘에 든다. 카펫은 낡았고 닳았지만 이곳의 역사를 느낄 수 있다. 밖으로 나갈 수 있는 로마풍 발코니가 있다는 사실이 맘에 든다. 여기 직원들은 심지어 중세 스타일의 유니폼을 입는다. 물론 서비스는 현대식이다. 그게 가장 마음에 든다. 결국 나는 진짜 로마풍 호텔에 묵기를 바라는 것은 아닌 것 같다.

화자는 호텔의 어떤 점을 가장 좋아하는가?

(A) 현대식 서비스
(B) 로마 스타일의 발코니
(C) 오래된 카펫
(D) 역사적인 주변 환경

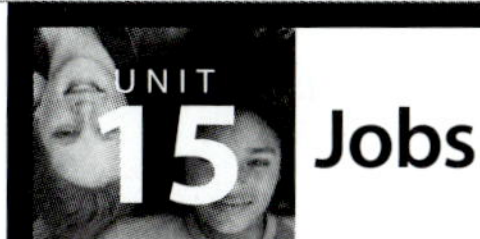

UNIT 15 Jobs

정답 answer

Key Expressions
1 1 chef   2 plumber   3 mechanic
    4 stylist   5 architect
2 1 train   2 poetry   3 grain   4 sew
    5 radio
3 1 ⓔ   2 ⓒ   3 ⓑ   4 ⓐ   5 ⓕ   6 ⓓ

Listening Practice
1 (B)   **2** (A)

Check Up
Listening Task 01   1 (C)   2 1) T   2) F   3) T   4) F
Listening Task 02   1 (B)
Listening Task 03   1 (A)   2 (D)
Listening Task 04   1 (B)

Listening Test
1 (D)   **2** (C)   **3** (C)   **4** (C)   **5** (C)   **6** (D)
7 (C)   **8** (A)

스크립트 & 해석 script & translation

Key Expressions

1 표에서 가장 적절한 단어를 골라 빈칸을 채우시오.
    1 주방장이 음식을 요리한다.
    2 배관공이 싱크대와 변기를 수리한다.
    3 수리공이 자동차를 수리한다.
    4 스타일리스트가 머리를 자른다.
    5 건축가가 건물을 설계한다.

2 해당 직업과 관계 없는 단어를 지우시오.
    1 파일럿: 기차 / 비행 / 비행기
    2 저널리스트: 시 / 보도 / 신문
    3 약사: 곡물 / 약 / 처방
    4 치과 의사: 칫솔 / 꿰매다 / 드릴
    5 사업가: 사무실 / 고객 / 라디오

3 다음 문장들을 가장 잘 어울리는 대답과 연결하시오.
    1 일주일에 몇 시간을 근무하나요?
      ⓔ 주당 최소 50시간은 근무해요.
    2 미안합니다. 당신은 해고됐습니다.
      ⓒ 왜요? 제가 뭘 잘못했나요?
    3 무슨 일을 하시나요?
      ⓑ 전 회계사예요.
    4 나 승진했어!
      ⓐ 축하해요!
    5 누가 절 인터뷰하나요?
      ⓕ 고객 서비스 부서의 부장님께서 인터뷰할 겁니다.
    6 일이 마음에 드세요?
      ⓓ 물론이죠. 연봉이 세요.

Listening Practice

1

I am Mr. Peter, and my job is teaching music to high school students. I teach the piano and violin. Before this job, I taught music courses at the local college. This is my first time teaching younger students. I start next week, and I am nervous about this new opportunity! However, I will do my best.

▶ local 지방의, 고장의

전 피터이고 제 직업은 고등학교 학생들에게 음악을 가르치는 것입니다. 전 피아노와 바이올린을 가르칩니다. 이 일을 하기 전에, 음악 과정을 지역 대학에서 가르쳤습니다. 어린 학생을 가르치기는 이번이 처음입니다. 전 다음 주에 일을 시작하는데 이 새로운 기회에 대해서 긴장하고 있습니다! 하지만, 전 최선을 다할 것입니다.

화자는 누구를 가르칠 예정인가?

(A) 대학생들
(B) 고등학생들
(C) 어린 아이들
(D) 중학생들

2

M   I have a job interview.
W   Good luck with that.
M   Can you give me some tips on how I should

dress?

W   Yes, you should dress neatly and look tidy.

M   So I should wear a formal dress?

W   If you want. But a suit will be enough.

M   Okay, thanks!

▶ **Good luck with...** ~에 행운을 빌어. **tip** 힌트, 조언, 비법
neatly 깔끔하게, 맵시 있게 **tidy** 단정한, 말쑥한
formal dress 정장 **suit** 슈트, 신사복 한 벌, 여성복 한 벌

남   나 면접 봐.
여   행운이 있길 바래.
남   무슨 옷을 입어야 할지 조언 좀 해 줄 수 있어?
여   응, 깔끔하고 단정하게 입어야 해.
남   정장을 입어야 하나?
여   원한다면. 하지만 양복도 괜찮을 거야.
남   알겠어, 고마워!

대화의 내용에 대해 사실인 것은 무엇인가?

(A) 남자는 면접을 보기 위해 어떤 옷을 입어야 할지 알기
    를 원한다.
(B) 여자와 남자는 데이트를 계획하고 있다.
(C) 남자는 여자가 그에게 양복을 사 주기를 원한다.
(D) 그들 둘 다 시간 외 근무를 해야 한다.

Check Up

Listening Task 01

M   How do you like my new office?

W   It's nice and big!

M   Yes. I have a larger work space and a new desk.

W   You're lucky.

M   Well, this comes after three years of hard work
    and dedication.

W   Yes, you deserved that promotion. I hope I can
    get promoted, too.

M   Thank you! And you will! Everyone knows
    that you're a hard worker.

▶ **work space** 작업 공간 **dedication** 헌신, 바침, 헌납
deserve ~할 만 하다, 가치가 있다 **promotion** 승진, 진급, 촉진
get promoted 승진되다

남   내 새 사무실 어때?
여   멋지고 큰데!
남   응, 난 더 큰 작업 공간과 새 책상이 생겼어.
여   운이 좋구나.
남   음, 이건 3년간 열심히 일하고 헌신한 결과야.
여   응, 넌 승진할 만했어. 나도 승진하면 좋겠다.
남   고마워! 너도 승진할 거야! 모든 사람들이 네가 열심히 일한다
    는 것을 알고 있어.

---

1   **남자는 자신의 승진에 대해서 어떻게 느끼고 있나?**
    (A) 실망한
    (B) 격노한
    (C) 좋아하는
    (D) 우울한

2   **맞으면 T, 틀리면 F에 체크하시오.**
    1) 남자는 3년간 일했다.
    2) 여자는 승진을 원하지 않는다.
    3) 남자의 새 사무실은 전보다 더 크다.
    4) 남자는 오래된 책상을 가지고 있다.

Listening Task 02

My dream job is to be a television news reporter.
But the women on television are so glamorous.
I don't think I would ever be good at that job
because I'm not like them. That's why I've decided
to become an accountant. Accountants work
hard, but they earn pretty good salaries. It's a
popular job because you can also work abroad.
That's what I want to do one day.

▶ **glamorous** 매혹적인, 매력에 찬 **accountant** 회계사, 회계원
work abroad 해외에서 일하다

내 장래 희망은 텔레비전 뉴스 기자가 되는 것이다. 하지만 텔레비
전에 나오는 여자들은 정말 매력적이다. 나는 내가 그 일을 잘 할 거
라고 생각되지가 않는다. 난 그들과 비슷하지 않기 때문이다. 바로
그 이유 때문에 나는 회계사가 되기로 결정했다. 회계사들은 열심히
일을 하고 월급을 꽤 많이 받는다. 해외에서도 일할 수 있기 때문에
인기 있는 직업이다. 그것이 바로 내가 앞으로 하고 싶은 일이다.

1   **왜 여자는 그녀가 좋은 TV 뉴스 기자가 되지 못할 것이
    라고 생각하나?**
    (A) 텔레비전에 나오는 것에 대해서 너무 긴장한다.
    (B) 충분히 매력적이지 않다.
    (C) 회계를 더 잘한다.
    (D) 월급에 만족하지 못한다.

Listening Task 03

W   I was thinking of becoming a veterinarian.
    What do you think?

M   It's a challenging job. Why are you interested
    in it?

W   I really love animals. But I know that it's hard
    work to become a veterinarian.

M   Yes, you have to study for a long time. But if it's
    something you really want to do, you'll do all
    right.

W Will you let me work here on weekends and during my vacations?

M Let's wait until you finish your first semester at university. If you get good grades, I'd be glad to offer you a job during your vacation.

▶ veterinarian 수의사 challenging 도전적인, 힘든, 자극적인

여 수의사가 될까 생각하는데요. 어떻게 생각하세요?
남 힘든 일이잖아. 왜 그 일에 관심을 갖게 됐는데?
여 전 동물들을 정말 좋아해요. 하지만 수의사가 되는 일이 어렵다는 걸 알고 있어요.
남 응, 넌 오랫동안 공부해야 해. 하지만 그게 네가 정말로 하고 싶은 일이라면, 괜찮을 거야.
여 제가 주말하고 방학 동안에 여기서 일해도 될까요?
남 대학교에서 한 학기 마칠 때까지만 기다려 보자. 좋은 점수를 받으면, 방학 동안에 일자리를 줄게.

1 이 상황을 가장 잘 나타낸 것은 무엇인가?

(A) 여자는 수의사가 되는 것에 관한 남자의 충고를 부탁하고 있다.
(B) 남자는 여자가 주말에 일해야 한다고 생각하지 않는다.
(C) 남자는 여자의 대학교 교수이다.
(D) 여자는 졸업하면 남자와 함께 일하고 싶어 한다.

2 대화에 대해 사실인 것은 무엇인가?

(A) 남자는 동물을 좋아하지 않는다.
(B) 여자는 동물을 좋아해서, 수의사가 되었다.
(C) 여자는 수의사 일이 지루하다고 생각한다.
(D) 남자는 수의사이다.

Listening Task *04*

My son wants to go to graduate school next year. I'm very disappointed. I want him to get a job. He's still young, and he needs to get work experience. If he studies for too long, he will end up working for a boss who is younger than him. But my son is not sure what kind of job he wants. That's why he wants to study for another year. I suppose it's his choice.

▶ graduate school 대학원 work experience 직장 경험
   end up 끝내 ~하게 되다, 결국 ~ 되다

내 아들은 내년에 대학원에 가고 싶어 한다. 난 너무 실망스럽다. 난 그가 취업하기를 원한다. 그는 여전히 어리고 직장 경험을 가질 필요가 있다. 만약 그가 오랫동안 공부한다면 결국 그보다 나이 어린 상사를 위해 일하게 될 것이다. 하지만 내 아들은 자신이 어떤 일을 원하는지 모른다. 그게 바로 그가 일년 더 공부하기를 원하는 이유이다. 난 그것이 그가 선택할 일이라고 생각한다.

1 화자는 그의 아들이 곧 취업을 하지 않으면 아들에게 무슨 일이 일어날 거라고 생각하나?

(A) 결코 부자가 되지 못할 것이다.
(B) 그의 상사가 그보다 더 어릴 것이다.
(C) 충분한 경험을 갖지 못할 것이다.
(D) 그의 아버지를 실망시킬 것이다.

Listening Test

1

Applying for a job is never easy. It requires time and patience. First, you should look at the requirements for the position you want. Don't bother applying if you don't qualify for the job. You will just be wasting your time. However, if you fulfill the requirements, fill out the application forms, send your resume, and be prepared to be rejected just in case. You may have to apply to a lot of jobs, but, if you don't give up, you will find something eventually.

▶ require 필요로 하다, ~을 요구하다 requirement 요구 조건, 요건, 요구 position 직, 직업, 위치, 지위 fill out 여백을 메우다, 기입하다 application form 신청 용지, 신청서 resume 이력서, 개요 just in case 만약을 위해서 eventually 결국, 마침내

회사에 지원하는 것은 결코 쉬운 일이 아니다. 그것은 시간과 인내를 필요로 한다. 먼저, 원하는 직종에 관한 자격 요건을 알아봐야 한다. 자격 요건을 충족시키지 못한다면 지원해서는 안 된다. 시간만 낭비할 뿐이다. 하지만 그 자격 요건을 만족한다면, 지원서를 작성하고서 이력서를 보내고, 만약의 경우 거절당할 것에 준비해야 한다. 당신은 여러 일자리에 지원해야 할 수도 있다. 하지만 포기하지 않는다면 결국 뭔가를 찾아낼 것이다.

일자리에 지원하기 위해 필요하지 <u>않은</u> 것은?

(A) 이력서 보내기
(B) 일자리의 자격 요건 확인하기
(C) 지원서 작성하기
(D) 자신감 갖기

2

M Your resume is very good.

W Thank you. I really think I am perfect for the position.

M Why?

W My qualifications are suitable, and I am a hardworking person.

M I'm sure you are. But we are looking for someone with more experience.

W I don't have a lot of experience, but I learn very fast.

▶ qualification 자격, 능력, 자격 부여
suitable 적당한, 적절한, 어울리는

남 이력서가 상당히 괜찮네요.
여 감사합니다. 전 제가 그 일에 적임자라고 생각합니다.
남 왜죠?
여 제 자격 요건이 그 일에 적합하고, 전 열심히 일하는 사람이에요.
남 전 당신이 그러리라고 확신합니다. 하지만, 우리는 경험이 좀 있는 사람을 찾고 있습니다.
여 전 경험은 많지 않지만 매우 빨리 배웁니다.

상황을 가장 잘 설명하는 것은?

(A) 남자는 여자가 인터뷰 준비하는 것을 돕고 있다.
(B) 남자는 여자가 새 직업을 시작하는 것을 돕고 있다.
(C) 남자는 여자를 인터뷰하고 있다.
(D) 남자는 여자와 함께 면접에 응시하고 있다.

3

W How do you like this job so far, Mr. Peter?
M I love it. The students are wonderful and eager to learn music.
W I am glad to hear that!
M I do miss my college students though. Sometimes the younger students here are too talkative with each other.
W Yes, but that's how younger people are.

▶ eager ~을 열망하는, ~에 열성적인
talkative 말이 많은, 수다스러운

여 지금까지 하신 이 일이 어떤가요, 피터 씨?
남 좋습니다. 학생들은 훌륭하고, 음악을 열심히 배우려고 합니다.
여 그렇다니 기쁘네요!
남 전 대학생들이 그립기도 해요. 때때로 이곳의 어린 학생들은 서로 너무 떠들거든요.
여 예, 하지만 어린 학생들이 다 그렇죠.

남자는 새 일에 대해서 어떻게 생각하고 있나?

(A) 그는 그 일을 좋아하지 않는다.
(B) 그는 대학생들을 더 좋아했다.
(C) 그는 지금 일을 좋아하지만 옛 일이 그립다.
(D) 그는 지금 초등학교로 옮기고 싶어 한다.

4

M I need a part-time job. I have to buy some textbooks.
W It's difficult to find a good job. Most part-time jobs are hard work, and they don't pay very well.
M I know that, but it doesn't matter. I'm a little desperate, but I don't have any experience.

W I'll ask my boss whether he needs another waiter.
M That would be great. I'm available to start this weekend if need be.
W I will let you know if he wants to interview you.

▶ desperate 필사적인, 절망적인
if need be 필요한 경우에는, 부득이하다면

남 나 아르바이트 자리를 구해야 해. 교재를 사야 하거든.
여 좋은 일자리를 구하는 건 어려워. 대부분의 아르바이트 일은 힘들고, 돈도 많이 안 주거든.
남 나도 알지만, 문제 없어. 난 조금 절실하지만 경험이 없거든.
여 다른 웨이터가 필요한지 사장님께 여쭤볼게.
남 그거 좋겠다. 필요하다면 이번 주말부터 일할 수 있어.
여 사장님이 널 인터뷰하시길 원하는지 알려줄게.

왜 남자는 아르바이트 일을 찾지 못했나?

(A) 그는 절실하다.
(B) 그는 학생이다.
(C) 그는 경험이 없다.
(D) 그는 열심히 일하고 싶어 하지 않는다.

5

When applying for a job, it should be something you enjoy and are good at. If you are good at writing, you should look for a job where you will do a lot of writing. Perhaps you have an interesting hobby, such as creating webpages. Then try to become a website and graphic designer. It is better to choose a job doing something you enjoy since you will be spending a lot of time at work.

▶ apply 지원하다, 신청하다

어떤 일자리에 지원할 때, 그 일은 당신이 좋아하고 잘하는 것이어야 한다. 만약에 글쓰기를 잘한다면, 글을 많이 쓰는 직업을 찾아야 한다. 당신은 웹페이지를 만드는 것 같은 재미있는 취미를 갖고 있을지도 모른다. 그럼 웹사이트와 그래픽 디자이너가 되도록 노력해라. 당신은 대부분의 시간을 일하는 데 보내기 때문에 당신이 즐겨하는 일을 선택하는 것이 중요하다.

이 이야기의 요지는 무엇인가?

(A) 당신이 글을 잘 쓴다면 작가가 되어야 한다.
(B) 웹페이지를 만든다는 것은 당신이 그래픽 디자인을 공부해야 한다는 것을 의미한다.
(C) 사람은 즐길 수 있고 흥미를 갖고 있는 분야의 일을 해야 한다.
(D) 당신이 알고 있는 것을 공부하는 것은 장래에 많은 돈을 벌게 해줄 것이다.

6

W So the computer is working now?

M Yes, I fixed it.

W How long did it take?

M Only about three hours.

W It was probably very complicated.

M Not really. I had fun.

W You must be good at your job.

M I do enjoy it. Besides, I studied really hard to do this well.

▶ fix 고치다, 수리하다, 정정시키다
complicated 복잡한, 풀기 어려운 besides 게다가, 또

여 그래서 지금은 컴퓨터가 작동되니?
남 응, 내가 고쳤어.
여 얼마나 오래 걸렸어?
남 한 세 시간 정도.
여 매우 복잡했을 텐데.
남 그렇지 않았어. 재미 있었어.
여 일을 잘하나 보네.
남 난 내 일이 정말 좋아. 그리고, 잘하기 위해서 정말 열심히 공부했어.

대화에 대해 사실인 것은 무엇인가?

(A) 남자는 그의 일을 좋아하지 않는다.
(B) 여자는 남자와 같은 일을 하기를 원한다.
(C) 남자는 컴퓨터 프로그래머이다.
(D) 남자는 세 시간 만에 컴퓨터를 고쳤다.

7

It could take months of hard work to find the job that you really want. If you already have a job, it may be easier to find information about job openings. You could speak to your co-workers in your company, for example. But it also means that you have less free time to search. If you are unemployed, you can treat your search like a full-time job. You can use newspapers, the Internet, or an employment service. With luck and hard work, you can soon find your dream job.

▶ job opening (직장의) 빈자리, 구인
unemployed 실직한, 일이 없는

당신이 정말로 원하는 일을 찾는 것은 수 개월이 걸리는 힘든 일일 수도 있다. 이미 일을 하고 있다면, 구직에 관한 정보를 찾는 게 더 쉬울지도 모른다. 예를 들면, 회사 동료에게 얘기할 수도 있다. 하지만 이는 직장을 찾을 시간이 더 적다는 것을 의미한다. 취업 상태가 아니라면, 풀 타임으로 찾을 수 있다. 신문, 인터넷, 고용 서비스 등을 이용할 수 있다. 운과 노력으로, 곧 당신이 꿈꾸는 일을 찾을 수 있다.

이 이야기의 요지는 무엇인가?

(A) 적절한 일을 찾기 위해서는 많은 운이 필요하다.
(B) 이미 일을 갖고 있다면 새 일을 찾는 것은 어렵다.
(C) 운과 노력으로 적절한 일을 찾을 수 있다.
(D) 직업을 찾기 위해서 당신의 인맥을 이용할 필요가 있다.

8

These days, it is common, when looking for a job, to get professional help. There are many companies offering to help people find suitable positions. They are called employment agencies or personnel placement services. If you are looking for a job though, be careful. While most of these companies will no doubt offer good services, the costs of getting their assistance are high. Often the company doesn't provide a guarantee that they will find you a job. You should be clear about what they are offering you before paying for their services.

▶ professional 전문적인, 직업적인, 프로의 placement 직업 소개, 배치 no doubt 의심할 바 없이, 물론, 필시 assistance 조력, 보조, 도움 guarantee 보증, 개런티

요즘에는 일자리를 찾기 위해 전문적인 도움을 얻는 것이 흔한 일이다. 사람들이 적절한 일자리를 찾는 것을 도와 주는 많은 회사들이 있다. 고용 에이전시나 인사 배치 서비스라고 불린다. 일자리를 찾고 있다면, 조심해야 한다. 이 회사들 중 대부분은 의심할 바 없이 좋은 서비스를 제공해 주는 반면, 그들의 도움을 얻는 데 드는 비용은 상당하다. 종종 회사는 당신이 직업을 찾는 것을 보장해 주지 않기도 한다. 그들의 서비스에 대해 돈을 지불하기 전에 그들이 당신에게 제공한 것에 대해서 명확히 해야 한다.

이 글의 목적은 무엇인가?

(A) 경고
(B) 설명
(C) 광고
(D) 분석

UNIT 16 Airport

Key Expressions

1　1 boarding pass　2 return
　　3 connecting flights
　　4 aisle seat　5 baggage

2　1 ⓓ　2 ⓔ　3 ⓐ　4 ⓒ　5 ⓑ

3　1 ⓑ　2 ⓐ　3 ⓒ　4 ⓔ　5 ⓓ　6 ⓕ　7 ⓖ

Listening Practice

1 (C)　　　　　**2** (B)

Check Up

Listening Task *01*　1 (C)　2 1) F　2) F　3) F　4) T
Listening Task *02*　1 (D)
Listening Task *03*　1 (B)　2 (C)
Listening Task *04*　1 (D)

Listening Test

1 (B)　**2** (B)　**3** (C)　**4** (C)　**5** (B)　**6** (C)
7 (C)　**8** (D)

Key Expressions

1 표에서 가장 적절한 단어를 골라 빈칸을 채우시오.

　1 탑승 게이트에서 탑승권을 준비해 두세요.

　2 편도 티켓입니까, 왕복 티켓입니까?

　3 비행기를 갈아타는 손님들은 11번 게이트로 가야
　　합니다.

　4 전 창가 쪽보다 통로 쪽 좌석이 더 좋아요.

　5 초과 수하물에 대해서 요금이 부과되지 않았으면
　　좋겠어요. 이 가방은 꽤 무겁거든요.

2 왼쪽에 있는 활동들을 오른쪽에 있는 올바른 장소와
연결하시오.

　1 비행기에 탑승하다
　　ⓓ 출발 게이트

　2 환전한다
　　ⓔ 환전소

　3 비행기 도착 후 친구를 만난다
　　ⓐ 도착 지역

　4 잡지를 산다
　　ⓒ 신문 판매점

　5 비행 후 가방을 찾는다
　　ⓑ 수하물 찾는 곳

3 다음 문장들을 가장 잘 어울리는 대답과 연결하시오.

　1 안녕하세요. 존슨이라는 이름으로 비행기 예약했는
　　데요.
　　ⓑ 아, 예, 오전 9시 도쿄 행이시죠.

　2 자리를 창가 쪽으로 드릴까요, 통로 쪽으로 드릴까요?
　　ⓐ 어느 쪽이든 상관 없어요.

　3 여권 볼 수 있을까요?
　　ⓒ 예, 여기 있습니다.

　4 비행기 출발이 1시간 늦어졌어요.
　　ⓔ 이제 우린 확실히 늦겠네요.

　5 피크 시즌 아닌가요?
　　ⓓ 사실, 한가한 시즌이에요.

　6 어느 비행기로 하시겠습니까?
　　ⓕ 6시 15분 걸로 주세요.

　7 이 표에 대한 지불은 언제 해야 하나요?
　　ⓖ 2주 안에요.

Listening Practice

1

In the past, people spent a lot more of their time getting from place to place. These days, many people choose to fly to their destinations. But those who fly frequently, such as businesspeople, complain that air travel is not fun. You have to book your ticket many days or even weeks in advance. There are frequent delays. Until there is a better alternative, however, air travel still offers the most benefits.

▶ **in advance** 미리, 앞서, 선금으로　**delay** 지연, 지체
alternative 대안, 다른 방도　**benefit** 이익, 이득

과거에 사람들은 이곳에서 저곳으로 가는 데 많은 시간을 보냈다. 요즘 많은 사람들은 그들의 목적지까지 비행기를 타고 간다. 그러나 사업가들처럼 비행기를 자주 타는 사람들은 비행기 여행이 재미없다고 불평한다. 당신은 며칠 전이나 심지어 몇 주 전에 비행기 티켓을 예약해야 한다. 종종 지체도 있다. 하지만 더 좋은 대안이 있을 때까지, 비행기 여행은 여전히 가장 많은 이익을 제공해 준다.

이 이야기의 가장 좋은 제목은 무엇인가?

(A) 비행기 여행의 발명
(B) 여행자들과 문제점들
(C) 비행기 여행의 도전 과제와 문제점들
(D) 목적지까지 가는 가장 빠른 방법

2

W May I see your ticket and passport please?
M Here you are.
W Only one bag? Just put it down there. Thanks.
M Will this bag be okay for carry-on luggage?
W That should be no problem, sir. And would you prefer a window or aisle seat?
M I'd like a window seat, thanks.

▶ **passport** 여권 **put down** 아래로 내려놓다
aisle seat 통로 쪽 좌석

여 티켓과 여권 좀 보여 주시겠어요?
남 여기 있습니다.
여 가방은 하나 뿐인가요? 그냥 거기에 두세요. 감사합니다.
남 이 가방을 기내 휴대 수하물로 가져가도 됩니까?
여 문제 없습니다. 창가 쪽 좌석과 복도 쪽 좌석 중 어느 쪽으로 드릴까요?
남 창가 좌석으로 주세요. 감사합니다.

상황을 가장 잘 나타낸 것은?

(A) 남자는 게이트를 통과하고 있다.
(B) 남자는 공항에서 수하물을 체크인하고 있다.
(C) 공항에 있는 세관 검색대를 통과하고 있다.
(D) 티켓과 여권을 잃어버렸다.

Check Up

Listening Task *01*

Kimpo Airport... I am currently sitting here waiting for my connecting flight. It was delayed, so I'll be here until 2 a.m. This is annoying. But, the flight from Beijing was great because, for the first time ever, I flew business class! From the second I sat down, they kept asking, "Can I bring you anything?"

▶ **currently** 지금, 현재, 일반적으로 **connecting flight** 갈아 탈 비행기
annoying 성가신, 귀찮은

김포공항... 난 지금 갈아 탈 비행기를 기다리면서 여기 앉아 있다. 출발이 지연되어서 새벽 2시까지 여기 있어야 할 것 같다. 정말 짜증난다. 하지만 베이징에서 오는 비행기는 아주 좋았다. 나는 처음으로 비즈니스 클래스에 탔다! 내가 앉자 그들은 "필요한 거 있으신가요?"라고 계속 물어 보았다.

1 **남자가 마지막에 할 말로 적절한 것은 무엇인가?**

  (A) 실망스러웠다.
  (B) 짜증나기 시작했다.
  (C) 최고였다.
  (D) 그건 날 화나게 했다.

2 **맞으면 T, 틀리면 F에 체크하시오.**

  1) 그는 프랑스에 있다.
  2) 그는 친구를 기다리고 있다.
  3) 그는 항상 비즈니스 클래스를 탄다.
  4) 그는 베이징에서 왔다.

Listening Task *02*

W Can you help me change the date of my return flight?
M Certainly. Do you have a reference number?
W It's nsaw59. I'd like to change my return date to tomorrow evening.
M I see. Unfortunately, the system shows me that the flights tomorrow are full. It's Sunday.
W What about Monday?
M It's almost the same situation. But there is a seat for Wednesday. Would you like to take it?
W Sure. Thank you.

▶ **reference number** 조회 번호, 정리 번호

여 돌아오는 비행 날짜를 바꿀 수 있을까요?
남 물론이죠. 조회 번호가 있나요?
여 nsaw59입니다. 돌아오는 날짜를 내일 저녁으로 변경하고 싶은데요.
남 알겠습니다. 불행히도 내일 비행기는 모두 다 찼네요. 일요일이라서요.
여 월요일은 어떤가요?
남 상황이 거의 비슷한데요. 하지만 수요일에는 좌석이 있어요. 수요일로 드릴까요?
여 네, 감사합니다.

1 **여자가 돌아오는 비행 날짜는 언제인가?**

  (A) 토요일   (B) 일요일
  (C) 월요일   (D) 수요일

Listening Task 03

M Excuse me, ma'am. What are the round things in your bag?

W What round things?

M There are five small round things about the size of a tennis ball showing on our x-ray machine. Are they balls?

W Ah, yes, sorry. I bought some juggling balls in Mexico.

M What are they made from?

W I don't really know.

M I'm afraid they might have grains or seeds, which are prohibited items, inside. Could you open your bag, please?

▶ grain 곡물, 낟알 seed 씨, 열매, 종자 prohibit 금하다, 금지하다

남 실례합니다. 부인. 가방 안에 있는 둥근 물건은 무엇인가요?
여 어떤 둥근 물건이요?
남 저희 X-레이에 테니스 공 크기의 둥근 물건이 다섯 개 보이는데요. 공인가요?
여 아, 네, 죄송합니다. 멕시코에서 저글링 공을 샀어요.
남 무엇으로 만들어졌나요?
여 잘 모르겠는데요.
남 그 안에 금지된 물품인 곡물이나 씨앗이 있을지도 모르겠어요. 가방 좀 열어 주시겠습니까?

1 이 대화가 일어나는 곳은 어디인가?

(A) 수하물 체크인에서
(B) 보안 검사에서
(C) 탑승 게이트에서
(D) 기내에서

2 대화에 대해 사실인 것은 무엇인가?

(A) 공들은 테니스 공이다.
(B) 공들은 곡물 공이다.
(C) 여자는 멕시코에서 공을 샀다.
(D) 여자는 공이 무슨 공인지 알지 못한다.

Listening Task 04

Whenever I try to catch a connecting flight, I seem to have a bad experience. Last week, I had one hour to catch my connecting flight in the Bangkok airport. They announced that my flight was boarding at Gate 3. I knew where that was, so I started rushing over with my heavy laptop computer. But I was halfway there when they announced that it was boarding at Gate 13. That's on the other side of the airport. By that time, I was so angry that I stopped a security guard and asked him to help me find my way before I missed my flight.

▶ board 탑승하다, 타다 rush 쇄도하다, 급히 달리다

나는 갈아 타는 비행기를 타려고 할 때마다, 안 좋은 경험을 갖는 것 같다. 지난 주에 방콕 공항에서 갈아타는 비행기를 타기 위해 한 시간을 기다렸다. 그들은 3번 게이트에서 탑승할 것이라고 방송했다. 하지만 그들이 13번 게이트에서 탑승한다고 방송했을 때에는 난 이미 반쯤 그곳에 갔다. 그곳은 공항의 정반대 쪽에 있었다. 나는 화가 나서 경비원을 붙들고 내가 비행기를 놓치기 전에 길을 알려 달라고 부탁했다.

1 남자는 왜 화가 났나?

(A) 공항이 너무 커서 길을 잃었다.
(B) 그의 비행기에 많은 연착이 있었다.
(C) 다른 항공사로 갈아 타야 했다.
(D) 그의 탑승 게이트에 대해서 항공사가 실수를 했다.

Listening Test

1

W Could I see your passport, please?

M Yes. Here is my passport.

W Are you coming here on business or on vacation?

M I have a short business meeting tomorrow, but I'm actually here on vacation.

W You have a tourist visa, but you're here on business? Please show me your return ticket.

M Here it is. I only have one business meeting, and the rest of my time will be vacationing.

W I see. Where are you staying?

M The Lotte Hotel.

W Do you have any company?

M No.

W Okay. Have a nice time.

▶ vacation 휴가를 보내다; 휴가 company 일행, 동료

여 여권 좀 볼 수 있을까요?
남 네. 여기 있습니다.
여 사업상 오셨습니까, 아니면 휴가차 오셨습니까?
남 내일 간단한 사업 미팅이 있긴 하지만 사실상 휴가차 왔어요.
여 여행 비자를 갖고 계시는데, 사업상 오셨다고요? 돌아가는 티켓을 보여 주세요.
남 여기 있습니다. 사업상 미팅은 한 번 있고, 나머지 시간은 휴가로 보낼 거예요.
여 그러시군요. 어디에서 머무르시나요?

남 롯데 호텔이요.
여 일행이 있으신가요?
남 아뇨.
여 됐습니다. 좋은 시간 보내세요.

대화에 대해 사실이 <u>아닌</u> 것은 무엇인가?

(A) 남자는 혼자 왔다.
(B) 남자는 머무르는 동안 몇 개의 사업 미팅을 할 예정이다.
(C) 남자는 롯데 호텔에서 머무를 것이다.
(D) 남자는 대부분의 시간을 휴가로 사용할 것이다.

2

M Hi, how was your flight?
W It was a little bumpy, but I guess that it wasn't too bad.
M Yeah, and your plane arrived on time as well. That's always nice.
W Totally. The last time I came here, I got delayed by a couple of hours. Do you remember that?
M Yes, I do. So, did you check any bags for this flight?
W Yeah, so I guess that we should go pick them up now.

▶ **flight** 비행, 비행기 여행 **bumpy** 덜컹거리는, 악기류가 있는

남 안녕, 비행기 여행 어땠니?
여 조금 덜컹거렸지만 나쁘지 않았어.
남 그렇구나. 또 네 비행기가 정시에 도착하기도 했고 말이야. 그건 늘 기분 좋은 일이지.
여 정말 그래. 저번에 여기에 왔을 때는 몇 시간이나 연착했었어. 그때 기억나니?
남 응, 기억나. 그래서, 너 이 비행기로 짐 부쳤니?
여 응, 그래서 지금 가서 가방을 찾아야겠어.

이 대화 후에 여자는 무엇을 할까?

(A) 호텔을 방문한다.
(B) 수하물 찾는 곳에 간다.
(C) 남자와 저녁을 먹는다.
(D) 다른 비행기에 탄다.

3

Most of us ignore the safety video that is played to passengers before the flight takes off. But, actually, we should take careful note of this video. It may be boring, but it is for our own safety. These are some of the safety tips. We are reminded to fasten our seat belts. All electronic equipment must be switched off during takeoff and landing. No one is allowed to smoke on the flight. Cell phones should remain off at all times. No sharp objects may be brought on board.

▶ **take off** (비행기가) 이륙하다 **take note of** ~에 주목하다, 주의하다 **fasten** 묶다, 단단히 고정시키다 **switch off** 끄다, (전류를) 끊다 **remain** 여전히 ~이다, ~대로이다

우리들 대부분은 비행기가 이륙하기 전에 승객들에게 보여 주는 안전 비디오를 무시한다. 하지만 사실 우리는 이 비디오를 주의 깊게 봐야 한다. 지루할지도 모르지만 그것은 우리의 안전을 위한 것이다. 다음 사항들이 안전 팁들이다. 안전 벨트를 매도록 상기시켜 준다. 모든 전자 장비들은 이착륙 동안에 전원이 꺼져 있어야 한다. 어느 누구도 비행기 안에서 담배를 필 수 없다. 휴대폰도 항상 꺼진 상태로 있어야 한다. 날카로운 물건을 휴대한 채 탑승할 수 없다.

이야기에 따르면 올바른 안전 팁은 무엇인가?

(A) 비행 중 휴대폰을 사용할 수 있다.
(B) 날카로운 물건을 가방 안에 가지고 올 수 있다.
(C) 비행 중에는 담배를 펴서는 안 된다.
(D) 이착륙 중에 컴퓨터를 사용할 수 있다.

4

W Can I help you, sir?
M I've just come in on KLM Flight 345. Do you know where I can collect my baggage?
W That's over on belt 12, sir.
M Oh, I see. Where everyone's waiting. I guess I should have looked carefully. Thanks.

▶ **come in** 도착하다, 입장하다

여 도와 드릴까요?
남 전 지금 막 KLM 345편에서 내렸어요. 제 짐을 어디서 찾아야 하는지 아시나요?
여 저쪽 12번 벨트로 가시면 됩니다.
남 오, 알겠습니다. 사람들이 기다리고 있군요. 제가 좀더 잘 찾아 봐야 했는데요. 감사합니다.

대화에 대해 사실인 것은?

(A) 남자는 비행기를 어디서 타야 할지 모른다.
(B) 남자는 KLM 345 비행기를 탈 것이다.
(C) 많은 사람들이 12번 벨트 근처에서 기다리고 있다.
(D) 여자는 그를 도울 수 없다.

5

W Do you have anything to declare?
M What do you mean?
W Are you carrying any plants or animals? Do you have items, such as alcohol or cigarettes, on which you must pay a duty?
M No, I don't have any of those items. I was only

on a business trip.

W   Very well. Please fill out this form, and walk through that gate.

M   Which gate is that?

W   The gate with the sign which reads, "Nothing to declare."

▶ declare (세관에서) 신고하다, 선언하다   duty 세금, 관세, 의무   read 나타내다, 읽다

여   신고할 게 있나요?

남   무슨 말인지요?

여   식물이나 동물을 동반하고 오셨습니까? 술이나 담배 같은 세금이 부과되는 물품들을 가지고 계시나요?

남   아뇨, 전 그런 물품들은 안 가지고 있는데요. 그냥 출장이었어요.

여   알겠습니다. 이 양식을 기입해 주시고, 저 문을 걸어 나가시면 됩니다.

남   어떤 문이죠?

여   '신고할 것 없음'이라고 쓰여져 있는 표지판이 있는 문이요.

이 대화 후에 남자는 무엇을 할까?

(A) 그의 짐에 대해 세금을 지불할 것이다.
(B) 서류를 작성할 것이다.
(C) 비행기에 탑승할 것이다.
(D) 공항에 도착할 것이다.

6

I had a very bad experience at the airport recently. I walked through the metal detector, and it went off. The security officer asked me to walk through the machine again after taking off my jacket. But he spoke very loudly, so many people turned to stare at me. I walked through the machine three times, and it still went off. More and more people stopped to see what was happening. Finally I took my shoes off and walked through. Everyone laughed at me.

▶ metal detector 금속 탐지기   go off (기계가) 작동하다, 울리다

최근에 공항에서 안 좋은 경험을 했다. 금속 탐지기를 지나가는데 경보기가 울린 것이다. 보안관은 재킷을 벗은 후 다시 기계를 통과하라고 했다. 그런데 그가 너무 큰 소리로 말해서 많은 사람들이 나를 쳐다보았다. 난 세 번이나 그 기계를 통과했는데 여전히 경보기가 울렸다. 더 많은 사람들이 무슨 일이 일어나는지 보려고 멈춰 섰다. 결국 나는 신발을 벗고 통과했다. 모든 사람들이 날 보고 웃었다.

화자의 감정을 가장 잘 나타내고 있는 단어는 무엇인가?

(A) 흥분한   (B) 우울한
(C) 당황한   (D) 만족한

7

I usually arrive at the airport two and a half hours early for my flight. But I still have to wait over an hour to check my bags in. It's very frustrating flying economy class. The business class counter is never busy. Business class passengers who turn up can just go straight there and check in while all of us have to wait. I'm not flying economy class any more if I can afford it.

▶ frustrate 실망시키다, 좌절시키다

난 보통 내 출발 시간보다 2시간 반 정도 일찍 도착한다. 하지만 내 가방을 체크인하기 위해서는 한 시간 이상을 기다려야 한다. 일반석으로 비행하는 것은 정말 실망스럽다. 비즈니스석 카운터는 결코 바쁘지 않다. 비즈니스석 승객들은 우리가 기다리는 동안 그곳을 곧장 지나가서 체크인할 수 있다. 만약 여유가 있다면, 난 더 이상 일반석을 이용하지 않을 것이다.

화자는 다음 번에 어떻게 할까?

(A) 좀 더 일찍 도착한다.
(B) 일반석을 이용한다.
(C) 비즈니스석을 이용한다.
(D) 기차를 탄다.

8

I was in the airport last year when I heard this announcement: "We regret to inform you that all scheduled flights to Seoul have been cancelled due to bad weather conditions." My son's birthday was the following day, and I had promised him I would be home. I went to the desk, but they could not help me. I couldn't help spending the next day in the airport wishing I was at home.

▶ announcement 발표, 공표   regret 유감으로 생각하다, 후회하다

난 작년에 공항에서 이런 방송을 들었다. "서울로 가는 예정된 비행이 악천후 때문에 취소되었습니다." 내 아들의 생일이 다음 날이었고, 난 그에게 집에 있을 거라고 약속했다. 난 데스크에 갔지만 그들은 나를 도울 수 없었다. 난 내가 집에 있었다면 좋을 텐데라고 생각하면서 다음 날 공항에서 시간을 보낼 수 밖에 없었다.

화자에 대해 사실인 것은 무엇인가?

(A) 그는 공항에 있어야 했기 때문에 피곤했다.
(B) 그는 항공사가 비행을 취소했기 때문에 화가 났다.
(C) 데스크의 직원이 그를 도울 수 없어서 화가 났다.
(D) 그는 아들의 생일에 집에 갈 수 없어서 실망했다.

LISTEN to the MAX

THE BEST PREPARATION AND PRACTICE FOR IMPROVING YOUR LISTENING SKILLS

Features

- 16 theme-based units with various topics that frequently appear on the listening sections of entrance exams for special-purpose high schools and universities
- Sound-based tasks to help students build their listening skills
- Intensive practice of all question types on listening exams
- Glossed vocabulary and collocations that help students understand each topic better
- Dictation practice to help students develop appropriate and correct listening skills
- Full answer key and Korean translations

Listen to the Max Series
Listen to the Max 1, 2, 3
Listen to the Max 실전모의고사 1, 2, 3

Scan this QR
code for online
resources.